D1082766

THE POLITICS OF CONTINUITY

The Goucher College Series

THE JOHNS HOPKINS UNIVERSITY PRESS
BALTIMORE & LONDON

THE POLITICS OF CONTINUITY

MARYLAND POLITICAL PARTIES FROM 1858 TO 1870

JEAN H. BAKER

Manufactured in the United States of America

The Johns Hopkins University Press, Baltimore, Maryland 21218
The Johns Hopkins University Press Ltd., London

Library of Congress Catalog Card Number 72-12354
ISBN 0-8018-1418-9

Library of Congress Cataloging in Publication data
will be found on the last printed page of this book.

Art provided courtesy of the
Maryland Historical Society, Baltimore

For R. R. B.

CONTENTS

LIST OF APPENDIX TABLES

ACKNOWLEDGMENTS

FITTINGLY, AUTHORS ACKNOWLEDGE the assistance of others, and such aid customarily falls into two areas: help with the practical aspects of research and contributions to the psychic and intellectual well-being of the author. In the former category, many kindly librarians and archivists have directed me to pertinent materials, and I am particularly grateful to Wayde Chrysmer and Page Swann Gillet for allowing me to see their collections. Two students of Maryland history—Gary Browne and Milton Henry—have generously shared their own findings with me.

In the latter category of acknowledgements, many years ago when I returned to college, the late William L. Neumann nurtured my interest in history. A successful scholar and teacher, Bill Neumann encouraged generations of Goucher women to combine different roles in their own lives. Later, David Donald of the Johns Hopkins University directed my dissertation, and while scholars admire his contributions to American history, reverential students marvel at his persistent and creative criticism of their own research and writing.

Finally, my family have contributed practically, intellectually, and psychically. Four young Marylanders who prefer change to continuity in their own politics—my children Susan, Scott, Robbie, and Jenny—have run the adding machines, counted the numbers, and listened to the revisions. To them and a sympathetic husband, I am grateful.

Change and decay
in all around I see
O thou who changest not,
abide with me.
H. F. Lyte

INTRODUCTION

THIS IS THE story of political parties during a time of great turmoil, confusion, and change. The years of Civil War and Reconstruction brought every form of disruption to Marylanders. Precariously balanced between North and South, the state became an important theater of battle as vast armies trooped across its territory. In addition to the thirty-one military engagements fought on Maryland soil, hundreds of minor raids and skirmishes made war more than a matter of reading newspaper accounts of distant battles. It was not by chance that the first casualties of the Civil War, in the spring of 1861, were Baltimore civilians. Later, spies, blockade runners, dealers in contraband goods, and bounty brokers—all the human impedimenta of war—found the state convenient for their operations. For four years, civilians also suffered the miseries of inflation, higher taxes, the disruption of the labor force, and the most final of all changes—the death of relatives in military service. Still, to some, the most significant change was the emancipation of nearly 90,000 slaves during the war, the doubling of the state's despised free Negro population, and the consequent derangement of racial patterns maintained for over two hundred years. The transformation of the Maryland Club, a meeting place for the gentry, into a rest home for blacks run by the Freedmen's Bureau symbolized, to many Marylanders, the calamitous changes of the war years.

In the view of many political scientists and historians, such social and economic alterations inevitably refashioned American politics, and hence to scholars like V. O. Key, Angus Campbell, and Philip Converse, the Civil War, like the Great Depression of 1929, represented a watershed in political history. Fitting the definition of a crisis which intimately touched the lives of most Americans—what Key has called "a drastic set of conditions"—war supposedly accomplished a durable realignment in both the anatomy and ideology of the Democratic and Republican parties. During Reconstruction, a new generation of political leaders, remembering the bitter war years, now appealed to constituents to "vote as you shot" or "vote for a white man's party." In the case of Maryland, these cataclysmic effects presumably produced a complete and enduring shift to the Democrats who, with rare exceptions, thereafter controlled the state.

On closer examination, this conventional wisdom hardly explains the Maryland experience. Throughout war and Reconstruction, the state staunchly maintained political parties established in the late 1850s, and these organizations used, even in 1870, almost the same issues, structures, and leaders as they had before the war. The basic realignment in Maryland politics, occasioned by fears of disruption of the Union, increases in the free Negro population, and the growing professionalism of the Democratic party, had occurred on the eve of the war. Postwar politics merely confirmed changes effected in the late 1850s.

In 1859, the Democratic party, reorganized and revitalized, became the majority party of the state. Stressing three basic themes—fear and hatred of the free Negro, the need for an end to election interference by Know-Nothing opponents, and the necessity of protecting "Constitution and Union"—Democrats lost control of Maryland during the war only because their supporters and leaders had left the state and not because a war-begotten party—the Unionists—replaced them in the affections of Marylanders. Democrats returned to power in 1866, their greatest strength in areas which had supported them before the war. Insisting that their opponents interfered with the right to vote by using military force and later by enforcing unfair registration laws, Democrats successfully created a response to the Republican "waving of the bloody shirt" in the "politics of the trampled ballot." Democratic politicians repeated the same themes that were popular before the war: the need to control Negroes, the need to protect the ballot, and the need to preserve "Constitution as it is and Union as it was"—all now threatened by the excesses of so-called Radical Republicans. With good reason, Marylanders described their political parties as "standing armies."

Similar continuity is apparent in the history of the opposition party. Despite a confusing name change from Know-Nothing to Union and finally, in 1867, to Republican, this political organization also maintained much the same structure, leaders, and constituency. While Democrats gained strength in the late 1850s, the Know-Nothings, their earlier xenophobic appeals now replaced by fervent Unionism, were disorganized and demoralized. Factionalism continued to weaken the party during the war years, and neither of the state's two most talented politicians—Congressman Henry Winter Davis or Montgomery Blair, Lincoln's Postmaster General—could unify the organization. By 1868, only the anticipation of Negro enfranchisement by constitutional amendment supported the fading Republican organization.

There were other constants in Maryland political life. The loyalty of legislative delegates to party, not section, continued unabated during the period, and membership in a party, rather than representation of a particular region, consistently determined voting behavior in the state legislature. As in the late 1850s, the treasured American notion of two-party competition usually remained an ideal and not a reality, for in most Maryland counties and Baltimore city one party controlled the political life of the community. War did little to shift the power of county government to the state, and both Democrats and Republicans continued to base their organization on the county unit. Certainly the rewriting of the Maryland Constitution in 1864, and again in 1867, produced few structural changes in state government. In addition, there was striking continuity in the attitudes and perceptions of Marylanders toward parties. While Democrats attempted to define the beneficial aspects of political institutions, Republicans, sounding much like their Federalist, Whig, and Know-Nothing ancestors, questioned the contributions of parties to American democracy.

Thus the war did not provide a convenient dividing point in the history of Maryland's political parties. The period of partisan realignment occurred before the war, and during the ensuing decade citizens clung doggedly to the allegiances forged in the 1850s. Though other monuments of the past disappeared as casualties of war and its aftermath, the political party remained a familiar guidepost of extraordinary durability. Parties came to play the role described by Graham Wallas in *Human Nature in Politics* as "something simpler and more permanent, something which can be loved and trusted and which can be recognized at successive elections as being the same thing that was loved before."

I. PATTERNS OF CHANGE: MARYLAND, 1840-1860

THE DAY OF PARTY DISCIPLINE is over. Men bolt parties with perfect consciousness of impunity and act without the least dread of ultimate retribution."[1] Thus William Preston—lawyer, sometimes officeholder, and dedicated Democrat—expressed his disgust at the disintegration of Maryland's party system in the 1850s. A fellow Baltimorean, Henry Winter Davis, agreed; noting a "breaking up in parties," Davis looked to the end of "old fogey" politics. From Salisbury to Cumberland, Maryland newspapers described the weakness of partisan allegiances and organizations. The *Cecil Whig* found "party ties loosened and party lines nearly obliterated," while the Baltimore *American* described the same transformation: "Everywhere people are coming together in their congressional districts, without reference to past distinctions."[2]

It had not always been so. In the 1840s Maryland politics displayed the characteristics of a stable party system. Although considerable power remained at the local level, both Democrats and Whigs achieved statewide organization and became part of a national party. This "second American party system" had its origins in contests for the presidency, as former Federalists and Republicans became Whigs and Democrats between 1824 and 1840. It was during this period that Maryland's political organizations adopted highly formalized ways of conducting campaigns, distributing power within the party, and choosing candidates.[3]

The voting behavior of Marylanders in the 1840s reflected the vitality of both political parties. In an admirable display of electoral equity, Marylanders of the 1840s chose one Whig and two Democratic governors; and of thirty-one congressmen who served during the decade, nineteen were Whigs. Democrats controlled the state legislature for three years, Whigs for six. Frequently only a few votes separated winner and loser in statewide elections. In 1841 Governor Francis P. Thomas's hairbreadth margin of 639 votes—out of 57,000

[1] William Preston to Madge Preston, August 25, 1855, Preston Papers, Maryland Historical Society (hereinafter abbreviated as MHS).

[2] Henry Winter Davis to Samuel F. Du Pont, October 1854, Du Pont Papers, Eleutherian Mills Historical Library, Wilmington, Del.; *Cecil Whig* (Elkton), April 30, 1859; Baltimore *American*, September 16, 1858.

[3] For an analysis of the competitive party system which followed the "Era of Good Feeling," see Richard McCormick, *The Second American Party System* (Chapel Hill: University of North Carolina Press, 1966). McCormick's interpretation of Maryland politics draws on Mark Haller's "The Rise of the Jackson Party in Maryland" (master's thesis, University of Maryland, 1953) and the same author's "The Rise of the Jackson Party in Maryland, 1820-1829," *Journal of Southern History* 28 (August 1962): 307-26.

cast—established the pattern for elections during the decade. Three years later Thomas G. Pratt, a Whig, won the governorship by 548 votes, and in 1847 Philip F. Thomas polled 638 more votes, of 68,000 cast, than his Whig opponent. National elections reflected this same intense competition. In the three presidential contests of 1840, 1844, and 1848, Marylanders split their votes so evenly that Whigs outpolled Democrats by only 11,241 votes of some 203,000 cast in the three elections.[4]

Such vigorous competition between Whigs and Democrats accounted, in part, for the high voter turnout. Encouraged by effective organizations, enthusiastic partisans implored party members "to take measures to bring every voter to the polls."[5] In many elections during the 1840s, 80 percent of the white adult males voted, while presidential elections brought an even greater number of voters to the polls. Marylanders have yet to match the election turnout of 1840 when 85 percent of the state's eligible voters cast ballots for either the Democratic candidate, Martin Van Buren, or the Whig, William Henry Harrison.

A new system of choosing candidates also helped to stimulate political interest in the 1840s. Gradually the party convention had replaced the legislative caucus. Under the older system, legislative leaders, without reference to other party channels, met before elections to choose candidates. The new arrangement required that delegates elected in ward and district meetings organize conventions where party nominees for national, state, and local offices would be selected. Using the same procedure employed in the national party conventions that met so often in their state,[6] Maryland Whigs and Democrats organized a hierarchy of such local conventions, thereby actively involving many citizens in politics.

Intense and competitive, the politics of the 1840s was also a highly sociable and pleasurable activity. In an age of few formal recreations, Marylanders enjoyed the steamboat rides, barbecues, and

[4]All election figures, unless otherwise noted, are from the Inter-University Consortium for Political Research, Ann Arbor, Michigan. In most cases I checked these statistics with the manuscript returns in the Executive Papers, Hall of Records, Annapolis, Maryland. For a statistical analysis of the Whig-Democratic vote during the 1830s and 1840s, see William J. Evitts, "A Matter of Allegiances: Maryland from 1850 to 1861" (Ph.D. diss., Johns Hopkins University, 1971), pp. 15–17.

[5]"Whig Central Committee of Maryland," October 23, 1844, Otho Scott Papers, Duke University Library, Durham, N.C.

[6]Of the six presidential nominating conventions held by Whigs and Democrats during the decade, four met in Baltimore.

dances organized by political parties. In 1840, according to one report, "an avalanche of people" attended a Whig meeting held north of Baltimore. "The assembly was one of much show—flying banners, clashing cymbals, restive horses, pretty girls, whole-souled politicians, log cabins, and hard cider."[7] Fall picnics were perhaps the most popular political activity. In 1844, 30,000 Baltimoreans crowded into Gibson's woods in Baltimore county to enjoy a Defender's Day picnic where Democratic appeals and speeches flowed as freely as the party's hard cider.[8]

As elections approached, such recreation gave way to more purposeful partisan activities. For the party faithful, frequent meetings of ward and district associations and of political clubs led to active electioneering.[9] For other Marylanders, the months of September and October brought an endless succession of processions, flag-raisings, and stump speeches. Irresistible to an ever-increasing number of participants, politics became unavoidable to others. "Even those who most closely confine their attention to their business," announced the Baltimore *Sun*, "cannot remain in ignorance [of politics] unless they bandage their eyes so that they may not read party papers nor see the poles, flags, and banners or stop up their ears and thus shut out the music accompanying the numerous processions."[10]

This flourishing period of party politics, marked by high voter interest, stable organizations, and close elections did not last. In 1852, for the first time in four presidential elections, Maryland cast her electoral votes for a Democrat, and the defeat of the Whig candidate General Winfield Scott led abruptly to the collapse of that party both nationally and locally. Regretfully, supporters like Jacob Engelbrecht, a Frederick farmer, mourned the end of an institution that they had supported all their political lives.[11] By 1855, Maryland Whigs found themselves members of what one called "the rump of broken down and discredited factions."[12] To Democrats, these 35,000 former Whigs represented an attractive and uncommitted constituency to be courted

[7] J. Thomas Scharf, *History of Maryland from the Earliest Period to the Present Day*, 3 vols. (1879; reprint ed., Hatboro, Pa.: Tradition Press, 1967), 3:198.

[8] Baltimore *Sun*, September 13, 1844.

[9] For an example of preparations for active electioneering, see George A. Frill, Henry Thomas *et al.*, to William Preston, July 2, 1846, Preston Papers.

[10] Baltimore *Sun*, August 29, 1844.

[11] Diary of Jacob Engelbrecht, June 4, November 8, 1852, MHS.

[12] Henry Winter Davis, *The Origin, Principles and Purposes of the American Party* (n.p., n.d.), p. 19.

throughout the decade; for other Marylanders the politics of the 1850s meant a confusing period of political transition marked by new parties, issues, and leaders.[13]

While the breakup of the Whigs signaled the beginning of a period of party instability, the rewriting of the Maryland Constitution further stimulated political change. This struggle to revise the state's seventy-four-year-old charter provided the occasion for a further weakening of party allegiances. When Marylanders joined organizations dedicated to calling a Constitutional Convention "without regard for partisan distinctions," political discipline suffered.[14] Gradually the fight over constitutional reform became a sectional, not a partisan, struggle with the northern and western counties of Maryland, along with the city of Baltimore, in favor of constitutional revision and the Tidewater areas opposed.

In 1851 Marylanders wrote and accepted a new Constitution, their first since the Revolution. The Constitution of 1851, by creating more elective offices, decreased the governor's appointive powers. Marylanders now elected judges, county commissioners, and clerks as well as a variety of other local and state officials. Recognizing the state's traditional regional allegiances, many of these offices, including the governorship, rotated successively among residents of the Eastern Shore, Baltimore and southern Maryland, and northwestern Maryland. Under a new apportionment system, Baltimore and the northwestern counties received a larger voice in the legislature, although disproportionate power still rested with the rural counties of southern and eastern Maryland, where each delegate represented 3,596 white citizens, compared with 7,300 for delegates from Baltimore and the northwest.

After the ratification of the Constitution and the disappearance of the Whigs, a new political party emerged, based on appeals to nativism and unionism. Almost overnight the American or Know-

[13]One statistical tool used to study voting patterns clearly reveals the change in Maryland's voting habits. Coefficients of correlation measure the relationship between variables. When Maryland election returns of the 1844 and 1848 elections are compared with those of 1856, there are no significant positive or negative relationships. Thus there is no significant correlation on a county-by-county basis between Maryland's vote for Henry Clay in 1844, General Zachary Taylor in 1848, and that for any of the three presidential candidates in 1856. Nor is there any significant correlation between the Democratic vote for James Polk in 1844 and Lewis Cass in 1848, and that for James Buchanan in 1856. See Appendix A for an explanation of coefficients of correlation.

[14]"Petition of Citizens of Maryland to the General Assembly for the call of a Convention to Reform the Constitution of the State," Preston Papers.

Nothing party—which was never able to shake the opprobrious nickname bequeathed by its opponents—became the state's leading party. In 1856, Maryland was the only state in the Union to vote for the Know-Nothing presidential candidate Millard Fillmore. A year later, Thomas Hicks, a Know-Nothing, became the governor of the state, and by 1858 the party controlled both statehouse and legislature. Elected to office on platforms that called for lengthened periods of naturalization and the prohibition of Roman Catholics from office-holding, the party did little to institute such policies when it was in power. Gradually, Know-Nothings dropped their xenophobic appeals and pleaded instead for the preservation of the Union and the support of the Republic.

The meteoric rise of Know-Nothings was the occasion for a dramatic shift in state loyalties. Baltimore, Democratic in the 1840s, became in the 1850s a political barony controlled by the Know-Nothings. Democrats, on the other hand, came to dominate previously Whig southern Maryland. During this period of shifting allegiances many Marylanders simply did not vote, and turnouts declined until, in 1856, only seven of ten eligible Marylanders voted.

The existence of regional pockets of one-party strength fostered corruption. Overzealous partisans found it easy to exert physical control over the state's wards and election districts. Particularly in Baltimore, but also in some county districts, guns, awls, and even cannons became popular weapons used to prevent opposition voters from reaching the polls. To the chagrin of many Marylanders, Baltimore's election riots soon earned the city a national reputation. Certainly the reputation was deserved, for some elections resulted in more casualties among Marylanders than the military engagements of the Mexican-American war.[15]

Largely a bipartisan affair, election violence grew out of the state's failure to regulate political parties and voting practices. It was virtually impossible for sixty Baltimore policemen—all patronage appointments—to prevent election riots among an urban population of 174,000. It was equally impossible, without a registration system, for county or city election judges to exclude from the polls repeat-voters, women dressed in men's clothing, or boys under twenty-one. Failure to increase the number of voting places or to erect fences to control crowds forced as many as 4,000 citizens to vote at one window. The popular practice of "striping" or coloring ballots cost Marylanders

[15]Scharf, *History of Maryland*, 3:250.

their political anonymity; only the intrepid—or politically orthodox—had the courage to walk through election day throngs and place their marked tickets in voting boxes. "I was mortified," complained one Marylander, "to hand in a ticket so marked on the outside that all would know who [*sic*] I was voting for."[16] Legislative dereliction in failing to regulate electoral practices almost guaranteed the political violence and fraud that Marylanders suffered during the decade.

Such corrupt proceedings led many citizens to question the role of political parties in a representative government. Uncomfortable with an institution suspect since the founding of the Republic, some voters responded enthusiastically to the Know-Nothing claim that theirs was a conservative reform organization dedicated "to cleans[ing] the Augean stable of politics, . . . prevent[ing] hordes of reckless prostitutes from plundering our offices, and stop[ping] the mercenary character of the foreign vote and the facility with which it can be influenced by the flimsiest demagogue."[17] In practice, Know-Nothings came to depend on the same type of coercion as their predecessors, but in theory nativist appeals raised hopes that elections could be more than the triumph of "raw force"[18] and that political parties could become responsible institutions.

☆ ☆ ☆

CHANGE WAS NOT CONFINED to the state's political life. From 1840 to 1860, Maryland's population increased by almost 50 percent, a rate of growth unmatched since colonial times.[19] Partly the result of natural increases, this expansion also reflected the arrival of the Irish and Germans, who by 1850 represented 11 percent of the state's

[16]Baltimore *American*, October 16, 1858. In 1857 Baltimore's police force was increased, but even 350 men were unable to forestall the election riots in 1858 and 1859. J. H. Hollander, *The Financial History of Baltimore*, Johns Hopkins Studies in Historical and Political Science, ser. 20 (Baltimore: Johns Hopkins Press, 1899), p. 223. For a description of one Baltimore election, see U.S. Congress, House, *Miscellaneous Documents*, "Papers in the Contested Election," 35th Cong., 1st sess., 1857–58, ser. 962.

[17]*Cecil Whig* (Elkton), November 3, 1855.

[18]*Der Deutsche Correspondent* (Baltimore), October 15, 1858.

[19]Statistics in the following pages are based on the Seventh and Eighth U.S. Census Reports. There are several useful compilations of the census for Maryland, among them Richard Edwards, *Statistical Gazetteer of the State of Maryland and District of Columbia* (Baltimore: J. S. Waters, 1856); R. S. Fisher, *Gazetteer of the State of Maryland, Returns of the 7th Census of the United States* (Baltimore: J. S. Waters, 1852); and Joseph C. G. Kennedy, *Preliminary Report on the Eighth Census, 1860* (Washington, D.C.: Government Printing Office, 1862).

white population. Many of these new Americans, so often the butt of Know-Nothing censure, settled in Baltimore and in the towns of the northwest. Consequently urban population soared during the period as Hagerstown, Frederick, and Cumberland more than doubled their population. While manufacturing flourished—its value tripled in twenty years and by 1860 was double that of the state's agricultural produce—the development of a sophisticated transportation system of railroads, canals, and clipper ships assured the state an important part in the commercial life of the country.

Change came more slowly to the state's farms. An agricultural revival during the 1840s helped to increase the value of the state's annual production. Gradually Maryland farmers turned to the profitable pursuit of truck farming. Thus, along with grain, potatoes, and tobacco, many Maryland farms in 1860 depended on the cultivation of orchard products and vegetables.[20] "I see," concluded one Eastern Shore farmer, "a spirit of improvement in every part of the county and the advancement must be rapid—for the people now begin to inquire about and think about the best modes of improving their lands."[21] The *Cecil Whig* concurred, noting the "rapid advance" of Maryland agriculture: "Where there was one blade of grass, now there are two. The thickets and swamps are disappearing."[22]

The eccentricities of Maryland's geography dictated that such changes would not be felt equally throughout the state. A cartographer's nightmare, Maryland is bisected by the Chesapeake Bay, "that noble sheet of water" which creates two Marylands.[23] On both sides of the Bay, the profiles of the eastern and western shores are pockmarked by rivers—many with names recalling the state's Indian heritage—the Patuxent, Patapsco, Nanticoke, and Potomac. To the west, Maryland's piedmont area gradually slips into another geographic barrier, that of the Appalachian mountains of western Maryland. By

[20]The classic study of the state's agricultural revival is Avery Craven, *Soil Exhaustion as a Factor in Virginia and Maryland, 1806-1860*, University of Illinois Studies, vol. 13 (Urbana: University of Illinois Press, 1925). Craven's conclusion, that Maryland experienced an agricultural revival about 1840, has recently been modified by Eugene Genovese in *The Political Economy of Slavery* (New York: Pantheon, 1965), pp. 124-52. Both studies suffer from the lack of basic research on Maryland agriculture and landholding. In part, Genovese and Craven differ because they fail to take into account the regional differences in the state's agriculture.

[21]William T. Goldsborough to Edward Lloyd VI, August 27, 1850, Lloyd Papers, MHS.

[22]*Cecil Whig* (Elkton), October 9, 1858.

[23]Edwards, *Statistical Gazetteer of Maryland*, p. 13.

1850 geography and tradition had combined to create four divisions within the state—the Eastern Shore, southern Maryland, northwestern Maryland, and Baltimore (Map 1).

Change came rapidly to the northwestern parts of the state. In the counties of Allegany, Frederick, Montgomery, Harford, Baltimore, Howard, Carroll, and Washington, there were fewer Negroes and fewer American and Maryland-born residents than in the southern and eastern parts of the state. The most advanced region agriculturally, this eight-county area produced more than one-half of the state's wheat crop as well as one-third of its corn and oats. The typical western Maryland farm was worth more, produced more, and used more agricultural machinery per acre than its counterpart in southern and eastern Maryland.

Yet the economy of western Maryland had an industrial base as well. Iron, coal, and flour mills as well as tanneries and coal mines attracted both foreign-born and out-of-state workers. In three coal-mining districts of Allegany county, nine out of ten coal miners were foreign-born.[24] By 1860, the northern and western counties attracted 42 percent of the state's investment capital, produced one-third of Maryland's annual industrial production, and employed one-fifth of the state's industrial force. Three important cities, Hagerstown, Cumberland, and Frederick, served the commercial needs of the area. Surely the state's motto, "Crescite et Multiplicamini," applied to this community among the rolling hills of western Maryland.

The most self-conscious of Maryland's regional divisions, the Eastern Shore lay separated from the rest of the state, like an arm thrust between the Chesapeake Bay and the Atlantic Ocean. Only a small spit of land connected this peninsula to Maryland, and the region's recurring threats to secede reflected its isolation. Even Governor Thomas Hicks, so adamantly Unionist during most of the national crisis of 1860–61, held secessionist dreams for the Eastern Shore. As a Dorchester county delegate to the Maryland Constitutional Convention of 1851, Hicks fought unsuccessfully for the inclusion of a clause giving "any portion of the people of this state . . . the right to secede and unite themselves and the territory occupied by them to such adjoining State as they shall elect."[25] Angry over the defeat of an internal improvements bill in 1858, citizens of the East-

[24]Katharine Harvey, *The Best Dressed Coal Miners: Life and Labor in the Maryland Coal Region, 1835–1910* (Ithaca: Cornell University Press, 1969), p. 20.

[25]*Debates and Proceedings of the Maryland Reform Convention to Revise the State Constitution*, 2 vols. (Annapolis: William McNeir, 1851), 1:150.

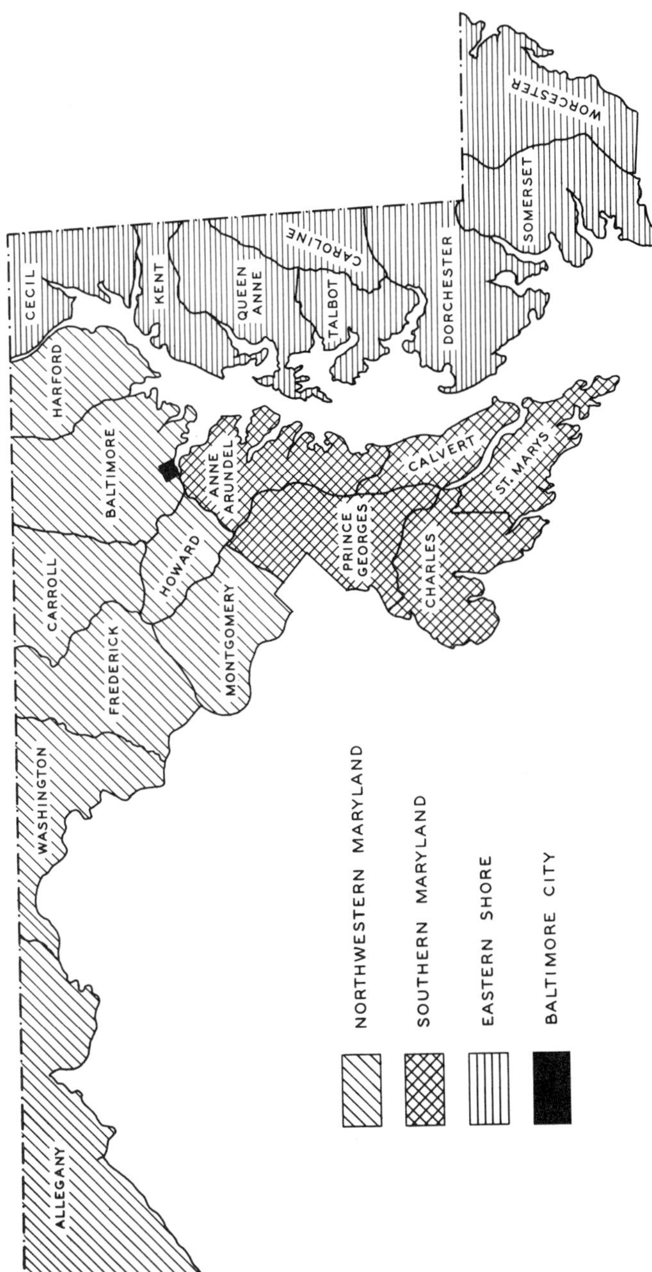

Map 1. *Maryland's Four Regions*

ern Shore displayed their persistent separatism by organizing a regional convention to advance their interests. Even the state's churches bowed to the facts of Maryland sectionalism by establishing separate dioceses on the Shore.[26]

Geographic isolation helped to reinforce a pattern of life quite different from that in western Maryland. On the flat, sandy farms of Kent, Dorchester, Worcester, Somerset, Queen Anne's, Cecil, Talbot, and Caroline counties, white and black farmers raised grains, fruits, and vegetables on agricultural units that ranged in size from Edward Lloyd's baronial 12,000 acres to the holdings, occasionally under ten acres, of Maryland's more modest farmers. The largest towns in this overwhelmingly rural area were Cambridge, Chestertown, and Easton. Little more than villages, none had a population in 1850 of over 2,000. Neither industry nor commerce flourished in such a setting. Only 5 percent of the state's capital was invested in the Eastern Shore's industrial establishments, which by 1860 produced a similar proportion of Maryland's industrial production.

While immigrants poured into Baltimore—as many as 12,000 disembarked in 1846—few chose to travel across the Bay to settle. One Baltimore ward—the Second Ward—contained more than three times the number of foreign-born as the entire Eastern Shore. Most of the region's white residents had been born in Maryland, presumably on the Shore itself, and static population figures suggest that some native sons and daughters chose to move away.

Ethnically homogeneous, the Eastern Shore held a more varied racial mix. With a fifth of the state's white population, the Shore contained one-third of Maryland's black population. Gradually, as slavery declined in economic importance, the number of free Negroes increased, until in 1860 almost one-half of the Eastern Shore's black population was free. Some slaves simply ran away and joined the large free Negro population living in the region. Others, like Frederick Douglass, escaped to free states north of the Mason-Dixon line. The unending complaints of the state's 14,000 slaveowners about "runaways" went unanswered,[27] and by 1860, Maryland had the largest free Negro population in the Union, and was second only to Kentucky in the number of fugitive slaves reported to census takers. Some slaves

[26]Baltimore *Sun*, February 25, April 19, 1858; *Cecil Democrat* (Elkton), April 21, 1858; Ezekiel F. Chambers to J. A. Pearce, March 30, 1858, Pearce Papers, MHS.

[27]Such complaints were numerous. For examples, see the Baltimore *American*, June 29, 1858; *Cecil Democrat* (Elkton), July 3, 1858; P. Bradley to Edward Lloyd VI, January 5, 1850, Lloyd Papers.

were quietly freed by their masters, and although the legal process of manumission became increasingly difficult after the 1830s, Maryland had almost double the number of manumissions than any other state in 1860. "The value of Negroes who have left the state and have never been recovered," one Baltimorean acidly remarked to a Massachusetts correspondent, "would probably endow a college as richly as Harvard."[28]

Across fifteen miles of the Chesapeake Bay lay another rural and agricultural region, southern Maryland, an area marked by its dedication to tobacco production and slavery. Of all Maryland's regions, the southern Maryland counties of Charles, Calvert, St. Mary's, Prince Georges, and Anne Arundel had changed the least since colonial days. The traditional commitment to tobacco still affected both the economic and social life. There were more planters with over twenty slaves than in any other region of Maryland; farms were larger, though worth less per acre, than the state average. From Annapolis to Leonardtown few villages, factories, or even mills intruded on this rural calm. Even the area's popular recreations—jousting and tournaments—were the amusements of an unchanging rural gentry.[29]

Similar to the Eastern Shore in its racial and ethnic composition, in 1860 southern Maryland held only 7 percent of the state's white population, most of whom were Maryland-born. Blacks outnumbered whites in the five-county region, for almost one-half of the state's slaves lived in southern Maryland. This was the work force that produced Maryland's famous oronoco tobacco. Yet for many planters, tobacco culture, even with the heavy use of marl and Peruvian guano, no longer was profitable. Some farmers struggled to alleviate the effects of soil exhaustion by raising grains, and the increasing production of wheat, corn, and oats demonstrated their success.[30]

The industrial and commercial hub of these disparate regions was Baltimore, third-largest city in the United States and for some Marylanders, "the soul of the state." Formed from an indentation of the Chesapeake Bay and a deep channel which connected its harbor to the Bay, Baltimore's port built the city. Cumberland coal, flour from local

[28] Frederick Brune to John Murray Forbes, June 21, 1861, Brune Papers, MHS.

[29] Mrs. Benjamin G. Harris of southern Maryland described such a tournament held near Leonardtown in 1859. "The Knights looked well and fought gallantly. Dr._____, being the victor presented the crown to_____, who made a grateful reply to his gallant address. The Knights rode in order to Town and the maids to their homes." Diary of Mrs. Benjamin G. Harris, September 26, 1859, Harris Papers, MHS; Port Tobacco *Times*, September 24, 1857.

[30] *The American Farmer* 14 (February 1859): 257.

mills, tobacco from Virginia and Maryland, Peruvian guano, South American coffee—all found their way to the busy docks along Pratt, Light, and Lancaster streets. This trade, valued at over $150 million by 1860, used the state's sophisticated transportation system of national roads, state-subsidized canals and railroads, and privately owned clipper ships.

The city's position as a port stimulated the related growth of industry until, by 1850, Baltimore produced more manufactured goods than any other southern city, including St. Louis. Baltimore's sugar refineries, tanneries, clothing and textile factories, iron mills, and a myriad of other concerns had tripled their output in the twenty years from 1840 to 1860. By 1860, "the queen city of the South," as Baltimore was called, employed over one-half of the state's industrial workers and produced an equivalent percentage of Maryland's annual industrial production. Yet even before the Civil War the state's recurring problem—a lack of financial capital—inhibited the growth of manufacturing.[31]

During the 1840s and 1850s the city's population changed dramatically. By 1860 one out of every four citizens had been born in Europe. The majority of these new Baltimoreans were German, not, as is often thought, the ubiquitous Irish. Another 12 percent of the city's population was black. The increasing competition between these two groups for Baltimore's unskilled jobs led to considerable violence among the city's workers, as Frederick Douglass had found in the 1830s when white workers ambushed him near the Fells Point shipyards. By the 1860s some slaveholders found their slaves displaced from profitable employment in the city's docks and factories by the burgeoning immigrant population.[32]

[31]The city suffered from a lack of both corporate and private capital. Although third in population, Baltimore was eleventh in bank capital. Furthermore, few Baltimoreans could match the private resources of New York, Philadelphia, and Boston millionaires. In fact, there were no individual millionaires in Baltimore, and only four citizens, including Johns Hopkins, claimed assets over $500,000, although the Garrett family had assets of over $1 million. Manuscript Census Returns, Eighth Census, 1860, vols. 4–6. See also *Real and Personal Assessments* (pamphlets), MHS; *Cecil Democrat* (Elkton), May 30, 1857; Baltimore *American*, February 12, 1858; William B. Catton, *John W. Garrett of the Baltimore and Ohio: A Study in Seaport and Railroad Competition, 1820–1874* (Ann Arbor, Mich.: University Microfilms, 1959), p. 82; Edward Pessen, "The Egalitarian Myth and the American Social Reality: Wealth, Mobility, and Equality in the Era of the Common Man," *American Historical Review* 76 (October 1971): 989–1034.

[32]M. Ray Della, "The Problems of Negro Labor in the 1850's," *Maryland Historical Magazine* 66 (Spring 1971): 14–32. See also Frederick Douglass, *Life and Times of Frederick Douglass* (New York: Collier, 1962), pp. 176–86, and the Baltimore *American*, October 11, 1858.

The size, growth, and composition of Baltimore's population frightened rural Marylanders, who considered the city an aggressive behemoth. Thomas Hicks expressed this sentiment when he asked whether "the people of the Eastern Shore [are] to be retained as serfs, hewers of wood and drawers of water for the city of Baltimore."[33] Under the Constitution of 1851, malapportionment, gerrymandering, and rotation of offices among the state's regions quieted such fears and guaranteed the protection of other Marylanders from "the power Baltimore would have under King Numbers."[34]

☆ ☆ ☆

DIVIDED BY POLITICAL AND economic changes, Marylanders still found much to unite them. One bond was a common past. Unique events from Maryland history—the state's tradition as a haven for Catholics, the attacks by colonial adventurers from nearby Virginia and Pennsylvania, the contribution of Maryland forces during the Revolution and the War of 1812—all served as the historical material of which collective pride is made. State histories and textbooks cultivated such feelings; one such account found "the people swelling with recollections of the past."[35] The loyalty many Marylanders felt toward their state was demonstrated during the secession crisis. According to Severn Teackle Wallis, a Baltimore lawyer, "whatever the decision of Maryland shall be, in that decision I shall acquiesce, for my home and destiny are here."[36]

By the 1860s Marylanders celebrated attachment to their state with a variety of symbolic rites. They observed special state holidays; a particular favorite was Defender's Day, the annual remembrance of the Battle of North Point, where in 1814 Maryland troops had defeated the British and saved Baltimore from the burning that Washington suffered. By 1850 many Marylanders recognized the unifying effects of such an experience, though few expressed their thoughts as

[33] *Debates and Proceedings of the Maryland Reform Convention*, 2:282.

[34] Frederick *Examiner*, March 17, 1858.

[35] James McSherry, *A History of Maryland from Its Settlement to the Year 1848* (Baltimore: John Murphy & Co., 1850), p. 378. McSherry's widely used account—with its lists of Maryland soldiers and officers of the Revolution—is an excellent example of the laudatory histories Marylanders read. For an example of a typical public address, see George William Brown, *A Sketch of the Life of Thomas Donaldson* (Baltimore: Cushings and Bailey, 1881), p. 22.

[36] Severn Teackle Wallis, *Writings of Severn Teackle Wallis*, 4 vols. (Baltimore: John Murphy & Co., 1896), 2:139, 140.

artistically as the Reverend J. N. McJilton in his poem in honor of a Baltimore monument to heroes of the War of 1812:

Thou art a sentinel standing amid
Civil contentions, and the waves have rolled
In party feuds around thy lovely plinth,
But they have fallen harmless.[37]

On many occasions patriotic speeches abounded with fervent rhetoric extolling the state. The virtuoso, dithyrambic performance of one Know-Nothing politician, who in a breath glorified all Maryland, was by no means unique:

> Americans of the everlasting Alleganian mountains dash down from your fortresses with irresistible force and gather new strength from the rich valley of the county honored by the name of the Father of his Country. . . . Then sweep through Montgomery's fair fields and land of Carroll endeared to us by revolutionary memories until you reach . . . Howard and Arundel. Your majority will meet with American voices from the land of pilgrims of St. Mary's, Prince Georges' dark forests, Charles' Potomac Shore and Calvert's broad fields, ennobled by memories of Baltimore's first proprietary. Meanwhile let the tide of American majorities from Worcester's Island roll us along the plains of the Eastern Shore swelled by voices of Somerset, Dorchester, Caroline, Queen Anne, Kent, Cecil, and Talbot, and wheeling around the head of our own noble bay be ready to join old Harford, and nicely balanced Baltimore, . . . and swell our own Baltimore majority.[38]

Along with the heritage of the past, Marylanders found common bonds in the problems of the present. Like many states, Maryland's financing of canals and railroads during the 1830s ended in debts and economic embarrassment. Echoing from Worcester to Allegany, the debate over how to repay this debt often transcended sectional lines and became a partisan issue. Southern Marylanders joined Frederick merchants in urging repudiation of the debt, while Baltimore manufacturers and Eastern Shore farmers insisted on increased taxation to pay the interest on state bonds. By the 1850s, despite the sectional roots of Maryland parties, there were still general issues such as the need for funding a public school system and the future of the state's free Negroes which diminished the centrifugal tendencies of Maryland regionalism.

Political parties organized, stimulated, and directed most of the discussion of state issues. No other organization—although by 1860 there were many statewide associations—cut across the regional paro-

[37] J. N. McJilton, *Poems* (Boston: Otis Broaders & Co., 1840), p. 227.

[38] *Cecil Whig* (Elkton), February 4, 1858.

chialism of Maryland as effectively as the political party, for few institutions were more directly involved in formulating, defining, and solving state problems. While there were some differences in party structures, both Democrats and Know-Nothings organized their political machinery on a statewide basis. Delegates elected at local meetings assembled in a state convention which in turn chose a president of the state central committee, the titular head of the state party. By the 1850s parties served as financiers of newspapers, committees of correspondence, initiators of debate, and supporters of political programs.

Every two years state concerns received formal legislative attention when the Senate and the House of Delegates met in the ancient Georgian capitol at Annapolis. By constitutional fiat and long precedent, the legislature held the power to enact laws for the counties and city of Baltimore,[39] and thus was greatly involved in local legislation relating to Maryland's subdivisions. Such an arrangement meant that even the most parochial issues found their way to Annapolis where, along with problems affecting the state as a whole, they became the concern of political parties. Legislators consistently responded to general issues as members of a political party rather than as representatives of a section. Even in the 1850s when parties were often debilitated, delegates still voted more frequently along party than sectional lines.[40]

Yet Marylanders found little to applaud in the performance of their political system in the late 1850s, and this distaste encouraged

[39]The power of the General Assembly to legislate for local subdivisions has been traced back to colonial times, when the Governor's Council held unusual powers over the counties. See Lois Green Carr, "County Government in Maryland, 1689-1712" (Ph.D. diss., Harvard University, 1968). See also V. O. Key, *The Problem of Local Legislation in Maryland* (Maryland State Planning Commission and Legislative Council, 1940).

[40]Using a program on file at the Johns Hopkins Computing Center, I determined the index of cohesion for forty-eight roll calls in the 1856 and 1858 legislatures. Indexes of cohesion measure the degree to which individual party members vote together on a scale of 1-100; the higher the index, the greater the degree of party cohesion and discipline. I also broke the state into regions and tested the degree of cohesiveness among members from the Eastern Shore, southern Maryland, Baltimore, and the northwest counties. My forty-eight roll calls were chosen for the following reasons: (1) they were roll calls that affected the state as a whole, not just one subdivision; (2) they were roll calls in which two-thirds of the House of Delegates participated; (3) on the basis of newspaper reports they were roll calls of general interest; (4) they were roll calls on a variety of different issues such as slavery, the status of free Negroes, corporations, education, etc. The highest index of cohesion—67—for members of a region in 1858 was that of delegates from the Eastern Shore, while that for members of the Democratic and Know-Nothing parties was 73 and 74, respectively. See Appendix B and Appendix Table D-1 for results of roll-call analysis.

the formation of new organizations and the improvement of old ones. While Know-Nothings made capital of this growing disenchantment by promising reform, Democrats complained that parties were corrupt and inept. Thus an increasing number of Marylanders found partisan politics "unnecessary, wholly injurious," "without principle, corrupted, perverted and absurd."[41] Only a few Democrats still recognized the contributions of parties; to most it seemed that "the age of virtuous politics" was past.[42] Philip Friese, the Baltimore author of one of the few systematic attempts to analyze American politics, agreed that abuses far outweighed the positive values of partisan organizations, and Friese therefore urged a new system of political parties.[43]

Thus the two decades before the Civil War brought rapid change to Maryland. By 1851 some complained of "the morbid love of change which has seized our people everywhere. . . . Change suggests change as rapidly and as recklessly as though the world was but beginning."[44] These patterns of change bore unequally on the state's disparate regions, and hence reinforced the mosaic of sections so long a part of Maryland tradition. Yet even during a period of fluctuation, the maligned political party served to unify a diverse and often divided state. Parties themselves were not immune from alteration, and on the eve of the Civil War, Marylanders attempted to refashion their political parties, as they had changed their society. In the words of Philip Friese, "parties cannot be fossilized. They are subject to an organic law of growth and decay."[45] In Maryland the time for a new political system had come.

[41] *Cecil Democrat* (Elkton), June 6, 1857; John P. Kennedy, "Journals," September 29, 1859; John P. Kennedy to Robert C. Winthrop, February 20, 1857, Kennedy Papers, Peabody Library, Baltimore, Md.

[42] Annapolis *Gazette*, July 19, 1860.

[43] Philip Friese, *An Essay on Party Showing Its Uses and Abuses and Its Natural Dissolution* (New York: Fowler and Welles, 1856). There are few systematic attempts to analyze American political parties before the end of the nineteenth century. Richard Hofstadter, while he reviews those of Francis Lieber, Alexis de Tocqueville, and Jabez Hammond, omits any consideration of Friese's perceptive and revealing monograph. Richard Hofstadter, *The Idea of a Party System* (Berkeley and Los Angeles: University of California Press, 1969), pp. 252–71.

[44] *Planter's Advocate* (Upper Marlboro), November 5, 1851, quoted in Evitts, "Matter of Allegiances," p. 30.

[45] Friese, *Essay on Party*, p. 41.

II. "A NEW TACK": THE TRANSFORMATION OF MARYLAND PARTIES, 1858-1860

ON A COLD JANUARY DAY IN 1860, Maryland legislators, lobbyists, and patronage seekers traveled to Annapolis for the biennial session of the legislature. Journeying by steamer, by the Baltimore and Elkridge's unpredictable railroad cars, and by innumerable horse carriages, these Marylanders crowded into the inadequate accommodations of the state capital. In a lengthy address to the delegates, Governor Thomas Hicks directed attention to a variety of state problems. The Know-Nothing governor gave particular emphasis to the need for a new penal code and militia system. Aware of the legislative penchant for local and special bills, Hicks warned against "the postponement and even exclusion of great public measures affecting the whole state."[1]

A typical group of Maryland legislators, delegates to the 1860 Assembly included "six planters, thirty farmers, five physicians, twelve lawyers, one lumber dealer, four merchants, one contractor, six mechanics, one student-at-law, one shipbuilder, one oyster packer, two manufacturers, three millers, and one mayor."[2] Over one-half of the seventy-four delegates were either lawyers or farmers, and a nearly equal proportion—52 percent—held slaves, although in the state as a whole, only 2 percent of the white population and 16 percent of Maryland's families held slaves. With median holdings of $18,000 in personal and real property, legislators were far wealthier than their fellow Marylanders and frequently were identified as "aristocrats." Although many had served in county political jobs before their election, only ten delegates had any legislative experience, a not surprising statistic for a group whose median age was 43 years.

Among this cross section of the Maryland gentry were forty-six Democrats, enough to give the Democracy control of the lower house. After six years of Know-Nothing domination, Democrats had com-

[1] "Message of the Governor to the General Assembly," Doc. A, *House Documents* (Annapolis, Md.: Beale H. Richardson, 1860), p. 4; Baltimore *Sun*, January 7, 1860.

[2] Easton *Gazette*, January 28, 1860. A broadside in the Maryland Historical Society, "A List of Members of the Maryland Legislature—Extra Session, 1861," also gives the occupations of these delegates. The following profile is based on the Manuscript Census Returns, Schedule No. 1, Free Inhabitants; Schedule No. 2, Slave Inhabitants, Eighth Census, 1860. I checked these findings with Ralph A. Wooster's "The Membership of the Maryland Legislature of 1861," *Maryland Historical Magazine* 56 (March 1961): 94–102. Wooster has also studied the legislatures of the lower South, and Maryland legislators were quite similar, socially and economically, to their counterparts in the South with two exceptions. There were more slaveholders and lawyers among delegates in the deep South. Ralph Wooster, *The People in Power: Courthouse and Statehouse in the Lower South, 1850–1860* (Knoxville: University of Tennessee Press, 1969), pp. 3–47.

bined new voters with defectors from the opposition to win fourteen of Maryland's counties. Only heavy Know-Nothing majorities from the city of Baltimore prevented a victory for the Democratic candidate for Comptroller, A. Lingan Jarrett. To encourage faithful workers in the counties, Democratic newspapers carefully omitted Baltimore from their election returns, and such statistics clearly exposed the Know-Nothing weakness outside of Baltimore. For many Marylanders, the election heralded the rejuvenation of the Democratic party. Chagrined opponents admitted a "sweeping Democratic triumph," while party members spoke with enthusiasm of "redeeming the past" and the "success of our new tack."[3]

This "new tack" represented the attempt by some Democrats to strengthen their organization by demanding loyalty from party leaders. While voting appeals continued to include exhortations to "Old Line Whigs," these same Whigs were increasingly excluded from party leadership. The Whig antecedents of U.S. Senator James A. Pearce, so helpful to Democrats in 1854, were no longer a benefit in 1859. In fact, friends warned Pearce that after twenty-two years of service in Congress and a voting record which would do credit to the most loyal Democrat, the 1860 legislature might oust him "for a straight out and old tried Democrat . . . to give confidence to the rank and file."[4] Henry Winter Davis, the Know-Nothing Congressman, happily observed "a pretty conflict between Old Line Whigs acting as Democrats who demand Pearce or Hambleton and the pure Democrats who will have nothing but a pure Democrat."[5] Pearce petulantly denied that he was not "candid" in his support for the party. "I have been," he declared in a statement published in many newspapers, "a Democrat since 1854."[6] Apparently such pronouncements of fealty were sufficient to convince Democrats in the legislature who returned him to the Senate, although not before a fight with a "pure" Democrat.

Intent on finding those "who have never swerved from or deserted their Democracy," party leaders had trouble discovering "pure" Democrats in a state where the political reshuffling of the early 1850s

[3]Baltimore *Sun*, November 11, 1859; Baltimore *American*, November 4, 1859; Frederick *Herald*, November 10, 1859.

[4]George Kane to Pearce, November 19, 1859, Pearce Papers, MHS.

[5]Davis to Samuel F. Du Pont, November 11, 1859, Du Pont Papers, Eleutherian Mills Historical Library, Wilmington, Del.; William Hamilton, whose name Davis misspelled, was a Democratic congressman from Washington county in the 1850s who became a Democratic senator during Reconstruction.

[6]Baltimore *Sun*, February 18, 24, 1860.

had produced "half-way politicians"[7] and where, as one disgusted Democrat said, "the ranks of the Democracy are studded with the brilliants of the Whig party."[8] By 1860, however, the Democratic search for the "untainted" produced a younger leadership than that of Know-Nothing counterparts.[9] Occasionally the youth of party candidates caused complaints from voters,[10] but such dissatisfaction was of secondary importance to Democrats intent on forming an effective political machine.

Virtually all Democratic leaders, whether legislators, holders of important patronage jobs, or members of the state central committee, came from well-known families, and many held surnames long familiar to Marylanders such as Dorsey, Brune, Bowie, Glenn, and Stewart. With wealth to match their social position, these gentlemen of property and standing owned sizable estates and claimed considerable assets at a time when the average Maryland family claimed $2,300.[11] Typical for nineteenth-century leaders, such privileged social and economic status was quite similar to that enjoyed by Know-Nothing leaders, although Democrats were more likely to own slaves and be planters than their opponents. In many cases, Democratic leaders had some family tradition of political service—a father or a grandfather, a brother or an uncle who had served in an appointive or elective public post. Because the same wealthy families provided leaders, Maryland politics often appeared the exclusive, and continuing, preserve of the gentry.[12]

In the late 1850s Democrats made several changes in their party structure to take advantage of the growing power of county governments. The Constitution of 1851, by increasing the number of elected officials, had correspondingly diminished the governor's patronage and by 1855, the governor's so-called "blue bag" of political favors held only 160 jobs. Meanwhile, local jobs had increased until the county commissioners often controlled over fifty appointments. The expan-

[7] Port Tobacco *Times*, March 17, 1859; Easton *Gazette*, December 18, 1857.

[8] *Maryland Union* (Frederick), November 25, 1858.

[9] See Appendix Table D-2.

[10] *Cecil Democrat* (Elkton), October 1, 1859.

[11] See Appendix Tables D-2, D-3, D-4, and D-5 for a profile of 106 party leaders. According to one newspaper, 64 percent of all Marylanders claimed assets valued under $2,000, while 11 percent claimed holdings of under $100. The average holding obtained by dividing the total amount of assets claimed by the number of free Marylanders is $695. *Cecil Democrat* (Elkton), July 2, 1858.

[12] Over 60 percent of the 106 leaders in the Democratic sample studied had a relative in politics.

sion in the number of elected officials, ranging from judges to clerks of the county court, combined with the increase in patronage, stimulated the development of local machines. Before 1851, the governor had simply appointed such officials; now local parties vigorously contested their election, and from such partisan competitions developed a strong county political system.[13]

Gradually, Democratic county organizations duplicated the structure of state parties. The same hierarchy of local meetings chose delegates to a county convention, which in turn made nominations and passed resolutions. In nearly all cases, these meetings focused on national rather than on local problems. Typical of such assemblies was an 1860 Frederick convention in which delegates resolved to support the national Democratic platform and to oppose congressional interference with slavery in the territories. The meeting ended, however, without mention or resolution of local or state issues.[14] Between elections, executive committees, chosen at such county meetings, represented the interests of the party and raised money by the traditional salary assessments on local officeholders.

By 1860, in the occasional confrontations between county and state organizations, it was usually the weaker state central committee which gave way. The head of the Democratic city organization, Joshua Vansant, a Baltimore hatmaker, admitted that the party was a collection of county units and urged that such local divisions be respected. Thus when the state central committee tried to change the slate of candidates chosen at a Frederick convention, angry local Democrats charged "interference."[15] Indeed, the state central committee, now appointed by the chairman of the state convention rather than elected by delegates, represented the choices of each county delegation within the legislature, and not the preference of the entire convention. Gradually the power of the county machines had grown to such an extent that the St. Mary's Democratic convention felt no incongruity in mak-

[13]James Wingate, *The Maryland Register for 1857* (Baltimore: Sherwood, 1857). The term "blue bag," of unknown origin, is still used to describe gubernatorial appointments, while the Mayor of Baltimore's patronage is referred to as the "green bag."

[14]*Maryland Union* (Frederick), March 15, 1860. This emphasis on national issues, partially the result of Maryland's location and consequent fears of war and Negro insurrections, and partially the result of the desire to avoid disruptive local issues, clearly separates Maryland from other states and cities. Even in the days just before the war, such communities as Pittsburgh were far more interested in local issues such as railroads than in national concerns. See Michael Holt, *Forging a Majority: The Republican Party in Pittsburgh, 1848–1860* (New Haven: Yale University Press, 1969).

[15]*Cecil Democrat* (Elkton), February 11, 1860.

ing a nomination for President. The man so honored was Roger B. Taney, a native of neighboring Calvert county and the author of the majority opinion in the locally popular Dred Scott decision.[16]

Both state and county organizations elected delegates to nominating conventions where, again by vote, party nominees were chosen. In the past, some candidates had simply announced their intention to run and because of their reputation, experience, or financial resources, the party placed them on Democratic tickets. In 1857, the party's central committee merely recommended the election of John C. Groome, its gubernatorial candidate, without a formal convention vote. By 1859, such politics of deference had disappeared, and William Preston, a prominent congressional candidate, learned to his dismay that no political aspirant should simply assume his party would support him. Refusing to contest his nomination in primary meetings, Preston insisted that the party make its choices without the candidates themselves contending for the nomination, a process which, in his view, only weakened the party. Such lofty principles, uttered while his opponent was busy lining up delegate support, led to Preston's defeat.[17]

Increasingly during the 1850s, Democrats found local issues divisive and replaced them with national appeals. The familiar campaign promises of earlier decades—to prohibit Virginia oystermen from Maryland waters, to end the lottery, and to repay the state's debts—disappeared and were replaced by national concerns. Even readers of small county newspapers found local news preempted by editorial debate on the Dred Scott decision and the future of Kansas. Indeed at the state convention in 1859, Democrats, after invocations to Jefferson, Madison, and Jackson, resolved to support Buchanan's policy on Kansas and work for "unity and liberty." A Democratic newspaper explained the reason for this new emphasis: "We trust the Democrats throughout the state will act as becomes a great national party and will not permit local matters to divide them."[18] By avoiding the distractions of local concerns, Democrats hoped to gain the votes of Marylanders sympathetic to their positions on national issues.

To counter growing division between North and South in the late 1850s, Maryland Democrats injected frequent appeals to the national symbols of Constitution and Union into their political campaigns. As

[16] Frederick *Examiner*, August 22, 1860; *St. Mary's Beacon* (Leonardtown), August 20, 1860.

[17] William Preston, "Scrapbooks," October 1857; Preston to the Editors of the *Sun*, September 1857; Preston to Henry Gifford, October 14, 1857, Preston Papers, MHS.

[18] *Cecil Democrat* (Elkton), February 21, 1857.

one prominent southern Marylander explained: "A glance at the platform of parties is sufficient to convince us of the importance of Democracy. Upon the success of the Democracy depends the preservation of Union, Liberty, and Constitution."[19] Using a theme that was to become even more important in the 1860s, Democrats accused Know-Nothings of violating the "Constitutional liberty" of Catholics and foreign-born.[20]

Such vague appeals to the symbols of nationhood served two party purposes—the need for issues which increased political harmony and concern in a border state for the future of the Union. Although Maryland Know-Nothings attempted to voice the same appeals, Democrats were more successful because they connected love of Union with defense of the South. In this way, Augustus R. Sollers, a former American party congressman, explained his defection from the party that had elected him:

> I am forced into the ranks of the Democratic party, despite prejudices engendered by twenty years of active opposition, because I behold in that party the only bulwark of Southern rights, the only political organization capable of stemming the tide of Northern fanaticism and of supporting in their integrity the Constitution and Union.[21]

From the perspective of Sollers and many other Democrats, Know-Nothings had joined the Republican party—an organization built by antislavery extremists and nurtured by antisouthern fanatics. "Married in Washington," announced one county paper, "Young Sam Know Nothing and Black Republican Widow Bloody Kansas." According to this dispatch, three Maryland congressmen, all Know-Nothings, had served as attendants of the groom. Such a liaison convinced Democrats that Know-Nothings had become "wooly heads who went all to Frémont and free Negroes."[22] As further evidence of the associations of Know-Nothings and abolitionists, Democrats pointed to the career of Henry Winter Davis, the Baltimore congressman who provided a continuing link between the two organizations. His votes

[19]Speech of Colonel William Coad, 1859, Coad Papers, owned by Charles Fenwick, Leonardtown, Md.

[20]James Raymond, *Political: Or, the Spirit of the Democracy in '56* (Baltimore: James Woods, 1857), pp. 22, 23, 25, and 66.

[21]Baltimore *Sun*, August 26, 1859. Cynics complained that Sollers's defection also stemmed from his anger at not having been nominated Comptroller by his party. Frederick *Examiner*, August 31, 1859.

[22]*Cecil Democrat* (Elkton), June 5, 1858; February 21, 1857. "Sam" was the nickname given to the Know-Nothing party during the 1850s, and Frémont was the Republican Presidential candidate in 1856.

for Northerners in the protracted speakership contests in 1856 and 1860, his intemperate attacks on Democrats, and his insulting assertion that Maryland should align herself with the North were evidence, for Democrats, "that Republicanism is marching Southward."[23]

Behind such attacks on the Republicans lay growing racial fears in a border state, where one of every five persons was a black and where the free Negro population had grown 20 percent in the decade 1840-50. Clearly Maryland's persistent attempts to colonize Negroes in Africa had failed to decrease the state's black population, and some Marylanders, frightened by the inexorable increases in the free Negro population, now concluded that blacks should choose between "going into slavery or leaving the state."[24] In 1859, a slaveholder's convention, organized by Democrats and chaired by James Pearce, Maryland's Democratic senator, explored the possibility of expelling free Negroes. Only the realization that such a law would remove a large part of the state's household and agricultural laborers forestalled a recommendation to the legislature that Maryland become a haven for white men.[25]

Shortly before the 1859 elections, events served to confirm Democratic fears for Constitution and Union, as well as party antagonism toward Republicans and free blacks. On an October night, just two weeks before the state elections, John Brown and his small band of eighteen followers, including five black men, stole from their hideaway in western Maryland and attacked the federal arsenal at Harpers Ferry. According to one account, "silently and stealthily descend[ed] upon Harpers Ferry under cover of darkness upon a Sabbath evening an armed band of murderous insurgents for the purpose of exciting a servile and bloody insurrection."[26] The intended purpose of Brown,

[23] *Cecil Democrat* (Elkton), July 10, 1857. For other Democratic complaints of the connections between Republicans and Know-Nothings, see *Der Deutsche Correspondent* (Baltimore), September 8, 11, 13, 1858; *Maryland Union* (Frederick), February 4, 1858; February 23, 1860; Easton *Gazette*, September 17, 1859.

[24] Baltimore *Sun*, November 6, 1858. See also Penelope Campbell, *Maryland in Africa: The Maryland State Colonization Society, 1831-1857* (Columbus: Ohio State University Press, 1971).

[25] Baltimore *American*, June 9, 1859; James M. Wright, *The Free Negro in Maryland, 1634-1860*, Columbia University Studies in History, Economics and Public Law, vol. 97 (New York: Columbia University Press, 1921), p. 311. Many Know-Nothings called this slaveholder's meeting a "partisan" movement by Democrats. Frederick *Examiner*, May 11, 18, 1859.

[26] *Cecil Democrat* (Elkton), October 22, 1859. The extensive bibliography on Brown has recently been enhanced by Stephen Oates's *To Purge This Land with Blood: A Biography of John Brown* (New York: Harper and Row, 1970).

who was acting for the abolitionist cause that consumed his life, was to seize arms for the liberation of Virginia's slaves. Captured quickly by federal forces under the future commander of the Confederacy, Robert E. Lee, Brown's trial and subsequent execution in Virginia hardly diminished the consciousness of Marylanders that a violent war against slavery had begun in their state. Though cooler heads realized that the event "dwindles into insignificance as literal facts are brought out," in the imagination of some, Maryland would soon take its place alongside Jamaica, Haiti, and Santo Domingo as the site of a bloody racial revolution.[27]

Brown's attempt to end slavery vividly illustrated the threat to Maryland by "fanatic Republicans" and was, in the partisan dialogue of 1859, "the legitimate fruit, the natural consequence and the inevitable result of Republican doctrine."[28] The national controversies over Kansas and Lecompton were no longer party abstractions. In the few weeks before the election, Democrats used Harpers Ferry to demonstrate a variety of partisan conclusions: the ineffectiveness of Governor Hicks and "the feeble Know Nothing allegiance to protect the South,"[29] the fanaticism of Northern Republicans, a few of whom had financed John Brown's raid, and the consequent need to support Democrats. One Democratic delegate predicted that the incident would ensure his election, and Henry Winter Davis admitted that Harpers Ferry was indeed the turning point of the campaign.[30] Angry Know-Nothings agreed and called the state assembly, elected in November, "the John Brown Legislature."[31]

☆ ☆ ☆

DEMOCRATS IN THE LEGISLATURE, owing their election to the renewed strength of their party and increasing fears of free Negroes, as well as to John Brown's fortuitous intervention, promptly moved to cement their new position. With the sure instincts of successful politi-

[27]Baltimore *Sun*, October 19, 1859.

[28]*Ibid.*, November 7, 1859.

[29]*Planter's Advocate* (Upper Marlboro), October 26, 1859. Hicks was accused of not sending the militia quickly enough, and in fact, as Robert E. Lee pointed out in his Letterbooks, the Maryland troops did little except to hunt for the carbines hidden by Brown. Lee to Colonel S. Cooper, December 24, 1859, "Letterbooks," Lee Papers, Historical Society of Virginia, Richmond, Va.

[30]Frederick *Examiner*, October 26, 1859; Davis to Samuel F. Du Pont, November 11, 1859, Du Pont Papers.

[31]Frederick *Examiner*, March 14, 1860.

cians, party members did nothing to intrude on the local issues which occupied over a quarter of the legislature's time.[32] County delegations, now largely controlled by Democrats, served as committees to draft legislation, receive petitions, and determine which bills should be sent to the Assembly. Few legislators, even from the opposition, quarreled with the prerogatives and power of local delegations who determined legislative policy toward their county; hence 48 percent of all roll calls passed unanimously.

Democrats excepted Baltimore from their prohibition on interfering in local matters. To free the city from its corrupt elections, unruly mobs, and, most particularly, its Know-Nothing rule became an essential part of Democratic strategy. With nearly one-third of the state's population, the city could not be neglected, for it had too many votes and too much patronage and power. In 1857, Democrats had helped organize a City Reform Association in order to attract Baltimoreans from their Know-Nothing attachments. The failure of the reformers to win in 1859 led Democrats to insist that the legislature serve "as a posse comitatus to free the city."[33] To this end, Democrats voted to restrict the city's control over its police force and to institute new judicial and election procedures. Furious, Henry Winter Davis complained that the legislature was trying "to yoke Baltimore" with "revolutionary" bills.[34]

United on such political matters, Democrats also voted together on a variety of issues ranging from internal improvements to changes in the judicial code and educational system. Despite their numerical dominance within the legislature—a status which sometimes threatens

[32]In 1860, 28 percent of the roll calls in the session involved local legislation affecting particular counties or subdivisions within counties, 46 percent involved special incorporations or legislation affecting particular individuals and interest groups, and only 25 percent of the bills voted on in the 1860 legislature affected the entire state.

[33]*Maryland Union* (Frederick), July 28, 1859; Baltimore *Sun*, July 22, 1859. According to a Know-Nothing newspaper, of 158 Reform leaders, 140 were "known" Democrats. Frederick *Examiner*, November 10, 1858; *Cecil Whig* (Elkton), October 30, 1858; Baltimore *American*, August 17, 1858; October 19, 1859. The Easton *Gazette* reached the same conclusion. "The Democracy has gotten tired of its old name and now clothes itself with reform, but that garment appeared to wear precious little in the last contest than its old coat." Easton *Gazette*, October 15, 1859. Henry Winter Davis agreed and called Reformers "loco focos and a few carping and timid and cranky merchants." Davis to Du Pont, October 20, 1859, Du Pont Papers. Among the reformers in 1859, I found fifty-four Democrats, including Adam Denmead, Charles Howard, Severn Teackle Wallis and George Brown, and only two former Know-Nothings. During the time the Reform League was active the Democrats made no nominations in the city.

[34]Davis to Du Pont, January 26, February 7, 1860, Du Pont Papers.

discipline—Democratic delegates found membership in their party a more important factor in determining their votes than their representation of one of the state's four regions.[35]

Democrats also achieved a surprising degree of unity on virtually all bills relating to free Negroes and slaves. Encouraged by various petitions to reduce the number of free Negroes, to make manumission more difficult, and even to auction Negroes to the highest bidder, the Democratic-controlled Committee on Colored Population presented a comprehensive legislative program designed to make it harder to be a free black man in the state. In the words of committee chairman Curtis M. Jacobs, an Eastern Shore planter who owned 200 slaves, "free negroism is an excrescence, a blight, a mildew, a fungus, hanging on to and corrupting the social and moral elements of our people."[36] By vote of the 1860 legislature, subject to county approval, manumission was prohibited; colonization and departure from the state were encouraged; free Negroes were entitled to renounce their freedom and choose their own masters; free Negroes, now required to be registered by county commissioners, could be sold into slavery for minor criminal offenses; and county commissioners were to register all free Negroes in their district. While Know-Nothings divided on these roll calls, all Democrats but one voted for the bills.[37] Aimed at controlling the free Negro population rather than strengthening the declining institution of slavery, such legislation earned Democrats the support of racially conscious Marylanders as well as the state's 14,000 slaveholders. "Nigger agitation," concluded the Frederick *Examiner*, "is the lifeblood of the Democratic party," and Democrats themselves admitted that the "colored question" was important to their interests.[38]

Democratic unity within the legislature was neither spurious nor coincidental. Democratic legislators, despite their inexperience, worked to increase the power of the caucus so that their fellow dele-

[35]The party's average index of cohesion for forty-eight roll calls, chosen according to procedures outlined in Chapter 1, was 75. The index of cohesion for the Eastern Shore was 65; for southern Maryland, 70; for Baltimore, 68; and for northwestern Maryland, 60. See Appendix B and Appendix Table D-1.

[36]Wright, *Free Negro in Maryland*, p. 315; Baltimore *Sun*, January 14, 1860; *Speech of Col. Curtis M. Jacobs on the Free Colored Population of Maryland, February 17, 1860* (Annapolis: Elihu S. Riley, 1860).

[37]On ten roll calls regarding slavery and free Negroes, the average index of cohesion among Democrats was 85. On the final bill voted on March 9, one Democrat voted against, twenty-nine for; Know-Nothings split nine for, thirteen against.

[38]Frederick *Examiner*, December 14, 1859; Baltimore *Sun*, March 5, 1860.

gates, some almost entirely immersed in county affairs, could learn the party's position on general legislation. In the past, such party assemblages were infrequent and, if held, were usually organized for some specific purpose, such as the dispensing of patronage or the election of a U.S. senator. In 1860 the Democratic caucus determined that Pearce would be the party's senatorial candidate, thus assuring his election; but at the same time, the caucus also decided a variety of party issues. So powerful was this body that Henry Winter Davis called it "the Legislature."[39] In the same vein, the Frederick *Examiner* complained that "King Caucus" had ended the independence of the legislature. "Now legislators must bow to the dictates of the party."[40] Democrats also developed another instrument of party discipline, the standing House committees, which in the past had merited so little attention that Speakers of the House sometimes overlooked party membership when making committee assignments. In 1860 Democrats controlled all twenty-two standing committees, and party leaders like Edward Long and John Thomas Ford ran the important Ways and Means Committee.

Democratic legislators turned to the Committee on Federal Relations for their direction in national affairs. In keeping with the party's focus on federal issues, the President's Kansas policy, his support of the controversial Lecompton Constitution, and the election of a Speaker of the House of Representatives became proper subjects for debate and resolution. Democrats, displaying their taste for political solutions of the past, voted support of the Missouri Compromise and the Compromise of 1850. Early in the session, party members passed a resolution to prevent Maryland congressmen from voting for any "radical" Republicans for Speaker of the House or for those who "endorsed" Hinton Helper's controversial *The Impending Crisis of the South*—a book which sought to prove that slavery had degraded and impoverished southern whites. Any congressman who so voted would "misrepresent the sentiment of his constituency and would justly forfeit the confidence and respect of the entire people of this state." In February, when Henry Winter Davis's vote for William Pennington elected the New Jersey congressman Speaker of the House, the Maryland General Assembly found Davis guilty of egregious error:

> Resolved, by the General Assembly of Maryland, that Henry Winter Davis, acting in Congress as one of the representatives of this state, by his

[39] *Congressional Globe*, 36th Cong., 1st sess., 1860, pt. 4, p. 119.

[40] Frederick *Examiner*, February 1, 1860.

vote for Mr. Pennington, the candidate of the Black Republican party for the Speakership of the House of Representatives, has misrepresented the sentiments of all portions of this state and thereby forfeited the confidence of her people.[41]

Never one to shirk controversy, Davis quickly lashed back at the Assembly from the floor of the House. Assuring his fellow congressmen that he had been "decorated with censure," Davis found the state legislature "deficient in practical common sense," "abounding in that genius . . . which enabled them to undertake to practice and teach, with the utmost confidence, arts and sciences of which they knew nothing," "inexperienced," and "responsible for despotic and oppressive measures." Warming to his indictments of the opposition party, Davis complained that the Democratic policies only increased sectional strife, "by agitation, clamor, vituperation, audacious [and] pertinacious."[42] The congressman made little public effort to hide his private conclusion that the legislature "had played the fool," and a Senate resolution appropriating $500 to send Davis to Liberia hardly hurt his case.[43]

Partly a battle between representatives of two opposing parties and partly a display of verbal intemperance, the controversy between Davis and the Democratic legislature involved the power of a constituency to instruct its delegates. The Maryland Assembly, led by a disciplined and aggressive force of Democrats, wished to control the actions of Marylanders in Congress. Convinced of their ability to fathom the wishes of their state, legislators did not hesitate to make judgments on national policy. Congressmen who failed to respond to such determinations acted "like European despots and Henry Winter Davis."[44] Davis, on the other hand, asserted that he had come to Congress as a "free man," and he therefore denied "the right of the Legislature to take away from me the confidence of that constituency that has stood by me."[45] Davis insisted that he knew "the people were pleased and contented except for a few jobbers in the Southern trade."[46] Despite a conviction that his supporters "applauded" his

[41] *Journal of the Proceedings of the House of Delegates, 1860* (Annapolis: Elihu S. Riley, 1860), pp. 16–17, 354.

[42] *Congressional Globe*, 36th Cong., 1st sess., 1860, pt. 4, pp. 117–20.

[43] Davis to Samuel F. Du Pont, February 29, April 1860, Du Pont Papers.

[44] Baltimore *Sun*, March 1, 1860.

[45] *Congressional Globe*, 36th Cong., 1st sess., 1860, pt. 4, pp. 117–20.

[46] Davis to Samuel F. Du Pont, February 3, 1860, Du Pont Papers.

actions, Davis had badly misread his district which, within fifteen months, was to elect Henry May, a former Democrat, to Congress.

☆ ☆ ☆

ON THE LAST DAY of the legislative session, Democrats voted to unseat the nine Know-Nothing delegates from Baltimore who, although they had served throughout the two-month meeting, were now considered unworthy beneficiaries of a corrupt election. With little ado, the seats of the Baltimoreans were declared vacant, the city delegation left the legislature, and a new election was called.

This casual expulsion of almost one-third of the Know-Nothing representatives in the Assembly was symbolic of the startling reversals that the Know-Nothing party had suffered—both locally and nationally. Despite their pleas for national unity, by 1855 the Know-Nothings were hopelessly divided over the issue of slavery. Sectional division had split the national party into two factions, and by 1857 a thinly attended national convention in Louisville turned the party back to the "state councils" or "any organization which may be best suited to the views of the party in their several locations."[47] Without any national organization, Maryland Know-Nothings, like the Whigs before them, suffered problems of finance and influence. Now the party could never hope to win the Presidency, control of Congress, or the patronage and power that such influence brought in a federal system. Nor could Know-Nothings offer aspiring young politicans membership in an institution whose policies and ideals would have national influence. The traditional taxes levied on congressional districts by the national committee and later disbursed to state organizations were no longer available to Maryland Know-Nothings. The distribution of pamphlets and the dispatch of speakers of national reputation to local political rallies, both functions of the national party, ceased. Even the anticipated advantages of rallying behind a popular national leader during the approaching presidential campaign were denied.

Yet not all the party's problems were national. While Maryland Know-Nothings used the same nominating machinery as did the Democrats, nativists continued to defer in both policy and tactics to the Superior Council composed of leaders from the old nativist socie-

[47]W. Darrell Overdyke, *The Know Nothing Party in the South* (Baton Rouge: Louisiana State University Press, 1950), p. 169.

ties. The Council's denunciations of Roman Catholics and foreigners embarrassed the more pragmatic state central committee, which argued that everyone opposed to the Democracy should join the American party. Such differences revealed a growing fissure between practical politicians who wished to win elections and members of the old secret societies who felt that the principles of nativism were more important than the practices of electoral strategy.

The Know-Nothings' attitudes toward their leaders increased the cleavage within the party. Some nativists, particularly former Whigs, complained that party politicians were little more than "hucksters" and "wire pullers." "We are," complained one Know-Nothing "drifting away from old landmarks. The pilots under whose care the ship of state has hitherto been safely navigated are dead."[48] Brantz Mayer, a well-known ex-Whig, agreed and saw a further danger: "The best men keep aloof from the political prizes to be won."[49] John Pendleton Kennedy, the prominent novelist and politician, described the party which his brother Anthony represented in the U.S. Senate "as without principle and composed of the worst and least capable men who have utterly disregarded and annulled by their course of proceeding every doctrine originally proclaimed by the party." In a letter to his uncle, Kennedy made the same point: "Do you remark on how lamentably destitute [we are] of men in public station of whom we can speak with pride?"[50]

As a group, Know-Nothing leaders had slightly less property than their opponents, and they were more likely to be men of business and commerce than the Democrats.[51] Although their economic holdings quite clearly placed them with Maryland's richest men, fewer names of the landed aristocracy appear among Know-Nothings. The fathers of Know-Nothings were often from more humble circumstances than

[48] *Cecil Whig* (Elkton), January 14, 1860.

[49] Brantz Mayer, "Address on True Americanism," February 21, 1860, Mayer Papers, MHS.

[50] John P. Kennedy, "Journals," September 29, 1859; John P. Kennedy to Philip Kennedy, September 29, 1859, Kennedy Papers, Peabody Library, Baltimore, Md. One of the most distinguished Marylanders of his time, John P. Kennedy combined a political career with that of a successful novelist. The author of *Swallow Barn, Quodlibet* and *Horse-Shoe Robinson*, Kennedy also served in the Maryland House of Delegates, in Congress, and as Secretary of the Navy in the Fillmore cabinet. For a perceptive biography of Kennedy as a man of letters, see Charles H. Bohnor, *John Pendleton Kennedy, Gentleman from Baltimore* (Baltimore: Johns Hopkins Press, 1961).

[51] For a more detailed description of these leaders, see Appendix Tables D-2, D-3, D-4, and D-5.

those of the opposition, and their sons were more likely to be in business, commerce, or a profession than the Democrats. A new political party in the 1850s, the Know-Nothing organization apparently served as a vehicle for young, self-made Marylanders eager for position, power, and prestige. In a state where only farming or the "learned professions" were considered suitable vocations for gentlemen,[52] social snobbery accounted for the opprobrium with which Know-Nothing leaders were held—even by some of their own constituents.

Many Maryland Know-Nothings found their most prominent national leader a continual embarrassment. Henry Winter Davis voted with the Republicans in Congress too often to vitiate the Democratic charge that he had joined that party. Furthermore, Davis's plan to reorganize the national party by joining Southern Know-Nothings, former Whigs, and Northern Republicans in a new coalition led by Edward Bates, the Missouri judge,[53] proved humiliating to Maryland nativists, who considered the Republican party a danger to any political success in Maryland. Yet such national aspirations did not deter Davis from playing an important role in local politics; the Baltimore congressman masterminded party tactics in the city,[54] and he frequently spoke at rallies throughout the state. By 1859 it was impossible to disassociate the Maryland party from the ubiquitous and vocal Davis, and when Davis voted for Pennington for Speaker of the House in 1860, twenty-five of twenty-six Know-Nothing delegates joined their Democratic colleagues to censure him.

These same Know-Nothing leaders had developed a less dangerous plan to revive party fortunes—without the Republicans. Gradually, the party had reduced nativism to a secondary place in its hierarchy of values. In 1855, William Alexander, a Baltimore lawyer and delegate

[52]Bernard Steiner, *The Life of Henry Winter Davis* (Baltimore: John Murphy, 1916), p. 42.

[53]Davis expressed his hopes for a new party with Bates as a presidential candidate in a series of letters to Samuel F. Du Pont. See Davis to Du Pont, December 20, 27, 1859, Du Pont Papers; and Davis to Justin Morrill, August 20, 1859, Morrill Papers, Library of Congress. As early as January 1, 1860, the Baltimore *Patriot*, a Davis organ, had put the Missourian's name on its masthead, and Bates himself was clearly aware of Davis's support. Diary of Edward Bates, January 9, 28, 1860, Bates Papers, Library of Congress. See also Gerald Henig, "Henry Winter Davis and the Speakership Contest of 1859-1860," *Maryland Historical Magazine* (in press).

[54]The extent of Davis's influence is apparent in two letters written to Thomas Swann regarding the Know-Nothing strategy to defeat, or at least to circumvent, the Baltimore police and election bills. Davis to Thomas Swann, n.d., and July 29, 1860, Swann Papers, owned by Mrs. Page S. Gillet, Glyndon, Md.

to the National Council, argued unsuccessfully that native-born Roman Catholics should be allowed to join the party.[55] In a state with a heavy Catholic population, the traditional appeal of the party to proscribe Roman Catholics disappeared, a victim of political expediency. By 1859, Know-Nothings invited all those opposed to the Democracy to join them, and a Democratic newspaper slyly noted that such a broad invitation included "foreigner, Roman Catholic, party Irish, and lop-eared Dutch"—groups previously unwelcomed in the party.[56] At the end of the decade, only the American Council, almost unheeded, continued to play on the strings of nativism. "Such," concluded a Democratic paper, "is the end of Sam."[57]

In the place of earlier, more xenophobic pledges, Know-Nothings now substituted appeals to form a Conservative party, based on the protection of Union and Constitution. Calling for a "union of conservatives," and a national party devoted to "Union and Constitution," Know-Nothing leaders encouraged the formation of a new party. As J. Morrison Harris, Baltimore congressman, told his constituents:

> From the ashes of this dissolving Democracy is to rise the phoenix of a new movement that will sweep the country. Already is the Southern sky bright with significant light. Already are the indications gathering strength and pointing to a union of all the elements of opposition . . . an opposition that rejecting all dangerous and useless dogmas, all questions of vain and irritating differences between sections and people will array itself firmly up on the platform of constitution and win by its moderation, its good sense, its high conservatism, its unquestioned nationality, the good and true men of all parties and sections. . . . I will try to be found always with those who must faithfully march under the flag and keep step to the music of the Union.[58]

By calling for a new party, Know-Nothings thus began the task of filtering their own organization into a new political beaker. Former appeals to protect America from foreigner and Catholic became calls to preserve the Union from extremists, both North and South. Leaders like Senator Anthony Kennedy, intent on a "union organization," insisted that the party stress Constitution and Union and exclude the slavery question.[59] "For all those who wish to uphold the Union,

[55] Overdyke, *Know Nothing Party in the South*, p. 129.

[56] *Maryland Union* (Frederick), January 6, 1859.

[57] *Ibid.*, January 6, 1859.

[58] Baltimore *Clipper*, September 14, 1859.

[59] Kennedy to John Crittenden, June 17, 1859, Crittenden Papers, Library of Congress. For references to the Union party, see the Baltimore *American*, March 31, May 27, 1858; Frederick *Examiner*, May 19, June 9, 1858.

defend the constitution, and respect states rights," declaimed the Frederick *Examiner*, "[must] join together, no matter whether the name is American, Know-Nothing, or Unionist."[60] Even before the presidential election of 1860 and the coming of the war, the Union party had begun in Maryland.

☆ ☆ ☆

THE ATTEMPT BY both Know-Nothings and Democrats to provide a "new tack" for politics in their state coincided with the presidential election of 1860. Four political parties had organizations in Maryland, but the outcome of the election clearly proved the power of the two established state parties, which, despite the complex electoral choices offered, managed to retain the allegiance of most Marylanders.

The Republicans of Maryland were at best a tentative organization. The hopes of some Marylanders, including Henry Winter Davis and Montgomery Blair,[61] that the Constitutional Unionists and Republicans could agree on a single candidate collapsed in June when the Republicans nominated Abraham Lincoln. Even after the nomination, Davis worked unsuccessfully to prevent "Lincoln's friends" from naming an electoral ticket in Maryland.[62] Actually Lincoln found few supporters in the state, where most agreed with the Baltimore *American* that "it is folly to organize the Republican party, it will only get a thousand votes in the state."[63] Even the German community, the vanguard of Republican support in some states, showed little enthusiasm for Lincoln. While one German language newspaper, *Baltimore Wecker*, came out for Lincoln, the other, *Der Deutsche Correspondent*, supported the Democrat John C. Breckinridge.[64]

[60] Frederick *Examiner*, May 19, 1858.

[61] Blair, the son of Francis Preston Blair, had moved to Maryland in 1853. He practiced law and dabbled in politics before his appointment to Lincoln's cabinet as postmaster general. In 1859 Blair wrote J. R. Doolittle of his interest in the Republican party, and his feeling that Negroes should go "where they can have political rights. If we can commit our party distinctly to this, I will undertake for Maryland in 1860. I am now a resident and voted there in the recent election." "Letters of Edward Bates and the Blairs," *Missouri Historical Review* II (January 1917): 137.

[62] Davis to David Davis, June 10, 1860, W. L. King Collection of David Davis Papers, Chicago Historical Society, Ill. See also Charles Branch Clark, "Politics in Maryland during the Civil War" (Ph.D. diss., University of North Carolina, 1940), p. 68.

[63] Baltimore *American*, April 27, 1860.

[64] *Baltimore Wecker*, October 13, 16, 1860; *Der Deutsche Correspondent* (Baltimore), April 15, December 15, December 22, 1860.

In some areas the party had no organization. One potential Republican wrote to Montgomery Blair, the party's Maryland leader:

> I hear indirectly that you are the candidate for Presidential elector on the Republican ticket. Will you please inform me on receipt of this if such is the fact and likewise give me your opinion about policy of voteing [sic] for the Republican nominee here.[65]

Another explained that the party had

> . . . but little strength in the counties and what little strength we have we have gained by a quiet action. But let Lincoln be once elected and then we can take a bold stand and measure swords with our enemies to good advantage but now we gain nothing but insult and abuse by holding public meetings and discussing the principles of the party.[66]

The expectation of Lincoln's election impelled Republicans, with little help from the national organization, to endure a campaign that at times involved physical humiliation and danger. Hostile Baltimoreans pelted the gaily-costumed Lincoln volunteers, the "Wide-Awakes," with eggs and bricks, while other Marylanders burned cayenne sticks, the nineteenth-century tear gas, to disrupt Republican meetings.[67] Such strong-armed tactics only hardened the fervor of that hardy band of Lincoln supporters who were shortly to find their rewards in the national patronage of the Republican administration.

At no time during the campaign were Republican appeals in Maryland even mildly tinged with antislavery sentiment. One of the state's first Republicans, William Ewing, a Free Soiler in 1848, explained that his support of the party came from a desire to protect working men from the competition of black labor. In 1857, Ewing, a Cecil county farmer, outlined his Republican credo:

> Why do you call upon the 16,000 slave owners and have no word to say to 410,000 free white men and women who eat their bread in sweat of their faces and don't own or expect even to own a single nigger? Republican [*sic*] does not wish to turn all the slaves loose and place them upon an equality with whites. It does not desire to interfere with slavery where it exists. Its only object is to give to whites complete and entire control of agricultural and mechanical pursuits.[68]

[65] N. Burnham to Blair, October 15, 1860, Blair Papers, Library of Congress.

[66] Jas. M. Palmer to Blair, October 22, 1860, *ibid.*

[67] Baltimore *American*, November 2, 1860; *Baltimore Wecker*, November 1, 1860; N. H. Pollack to Blair, October 23, 1860, Blair Papers.

[68] *Cecil Democrat* (Elkton), July 25, 1857. In 1860 there were 14,000 slaveholders in Maryland.

Such sentiments, those of a minority in Maryland, nonetheless expressed an important part of the Republican appeal to white farmers throughout the country.[69]

During the fall of 1860, Montgomery Blair established campaign themes which softened the national Republican party's commitment to antislavery in the territories. In a speech in Montgomery county, Blair attacked "firebrand" Democrats for their extremism and appealed to southern men who loved the Union, Henry Clay, and Andrew Jackson. Denying that Republicans would outlaw slavery in states where it was already established, Blair concluded that "any law of the Federal government abolishing slavery in Maryland would be as void and nugatory as an act of the British Parliament."[70] Other Republicans, perhaps conscious of their own investment in slaves, announced their opposition to personal liberty laws that helped protect fugitive slaves in the North and their support of the state-subsidized Maryland Colonization Society, which had long sought to resettle American blacks in Africa.[71]

In an effort to avoid the possible embarrassments of national issues, some Republicans focused on local concerns. Thus the Republican state convention stressed the importance of Baltimore as a commercial center. In a bid for Know-Nothing votes, party spokesmen defended the city's previous administration and urged legislative reapportionment to protect Baltimore's interests. Apparently such attempts to avoid the issues raised by slavery were unsuccessful for Republicans never did dispel the feeling that they were, as one southern Marylander insisted, "the spirit of John Brown."[72] Only two weeks before the election, a Democratic speaker at Baltimore's Richmond market asked who the Republicans were, and the answer came back in unison: "The niggers."[73]

[69]Both Eugene Berwanger and Eric Foner have recently demonstrated the antiblack prejudices of early Republicans whose antislavery sentiment was basically an attempt to prevent black slaves from sullying their states and to advance the conception of a progressive free society, as distinct from a reactionary slave one. See Eugene Berwanger, *The Frontier against Slavery: Negro Prejudice and the Slavery Extension* (Chicago: University of Illinois Press, 1967), and Eric Foner, *Free Soil, Free Labor, and Free Men: The Ideology of the Republican Party before the Civil War* (New York: Oxford University Press, 1970).

[70]Speech at Iddin's Store, October 13, 1860, Blair Papers.

[71]I found six slaveholding Republicans among twenty-seven leaders. This does not include Montgomery Blair's father, Francis P. Blair, who, in 1860, owned fifteen slaves, only one of whom was over fifty years of age. Manuscript Census Returns, Schedule 2, Eighth Census, 1860.

[72]Port Tobacco *Times*, May 3, 1860.

[73]Annapolis *Gazette*, November 1, 1860.

Certainly the party's miniscule 2 percent of the state vote in 1860 reflected the association of the party, in the minds of Marylanders, with sectional agitation and radical antislavery. Before the election, some newspapers predicted that the Republican vote would come from the Know-Nothings; others, assessing the party's support after the election, concluded that the Republican constituency was made up of formerly Democratic Germans.[74] In fact, Lincoln did not carry the Baltimore wards with heavy German populations, such as the First—where 2,767 German-born lived in 1850—or the Second—with 1,857 German-born.[75] In these two wards, Lincoln received only 47 and 57 votes, results which Henry Winter Davis attributed to "the [Germans'] employers [who] required them to vote for Breckinridge and they did so."[76] One-half the Republican vote was spread throughout the city, and the rest came from the state's northwestern counties.

The split in the national Democratic party in Charleston, and later in Baltimore, created Maryland's second minor party, the National Democrats who supported Stephen A. Douglas of Illinois for President and Georgia's Herschel Johnson for Vice President. Maryland's delegation to Charleston divided during the convention over the issue of federal protection of slavery in the territories, and when the convention adjourned to Baltimore in the June heat, the city had a first-hand view of the deep discord within the Democratic party and its own Maryland delegation. After the nomination of Douglas in the Front Street Theatre, eight Maryland delegates joined those from other states who adjourned to the nearby Maryland Institute Hall. Here John C. Breckinridge of Kentucky and Joseph Lane of Oregon became the candidates of the Democratic National party. Some Mary-

[74]Frederick *Examiner*, October 31, 1860. Overly optimistic Republican leaders had hoped that two-thirds of Maryland's Know-Nothings would vote Republican, although a tentative agreement that Republicans would support American state and local candidates in return for American support of the Republican national ticket failed. William Marshall to Montgomery Blair, May 5, 30, 1860, Blair Papers. Henry Winter Davis concluded that the Lincoln votes came from former Know-Nothings. Davis to David Davis, November 8, 1860, W. L. King Collection of the David Davis Papers. See also the Baltimore *American*, November 3, 8, 1860.

[75]There is no breakdown of the number of foreign-born per ward in the 1860 census. The coefficient of correlation between the percentage of the Republican vote in 1860 by ward and the percentage of the German-born population in 1850 is $-.1549$.

[76]Davis to David Davis, November 8, 1860, W. L. King Collection of the David Davis Papers.

landers saw this split as "rendering the election of Lincoln a certainty," and Henry Winter Davis exulted that "here in Maryland the division of the Dems is complete, hearty, rancorous, and satisfactory."[77]

Davis's judgment was, however, premature. From the first, the Douglas party had very little support in the state. Breckinridge Democrats led by Bradley T. Johnson, the handsome, goateed Frederick county newspaper editor and future Confederate general, controlled the state and local apparatus, with the exception of Allegany county. In a series of swift removals, Breckinridge's supporters replaced Douglas men on county executive committees. For all the barbecues, mass meetings, pole-raisings, and torchlight parades of the Douglas Invincibles, the party had few ward campaign funds, and little of the support from any cadre of dedicated officeholders, politicians, and newspaper editors so necessary to successful campaigns. The national Douglas organization, faced with its own financial embarrassments, helped little.[78]

The supporters of Douglas spent little time on the national party platform, which called for support of the Cincinnati platform,[79] acceptance of the decisions of the Supreme Court, and the enforcement of the Fugitive Slave Law. Indeed, an address by Douglas to a Baltimore audience in September was one of the few extended examinations given the doctrine of "popular or squatter" sovereignty associated with the Illinois senator. Instead, with all the bitterness of a family argument, the Maryland Douglas faction attacked their Democratic opposition for division of the party, southern extremism, and denial of the Union. In a speech that lasted over three hours, Governor Francis Thomas, recently returned to politics after a private scandal, excoriated the Breckinridge Democrats for "intrigues, nullification and Lecompton, . . . a record of disunion."[80] With more brevity, political transparencies simply proclaimed: "If you desire dissolution of

[77]*Ibid.*, June 27, 1860; Davis to Samuel F. Du Pont, July 1860, Du Pont Papers.

[78]For a study of August Belmont, Democratic party chairman, and his problems in managing the Douglas campaign, see Irving Katz, *August Belmont: A Political Biography* (New York: Columbia University Press, 1968), pp. 75-83. The national committee assessed every congressional district $100, but in 1860 few Maryland districts paid this levy.

[79]The Cincinnati platform of 1856 stated that "Congress had no power under the Constitution to interfere with or control the domestic institutions of the several states" and decried attempts to induce Congress to interfere with questions of slavery.

[80]Thomas's divorce from his young wife had titillated Marylanders since his retirement from the governorship. For his speech, see the Baltimore *American*, October 6, 1860. See also Francis Thomas, *Statement of Francis Thomas*, MHS.

the Union, vote for Breckinridge; if you desire the disruption of democracy, vote for Breckinridge."[81]

Such negative appeals were unsuccessful, for only 6 percent of Maryland's electorate voted the Douglas ticket with its dramatic etchings of Andrew Jackson and the American flag. Half of this vote came from Baltimore city and Allegany, the only county that Douglas carried. The surprising returns in Allegany were the result of the coal-mining interests' satisfaction with Douglas, their ability to "influence" the miners' votes, and the control of the county machinery by National Democrats.[82]

The real contest for Maryland's eight electoral votes was between the Constitutional Unionists led by John Bell, the Tennessee senator, and the Democrats of Kentuckian John C. Breckinridge, both of whose organizations controlled the machinery and constituency of the state's established parties. Throughout the hot, dry summer and fall of 1860, supporters of Bell and Breckinridge argued, cajoled, and finally demanded, "for the sake of the Union and Constitution," the votes of their fellow Marylanders.

For those who supported Bell, the task of merging the Know-Nothing organization into a national Union party had begun as early as 1857. By the summer of 1860, almost without exception, Know-Nothing leaders supported Bell who in the past had shown sympathy toward the American party. County conventions and most ward clubs found no difficulty in transferring their allegiance from the Know-Nothing to the Constitutional Union party.[83] Even John Pendleton Kennedy, the distinguished and aging head of the Constitutional Union organization in Maryland and a Know-Nothing voter despite his occasional objections to the party, worked closely with Charles C.

[81] *Maryland Union* (Frederick), November 1, 1860.

[82] *Cecil Whig* (Elkton), October 27, 1860. C. B. Thruston to James Partridge, January 7, 1860, Hicks Executive Papers, Hall of Records, Annapolis, Md.

[83] Two sets of Baltimore delegates—one chosen at a Constitutional Union mass meeting, the other elected by the Know-Nothing City Convention—fought to represent the city at the first statewide convention of the Constitutional Unionists. Actually, both these delegations were made up of former Know-Nothings. As early as 1858, Henry W. Hoffman had attended meetings in Washington aimed at the formation of a new Conservative party. Baltimore *Sun*, April 20, 1860; John B. Stabler, "A History of the Constitutional Union Party: A Tragic Failure" (Ph.D. diss., Columbia University, 1954). As Stabler points out, the demand for a new Union party came not from national caucuses, but rather from state party organizations and newspapers. Stabler also notes the determination of the Know-Nothing party to control the new party, and concludes that the new Constitutional Union party was a direct descendant of the Maryland Know-Nothings. Stabler, pp. 178, 370, 373, 728.

Fulton, editor of the *Clipper* and a leader of Maryland's nativists. Kennedy admitted that he deferred greatly to Fulton, and both men worked out a formula to allot most of the places on election committees to Know-Nothings.[84] By the summer, Kennedy had finished much of the difficult work of channeling American support into the new party, and even opponents admitted his success in "the transfer of the defunct Know Nothing carcass to the Constitutional Unionists."[85] Complaining that "this matter takes up too much time,"[86] the weary, rheumatoid Kennedy summered on his Patapsco estate, while Know-Nothing district and ward clubs campaigned for John Bell.

For Bell supporters, the greatest challenge to their organization came from those who wished to include Douglas Democrats in a new Unionist coalition. In some states, such as New Jersey, a fusion ticket between Douglas and Bell electors was accomplished with ease, but in Maryland, party loyalties were too strong to permit any such merger between the two organizations. By early autumn Douglas's personal intervention "to bring about a good understanding between his friends and those of Bell and Everett" failed.[87]

The organization that Kennedy had helped to fashion continued the hard work of gaining the support of Maryland voters during the fall. At an array of picnics and mass meetings, Unionists repeated a familiar message: opposition to the sectionalism of fanatics and support of Constitution and the Union. In the words of the inevitable pun, "Our Bell rings to the sound of Union. Try it."[88] Encouraged by Kennedy, who saw the party as a "great body of friends of Union, now so madly threatened by the exasperation of slavery,"[89] Constitutional Unionists diligently avoided any specific platforms and kept faithfully to the abstractions of the party's slogans:

> Union of Lakes, the Union of Lands
> Union of states, none shall sever
> Union of hearts, and Union of hands.
> And the flag of the Union forever.[90]

[84]Kennedy, "Journal," May 9, August 2, 1860, Kennedy Papers.

[85]*Cecil Democrat* (Elkton), April 14, 1860.

[86]Kennedy, "Journal," July 10, 1860, Kennedy Papers.

[87]George Steuart to C. D. Steuart, August 31, 1860, George Steuart Papers, Duke University Library, Durham, N.C.

[88]Baltimore *American*, May 15, 1860.

[89]Kennedy, "Journal," January 25, 1860, Kennedy Papers.

[90]Baltimore *American*, July 19, 1860.

At a Bell meeting in Talbot county the roasted ox and hams, savoring of the trees on which they cooked, were more spicy than the repetitious platitudes of speakers proclaiming for Union and Constitution.[91]

This attempt to dampen the fiery issues of 1860 occurred in all four political campaigns, but it was most obvious among the Unionists. As John P. Kennedy explained:

> Is there a man of any intelligence North or South who does not see that irrespective of the merits of the candidates and altogether apart from the question of which party is right or wrong, the election of either Lincoln or Breckinridge to say nothing of Douglas, for he seems out of the question, must be followed by four years of such exasperation of parties, such reciprocal vituperation and such intense sectional hostility as will shake society to its center.[92]

In the view of some party members this constant reiteration of the dangers of the future helped the Breckinridge party. If, as the Baltimore *American* put it, "the Republic is on the verge of a precipice,"[93] and if the threats to Union were as real as the Unionists implied, many Marylanders reasoned that it was time to unite with the South. While Henry Winter Davis scarcely agreed with such sentiments, he succinctly explained the reasoning of other Marylanders: "If the danger be so great of Lincoln's election and war afterwards, we had better help the Democrats who alone have the power to encounter him."[94]

The task of political organization was somewhat easier for the Breckinridge Democrats, who successfully controlled the revived Democratic machine in Maryland. The defection to Douglas of a few prominent state leaders such as Reverdy Johnson, the partially blind former U.S. Attorney General, and William Maulsby, a Bel Air lawyer and president of the Chesapeake and Ohio Canal, counted little when the support of newspapers and beneficient officeholders, many recently appointed by Buchanan, was so enthusiastic. Federal patronage holders, particularly in Baltimore's Custom House, contributed so handsomely that the city party ended the campaign in the black.[95]

Breckinridge partisans appealed to voters in much the same way as the other three parties. These self-described National Democrats endorsed the Dred Scott decision, protested northern agitation against

[91] *Ibid.*, October 27, 1860.

[92] Kennedy to Robert C. Winthrop, October 20, 1860, Kennedy Papers.

[93] Baltimore *American*, August 16, 1860.

[94] Davis to Samuel F. Du Pont, November 7, 1860, Du Pont Papers.

[95] Baltimore *American*, November 16, 1860.

"the institutions of slave states," and insisted that the provisions of the Fugitive Slave Act be upheld.[96] Instead of emphasizing tendentious issues such as the status of slavery in the territories, Democrats preferred to stress the popularity of both their candidate and party as well as the importance of Constitution and Union. Thus the Breckinridge ticket displayed, beneath an etching of George Washington, the legend "One Constitution, Union, and the Equality of States," sentiments which were, to the uninitiated, almost unrecognizable from the Bell and Everett ticket which proclaimed "Union, Constitution, and the Enforcement of Laws."[97] Democrats varied such appeals with charges that their opponents were, in varying degrees, abolitionists, and even Bell was found guilty of this heresy late in the campaign.

The distraction of a presidential election did not deter the Breckinridge and Douglas Democrats from uniting to wrest control of Baltimore from the Know-Nothings. Under the guise of a nonpartisan reform party first organized in 1857, Democrats appealed for good government, honest elections, and an end to party control over cities. Insisting that local concerns be kept separate from national issues, reformers demanded more polling places within each ward and better police control of elections. Overwhelmingly patrician and Democratic in background,[98] reformers gave the mayoral nomination to George W. Brown, a well-known attorney and member of the famous banking family whose political allegiance had long been Democratic. Brown insisted in September that he would be elected by "a large majority,"[99] and his predictions proved correct, as Democrats returned to power in Baltimore for the first time in six years.

A few weeks after Brown's victory, citizens voted again, this time for their presidential choice. When the polls closed on election day, Baltimoreans crowded into the Holliday Street Theatre and around the city's newspaper offices to learn that Breckinridge had carried the state by less than a thousand votes and that Maryland's last choice—Abraham Lincoln—was President of the United States. The Breckin-

[96]Port Tobacco *Times*, October 11, 18, 1860; Baltimore *Daily Exchange*, November 5, 1860.

[97]Jarboe Election Tickets, 1860, MHS.

[98]See p. 27 above. My study of sixty-four leaders of the party reveals that fifty-two were businessmen, lawyers, or professional men, and one-third were members of the prestigious Board of Trade. Of 141 leaders, Evitts finds 65 proprietors, 40 professional men, 6 clerks, 29 skilled laborers, and 1 unskilled laborer. William J. Evitts, "A Matter of Allegiances: Maryland from 1850 to 1861" (Ph.D. diss., Johns Hopkins University, 1971) p. 184.

[99]Brown to Frederick Brune, September 4, 1860, Brune Papers, MHS.

ridge Democrats, who gained 45 percent of the state's popular vote, lived in every part of the state, but were strongest in areas where the black and slaveholding population was highest.[100] Their political heritage was Democratic, although certainly many ex-Whigs voted for Breckinridge.[101] In Baltimore, Democrats who voted in October for George Brown voted for Breckinridge three weeks later—a pattern which the acerbic Davis compared to a horsebreaking technique called "the Reary process . . . his will is his master's ever after."[102] The combined Douglas and Breckinridge vote was a majority, not just a plurality of the state's electorate, and this majority represented the triumphant resurrection of the Democratic party.

The Constitutional Unionists, on the other hand, ran far ahead of that party's weak vote of 12 percent in the country as a whole. With 44 percent of Maryland's vote, the party was particularly strong in areas of former Know-Nothing strength; in fact, 80 percent of the election districts that voted for Bell in 1860 had supported Know-Nothing candidates in the two preceding statewide elections.[103] For some, the voting habits of the past determined the attitude of Marylanders toward Bell's party. Thus, while one Baltimorean explained that he voted against "the Constitutional Unionists because the party that supports [Bell] was composed of the Know Nothing organization,"[104] others like Henry Winter Davis voted for Bell, not with any expectation of making him president, but "to exclude the democrats from power in Maryland."[105]

[100]The coefficient of correlation between the percentage of the Breckinridge vote and the percentage of black population on a county-by-county basis is +.6573. The coefficient of correlation between the percentage of whites owning slaves and the Breckinridge vote is +.6896. Breckinridge carried most of the Maryland counties with a Negro population over 35 percent—Charles, 64 percent black; Prince Georges, 58 percent black; St. Mary's, 60 percent black; Talbot, 49 percent black; and Worcester, 35 percent black. See Evitts, "Matter of Allegiances," p. 221.

[101]Charles Howard to Benjamin Chew Howard, February 5, 1861, Bayard Papers, MHS.

[102]Henry Winter Davis to Samuel F. Du Pont, November 7, 1860, Du Pont Papers. The reference is to a method of breaking horses developed by John Solomon Rarey whose name Davis misspelled. The coefficient of correlation between the percentage of the Breckinridge vote and the percentage of the Democratic vote in 1859 for Comptroller is +.6367 and between the Breckinridge vote and the Brown vote in October 1860, is +.8379.

[103]The coefficient of correlation between the percentage of the Know-Nothing vote in 1859 and the Bell vote in 1860 is +.8326. See Evitts, "A Matter of Allegiances," pp. 224, 225.

[104]Baltimore *American*, November 7, 1860.

[105]Davis to Samuel F. Du Pont, July 1860, Du Pont Papers.

The presidential election of 1860 capped a period of political transformation in Maryland. Despite the excitement of four different parties and candidates and despite frequent acknowledgment of the dangers of the future, the election did not bring many new voters to the polls, as had the elections of 1840 and 1856.[106] Indeed, at least one-half of the nearly 6,000 Marylanders who voted for the first time in 1860 were newly naturalized citizens, and natural increases in population accounted for the rest. The 70 percent of the eligible voters who did vote overwhelmingly supported the two candidates, Bell and Breckinridge, who controlled the state political machinery.

By 1860, the rapid collapse of the Know-Nothings, the pernicious fear of free Negroes, and the growing alarm for the Union had accomplished a realignment in Maryland politics. Equipped with new appeals, a strengthened organization, and loyal leaders, Democrats had embarked on their "new tack." Know-Nothings, on the other hand, had completed their own new strategy—the transformation of political nativism into Unionism.

[106] The average quadrennial increase in turnouts from 1836–60 was 11 percent, but in 1840 the increase was 29 percent, and in 1856, 15 percent. In 1860, 6 percent more Marylanders voted than had in 1856.

III. THE POLITICS OF LOYALTY AND THE TRAMPLED BALLOT: MARYLAND PARTIES IN 1861

WITHIN WEEKS OF LINCOLN'S ELECTION, Marylanders faced the prospects of secession, disunion, and war. Convinced that the election of 1860 represented, at best, a sectional victory of the Republican party and, at worst, "the victory of fanatics," some communities banished Republican voters, while others urged the calling of a convention "to secure the constitutional rights of Maryland within the Union." A few Marylanders encouraged more radical action: "Up Southians," announced a card in the Frederick *Examiner*. "The tocsin sounds! Will ye be mere submissionists? Cavaliers to the rescue!"[1] The secession of South Carolina in December, followed by that of six other southern states in the early winter of 1861, only heightened the feverish anxiety. Throughout the state, Marylanders, as they had so often in the past, met to debate the choices available to their border state. Should Governor Hicks convene the state legislature? Should Maryland secede? Should delegates be elected to a "sovereign convention" empowered to pass a secession ordinance? Should Maryland follow the course of neighboring border states? Excited public debate in newspapers, pamphlets, and conventions resounded throughout the state during the famous "secession" winter of 1861. According to one Marylander, "no one who did not live South of the Mason-Dixon Line can comprehend the feeling ftom the election of Lincoln to the beginning of March."[2]

Marylanders did not make their choices independently. In December, the first of a series of emissaries from the South arrived to see Governor Hicks. When the governor refused to grant an interview to his old friend Alexander Handy, the Maryland-born Mississippian renewed important contacts among friends who favored the secession movement. Supporters arranged a public meeting, and Handy's fervent defense of the rights of the southern states brought loud cheers for the South as well as a spate of "palmetto" flag raisings. Shortly thereafter, commissioners from Pennsylvania arrived to present the merits of

[1] Frederick *Examiner*, November 28, 1860; for references to the reaction of Marylanders to Lincoln's election, see Lewis Wheeler to John Pomeroy, December 22, 1860, January 3, 1861, Baker-Wheeler Papers, University of Virginia Library, Charlottesville, Va. Out-of-state Republicans tried vainly to quiet border-state fears of their party. As Richard Henry Dana, Jr., explained to his friend Frederick Brune, "You gentlemen of the South naturally and properly attach more weight to speeches which we Republicans make at home to our own people rather than those we may put in our letters or even speak in Washington." Dana thoughtfully included a speech of his own so that Brune could see how "conservative and moderate we are." Dana to Brune, February 20, 1861, Brune Papers, MHS.

[2] Libertus van Bokkelen, "Memorandum on the Civil War," Van Bokkelen Papers, MHS.

common action by the states astride the Mason-Dixon line. In return, a number of Marylanders, some with commissions from the governor, others with no such official credentials, traveled to Washington, to the Confederate capital in Montgomery, Alabama, and to northern states.[3]

By winter, discussion in Maryland, entirely oblivious to questions of slavery, Kansas, and the controversies of 1860, had narrowed to one issue—the calling of the state legislature into special session. Although leaders of both sides emphatically affirmed the need to forget former party distinctions, the struggle developed within the framework of partisan politics—a fact recognized by most realists.[4] Democrats favored convening the legislature, which they controlled, while Know-Nothing-Unionists vigorously opposed such a session. One meeting, organized by Democrats in Frederick, urged the people of Maryland to speak through the ballot box. "If the Governor fails to convene the Legislature, the people shall act for themselves for the preservation of their rights."[5] By March, sentiments for a "people's assembly" were statewide, and the delegates elected at local meetings met in Baltimore to urge the formation of a "sovereign convention." Insisting that the governor no longer represented the state, a predominantly Democratic convention argued that representatives from Maryland should confer with "sister states of the South" and recommended that if the governor did not act and if Virginia seceded, the Conference Convention would reassemble "with a view toward recommending to the people of the state, the election of delegates to such a Sovereign Convention."[6]

Despite continued pressure from Democrats and even occasional physical threats, Hicks, with the support of his party, refused to convene the legislature. Fearing "a party trick," the governor insisted that such a session would be unnecessary, expensive, and aimed at "increasing and reviving the excitement."[7] Such sentiments did not mean that

[3] Baltimore *Sun*, December 19, 20, 1860; Baltimore *Clipper*, March 18, 28, 1861.

[4] Baltimore *Sun*, January 11, February 9, 1861. Diary of Allen Davis, January 19, 1861, Allen B. Davis Papers, MHS; Anthony Kimmel to Governor Hicks, January 26, 1861, Hicks Papers, Hall of Records, Annapolis, Md.

[5] Broadside, "To the People of Frederick County," Civil War Papers, Record Group 59, Records of the Department of State, National Archives. Hereinafter cited as State Department Records. See also Levi K. Bowen to Howell Cobb, March 14, 1861, Cobb-Erwin-Lamar Papers, University of Georgia Library, Athens, Ga.

[6] Baltimore *American*, February 20, 1861; Civil War Diary of William Glenn, January 1861, Glenn Papers, MHS.

[7] The best study of Thomas Hicks and the secession crisis is George Radcliffe, *Governor Thomas H. Hicks of Maryland and the Civil War*, Johns Hopkins University Studies in Histori-

Hicks was unconditionally committed to the Union. In a letter to a Democratic friend, the governor argued that "if the Union must be dissolved, let it be done calmly, deliberately, and after full reflection on the part of a united South."[8] To his friend, Congressman Edwin H. Webster, an officer in the Maryland militia, Hicks displayed his erratic attachment to the Union and its President:

> [I have] no arms at hand to distribute, at earliest possible moment you shall have arms. . . . Will they [your militia company] be good men to send out to kill Lincoln and his men. If not, I suppose the arms would be better sent South.[9]

Gradually, Hicks's views shifted, not perfidiously as opponents charged, but rather in accordance with conditions in both his state and nation.

To some, Hicks's stubbornness on the convention issue was entirely in keeping with his character. The son of a prosperous Dorchester county slaveholder, Thomas Hicks had worked up Maryland's political ladder, slowly and tenaciously. He began his ascent as a sheriff in 1824; by the 1830s he represented his district in the state legislature, and in 1850 he was chosen as a Whig delegate to the Constitutional Convention. An abrupt shift to the Know-Nothings hardly interrupted his career, and by 1857 the short, ruddy-faced politician was governor of Maryland. Despite chronic ill-health, the death of several children, and economic difficulties, the governor paid close attention to his public obligations, only rarely giving way to the private chagrin that his "duties would perplex a saint."[10] The nickname "Old Caesar" was the state's grudging recognition of the governor's determination, his independence, and, according to some, his stubbornness.

---

cal and Political Science, ser. 19 (Baltimore: Johns Hopkins Press, 1901). Radcliffe had access to many of the Hicks papers which have since burned. The quotation is from the "Proclamation to the People of Maryland," January 3, 1861, Executive Papers, Hall of Records, Annapolis, Md.

[8]Hicks to John Contee, cited in J. Thomas Scharf, *History of Maryland from the Earliest Period to the Present Day*, 3 vols. (1879; reprint ed., Hatboro, Pa.: Tradition Press, 1967), 3: 367; Baltimore *American*, December 19, 1861.

[9]A copy of this controversial letter dated November 9, 1860, and not in Hicks's handwriting, but evidently copied from the original, found its way to the Baltimore *Daily Exchange* and is in the State Department Records. Radcliffe dismisses the letter as an imprudent attempt at humor between Governor Hicks and an intimate friend. If so, it is the only example of such humor I have found among many letters the governor wrote to his close associates. Furthermore the punctuation, ellipses, vocabulary, and syntax seem consistent with Hicks's style.

[10]Hicks to James Dorsey, March 22, 1861, Dorsey Papers, MHS.

While Hicks vacillated on Maryland's proper relationship to both Union and Confederacy, he remained firmly convinced of the need for common action by the border states. Shortly after Lincoln's election, the governor explained his position:

> I shall be the last one to object to a withdrawal of our state from a Confederacy that denies to us the enjoyment of our undoubted rights; but believing that neither her honor nor interests will suffer by a proper and just delay, I cannot assist in placing her in a position from which we may hereafter wish to recede. When she moves in the matter, I wish to be side by side with Virginia—our nearest neighbor—Kentucky and Tennessee.[11]

Hicks often repeated this theme of cooperation among border states in the coming months. In January, he described a

> full interchange of views with the Governors of Virginia, Kentucky, Tennessee, and Missouri with a view to concerted action upon our part. . . . I believe firmly that the salvation of the Union depends upon the Border slave states. Without their aid, the Cotton States could never command the influence and credit and men essential to their existence as a nation. Without them, the Northern half of the republic would be shorn of its power and influence.[12]

In a private letter to John Crittenden, the Kentucky senator who was himself engaged in finding a compromise for the crisis, Hicks quoted the old Methodist hymn—"unless the fold he first divide, the sheep he never can devour." According to the governor, "this applies to our border slave states, the sheet anchor of the stranded ship of state."[13]

Often forgotten amid the polarities of North and South, this movement for a regional alliance to counteract sectional extremism attracted numerous Marylanders. Men as diverse in their politics as John Pendleton Kennedy and Benjamin Chew Howard, son of the famous Revolutionary general, saw the salvation of the Union in the border states. Mediation by these states served as the theme for Kennedy's widely circulated pamphlet, *The Border States: Their Power and Duty in the Present Disordered Condition of the Country.*[14] Howard, while he seldom agreed with Kennedy's politics, con-

[11]Hicks to John Contee, cited in Scharf, *History of Maryland*, 3: 367.

[12]"Address to the People of Maryland," January 3, 1861, Executive Papers.

[13]Hicks to John Crittenden, January 5, [1861], Crittenden Papers, Library of Congress. This letter is misdated 1860.

[14]According to Kennedy, if the border states failed to bring about the restoration of the Union, they should form their own Confederacy. As late as April 1861, Kennedy saw an important role for such a confederation in the reconstruction of the Union. Kennedy to Salmon P. Chase, April 24, 1861, Chase Papers, Historical Society of Pennsylvania, Philadelphia, Pa.

curred; in his view, the border states must find a way to prevent the division of the United States "into parallel slices."[15] Even at the Conference Convention, a meeting of Democrats who wanted Hicks to convene the legislature, there was support for united action with "sister states." An anonymous letter to the editor of the Baltimore *Daily Exchange* summed up the feeling of many Marylanders:

> The border slave states will form a wall of brass which neither the fire at the North nor the fire at the South will be able to overleap. Border slave states may arrest the conflagration and quench the fire. For they can say to the North, Hands off—Restore to the South her just rights. This voice . . . will be heard and their patriotic action may be successful, when peace and harmony will reign again throughout the Union.[16]

Such expressions of hope came naturally in a state whose frontiers were plainly exposed to the dangers of civil war. Geographical position made Marylanders fear, quite correctly, that their homes and farms might become a military proving ground. The desire to maintain the Union was more than just patriotic sentiment, as Thomas Swann pointed out to the Ohioan Salmon Chase:

> Maryland of all her sister states occupies a position the most delicate. Situated upon the borders of Pennsylvania, exposed upon an extent of coast beyond her ability adequately to protect—drawing her supplies mainly from the West by a line of intercommunication which has cost her more than $30,000,000, she may well look to her safety in the event of the severance of the Union.[17]

Merchants and businessmen in Baltimore used much the same logic to argue that destruction of the Union, no matter which side Maryland chose, would disrupt the state's trade, and the economic recession of 1860-61 doubtless gave some Marylanders a taste of what such a future could bring.[18]

[15] Howard to J. P. Kennedy, December 26, 1860, Kennedy Papers, Peabody Library, Baltimore, Md.

[16] "The Union and the State of Maryland," unsigned letter to the Editor of the Baltimore *Daily Exchange*, 1861, State Department Records.

[17] Swann to Chase, January 28, 1861, Chase Papers.

[18] For a detailed analysis of the reactions of the Baltimore business community in 1860-61, see William B. Catton, "The Baltimore Business Community and the Secession Crisis, 1860-1861" (master's thesis, University of Maryland, 1952). Catton demonstrates conclusively that "the North was the most important section in Baltimore's trading life." Catton, p. 41. For other evidence of the economic difficulties of the state, see the letters of a Baltimore agent of the Baring Brothers, George W. Lurman, to various members of the firm, including Thomas Baring in Canada. According to Lurman, the state's economic difficulties were the result of a lack of capital, the failure of economic institutions to recover from the 1857 depression, and the reluctance of businessmen to undertake any commitments in the

Hopes for such a counterforce were sadly misplaced, however, for the border state movement never developed into anything more than the abstraction of pamphleteers. While Maryland commissioners shuffled back between various state capitals, Hicks enthusiastically supported the Washington Peace Convention, called by the Virginia legislature, and he therefore appointed men of diverse political background, but of uniformly high reputation, to represent Maryland at the convention. Yet even the talents of John Pendleton Kennedy, Augustus A. Bradford, Benjamin Howard, and three other distinguished Marylanders failed to make "the old gentlemen's convention" any more than another unsuccessful attempt to allay disunion. High January hopes to preserve the Union ended in late February when the convention recommended that a badly divided Congress frame amendments extending the Missouri Compromise line, outlawing the foreign slave trade, and protecting slavery from congressional interference. One weary Maryland delegate complained: "Little by little hope has faded. What good can come of these deliberations when upon every question which is presented the lines of sectionalism are tightly drawn. . . ."[19] Expectations for an independent force to check the division of the Union collapsed with the failure of the conference. Only the voting unity among border state representatives in wartime Congresses remained to remind Marylanders of their hopes for a "wall of brass."

Just weeks after the collapse of the conference and the inauguration of Lincoln, the war began. Still divided as to her proper course, Maryland took momentary refuge in "armed neutrality," a policy honored by Virginia commissioners authorized to negotiate a "defensive" alliance.[20] Yet within the state there was little neutrality in the fierce street-corner arguments among former friends, the pro-Confederate

---

uncertain days of 1861. Gary Browne of Wayne State University kindly lent me transcriptions of these letters, which are in the Foreign Offices, British Consular Reports, Public Archives of Canada, Ottawa, Canada.

[19]L. E. Chittenden, *A Report of the Debates and Proceedings in Secret Sessions of the Conference Convention* (New York: D. Appleton & Co., 1864), p. 386. Some Democrats were furious when party members like B. C. Howard accepted Hicks's commission to serve as delegates to the conference. Benjamin Presstman to Howard, February 3, 1861, Bayard Papers, MHS. For a study of the "old gentlemen's convention," see Robert Gunderson, "William C. Rives and the Old Gentlemen's Convention," *Journal of Southern History* 22 (November 1956): 459–76; Robert Gunderson, *Old Gentlemen's Convention: The Washington Peace Conference* (Madison: University of Wisconsin Press, 1961).

[20]George W. Brown, *Baltimore and the Nineteenth of April, A Study of War* (Baltimore: N. Murray, 1887), p. 84. Civil War Diary of William Glenn, April 17, 1861, Glenn Papers.

red-and-white cockades worn by many Maryland women, and the raids on federal armories by militia sympathetic to the South. Schools closed, trade halted, and in the words of one Marylander, "the world's Saturday night had come."[21]

Official neutrality soon gave way to armed clashes when Baltimoreans denied the right of the federal government to march troops through their state. Zealous partisans of state sovereignty hastily burned bridges and destroyed roads, as northern troops en route to Washington approached the Mason-Dixon line. On April 19 a regiment of Massachusetts soldiers, forced to change railroad terminals to continue their journey to Washington, found the streets of Baltimore barricaded with hastily erected obstacles of lumber, rocks, and railroad track. Passing between sidewalks lined with southern sympathizers cheering for Jefferson Davis, South Carolina, and the Confederacy, troops heard "hisses and groans" for Lincoln and the North.[22] Amid a hail of rocks, shooting began, and while the disagreement over responsibility for the first shot was never resolved, both sides agreed that sixteen men had been killed—twelve Marylanders and four federal soldiers. The streets of Baltimore had claimed the first casualties of the long war.

This Baltimore riot of April 19, which followed by one day the secession of Virginia, convinced many Americans, some for the duration of the war, of the state's disloyalty.[23] Yet Marylanders, more accustomed to the subtle nuances of state opinion, noted that the Baltimore mayor, George Brown, had marched at the head of the line of federal troops with the police commissioner at the rear, and that Governor Hicks, although he asked for a halt to federal recruiting and the passage of troops across the state, removed arms from southern sympathizers and conferred with Lincoln. Many Marylanders agreed with the President's own view, that "if quiet was kept in Baltimore a little longer, Maryland might be considered the first of the redeemed."[24]

[21]Hester Davis to Rebecca Davis, April 1861, Allen B. Davis Papers.

[22]Brown, *Baltimore and the Nineteenth of April,* p. 46. See also William J. Evitts, "A Matter of Allegiances: Maryland from 1850 to 1861," pp. 273–81, and for a neglected eyewitness account, Lewis Wheeler to John Pomeroy, April 20, 1861, Baker-Wheeler Papers.

[23]For examples, see J. H. Jordan to Nathaniel P. Banks, July 1, 1861, Banks Papers, Duke University Library, Durham, N.C.; and Thurlow Weed to Lincoln, May 4, 1861, Robert Todd Lincoln Collection of Abraham Lincoln Papers, Library of Congress. Hereinafter cited as Lincoln Papers.

[24]Tyler Dennett, ed., *Lincoln and the Civil War in the Diaries and Letters of John Hay* (New York: Dodd, Mead & Co., 1939), p. 16. See also John Pendleton Kennedy's "Journal,"

Aided by the governor's revived Unionism, economic ties with the North and West, and the appearance of federal troops, Maryland chose the Union. Southern sympathizers have insisted that only the appearance of federal troops saved Maryland for the Union, but most contemporaries agreed with William Schley, a Baltimore lawyer, that "there never was a moment when Maryland could have been forced into secession."[25] The high tide of southern sentiment had receded and left the state on Union ground.

The movement for secession now became the concern of a small band of conspirators whose activities continued, in varying forms and intensity, throughout the war. The most serious Confederate sympathizers fled across the Potomac, using in some cases the same routes as slaves fleeing northward to freedom. In May, Bradley Johnson marched a company of Marylanders across the border to join Stonewall Jackson at Point of Rocks, Virginia. Others followed the plaintive commands of Virginia friends:

> Fly to the South, fly with men,
> In Richmond, there's a home for thee.[26]

A quizzical General Benjamin F. Butler, stationed in Annapolis, questioned his superiors about the proper course toward these companies of "volunteer troops which are passing within six miles of me daily. I have been in doubt whether or not to stop them—[and] what we should do with them after we have detained them."[27] Subsequently, Butler received orders to stop provisions, but not men, headed South. Meanwhile the recruiting of Confederate troops continued in Baltimore. Under the direction of three prominent citizens, broadsides urging the formation of a Maryland line for the Confederacy appeared

---

April 29, 1861; Diary of William Price, April 1861, owned by Truman Semans, Brooklandville, Maryland. Henry Winter Davis expressed the feeling of Unionists when he wrote: "We are now up and doing and feel that we are still masters of the state." Davis to Samuel F. Du Pont, April 29, 1861, Du Pont Papers, Eleutherian Mills Historical Library, Wilmington, Del.

[25]For examples of similar attitudes see John W. M. Williams, "The Crisis, 1861," Southern Historical Collection, University of North Carolina Library; Reverdy Johnson to S. P. Chase, May 8, 1861, *Annual Report of the American Historical Association* 2 (1902): 497; Brown, *Baltimore and the Nineteenth of April*, p. 77. The quotation above is from *The War of the Rebellion: A Compilation of the Official Records* (Washington, D.C.: Government Printing Office, 1894), 2d ser., 1:610. Hereinafter cited as *O.R.*

[26]"A Virginia Girl's Address to her Lover" (1861), State Department Records.

[27]Butler to General Scott, May 8, 1861, Butler Papers, Library of Congress. For evidence of similar movements, see Henry Love to John Judge, May 9, 1861, Judge Papers, Southern Historical Collection, University of North Carolina Library.

on trees, courthouse doors, and even private homes.[28] Such activities insured that the most fervent young Confederates were not in Maryland during the war.

Older southern sympathizers found their own ways to test the state's devotion to the Union. Some manufactured pikes and cast cannon for the South; some raised the Confederate flag and used envelopes proclaiming "Our Destiny is with the South" and "Jefferson Davis, why don't you come?" Still others, of more devious mind, may have tried to poison federal provisions and to plan the kidnapping of Maryland officials.[29] Indeed, such a plot precipitated the arrest of Maryland officials in September.[30] The activities of a minority of the state's population convinced some federal officers that "the demon is here and will rise at the moment an opportunity offers . . . ,"[31] and such sentiments occasionally led to unnecessary interference in civilian life.

At the end of April, Hicks convened the legislature in Frederick "for the safety and comfort of members." Many Unionists applauded the governor's decision to avoid Annapolis, where there was considerable southern sympathy, but the removal of the legislature was primarily the result of Hicks's disagreement with military officials who had commandeered the railroad lines and whose troops now trained outside the state capital. Furthermore, with federal forces stationed in an area of heavy black population, Hicks feared the meeting of the legislature might precipitate what many Marylanders dreaded above all: a Negro insurrection.[32]

When the legislature finally organized in the unfamiliar surroundings of western Maryland, Democrats, who now controlled fifty-six of seventy-four seats in the General Assembly, promptly proved their loyalty to the Union. Viewing their role as that of watchful critics, not secessionists, Democrats denied the right of the legislature to pass an

[28]For evidence of this recruiting organization, see an unsigned letter to the Maryland brigade in Virginia, summer of 1861, State Department Records; Louis Wigfall to General Beauregard, March 12, 1861, cited in John Robinson, "Baltimore in 1861," *Magazine of American History* 14 (September 1885): 260.

[29]Stinnecke Scrapbook, Peabody Library, Baltimore, Md.; Special Brigade Order, May 1861, Department of Annapolis; H. H. Grove to Simon Cameron, May 4, 1861, Butler Papers; Edward Thomas to Hicks, June 7, 1861, Hicks Papers.

[30]*O.R.*, 2d ser., 1: 562–748.

[31]Nathaniel P. Banks to Salmon P. Chase, June 15, 1861, Chase Papers.

[32]Hicks to Butler, April 23, 24, 1861, Butler Papers; "Message to the Maryland Legislature," April 1861, Hicks Executive Papers, Hall of Records, Annapolis, Md. See also Butler to Hicks, April 23, 1861, *O.R.*, 2d ser., 1:567. The convening of the legislature was not the

ordinance of secession. When residents of Prince Georges petitioned for such a resolution, only Delegate William Bryan of that county supported their request. When State Senator Coleman Yellott introduced a bill to form a Committee of Public Safety whose powers over the militia would supersede those of the governor, Democrats buried the bill in the Committee on Federal Relations.[33] Noting the administration's exaggerated fears about the legislature, Senator James Pearce was as "confident as of my existence that this is the result of false statements made to the President. They [the legislature] were pledged by formal vote at a former session to the declaration of their want of authority to do such a thing."[34]

Unquestionably loyal to the Union, Democrats were nonetheless critical of Lincoln's war policies. Consistent with their recent emphasis on national issues, the party tirelessly complained of "the unconstitutional and arbitrary proceedings of the Federal Executive." Among such arbitrary proceedings, Democrats included Lincoln's April 1861 proclamation calling up the militia, the deployment of federal forces within Maryland, and the arrest of state legislators. Without a single Democratic dissent, resolutions passed protesting the suspension of the writ of habeas corpus, the violation of state rights, and the arrest of Maryland officials.

Convinced of Lincoln's abuse of his authority, Democrats still had considerable difficulty determining the state's proper relation to the South. In May the party urged the recognition of the Confederacy, an end to the war, and abstinence "from all violent and unlawful interference with troops in transit through our territory or quartered among us."[35] This compromise resolution temporarily satisfied both pro-southern Democrats who were delighted with the party's support

---

result of military pressure; indeed federal authorities were irritated when Hicks made his decision. Rather, Hicks, convinced that Maryland was a Unionist state and that the opposition party was loyal, wished to undercut the appeals of Marylanders who still threatened "a sovereign convention." See John Dent to Hicks, April 17, 1861, Hicks Papers. Lincoln certainly feared the assembling of the legislature, although in a letter to General Winfield Scott, he defended its right to convene. Roy P. Basler, ed., *Collected Works of Abraham Lincoln* (New Brunswick, N.J.: Rutgers University Press, 1953), 4: 344. See also Radcliffe, *Governor Thomas H. Hicks*, pp. 27, 55, 62–63, and Charles Clark, "Politics in Maryland during the Civil War" (Ph.D. diss., University of North Carolina, 1940), pp. 155–65.

[33] *Journal of the Proceedings of the House of Delegates, Extra Session, 1861* (Frederick: Elihu Riley, 1861), p. 23; *Journal of the Proceedings of the Senate* (Frederick: Elihu Riley, 1861), p. 67.

[34] Pearce to William Fessenden, September 25, 1861, Fessenden Papers, Library of Congress.

[35] These so-called Wallis resolutions passed by a strict party vote of 50–11. *Proceedings of the House of Delegates, 1861*, pp. 107–8.

for recognition of the Confederacy, and Union Democrats who now had the party's denial of the right to interfere with federal troops. Such a flimsy agreement soon proved unsatisfactory, however, and in June, Democratic delegates from northwestern Maryland balked when party members from Baltimore and southern Maryland wished to "instruct" their senators to support recognition of the Confederacy.[36] By August, roll calls relating to the Confederacy and war policy found the Democratic party divided.

Gradually the leadership of the Democratic caucus slipped into the hands of the newly seated Baltimore delegation. Elected without opposition after the April riot, these ten Baltimore delegates were prominent businessmen, doctors, and lawyers who, without exception, had strong personal and business ties with the South.[37] While all were Democrats—and had been nominated by this party—none previously had held elective office. With little reverence for the Democratic label or the civilities of political practice, most preferred to be known as members of the Southern and States' Rights party. High-minded, consistent, and inflexible, the Baltimore delegation achieved a remarkable degree of voting unity during the special session of 1861, and such constancy helped to foster the growth of a new political organization—the States' Rights party.[38]

Despite the existence of this organized faction, Democratic voting behavior in the House of Delegates was quite similar to that of the prewar party. Assured of virtual unanimity on local issues, criticism of Lincoln, and changes in state law, Democrats consistently divided on roll calls relating to the Confederacy. On issues involving free Negroes and slavery, Democrats, unlike the opposition Know-Nothing-Unionists, were united. As in 1858 and 1860, the key to a delegate's voting stance, with the exception of the Baltimore delegation, remained membership in the Democratic party and not representation of one of Maryland's regions.

[36]A reflection of the continuing attempt by local Democrats to influence national policy, the wording of this resolution was later changed to "request" and in this form narrowly passed the legislature. *Proceedings of the House of Delegates, 1861,* pp. 220-21. Opponents complained that this insistence on the right of legislative instruction was a "shibboleth" of the Democratic party. Baltimore *Sun*, June 12, 1861.

[37]At the end of the 1860 session, the Baltimore Know-Nothings had been expelled from the legislature. For a description of the nomination of the Baltimore delegation, see Civil War Diary of William Glenn, April 22, 1861, Glenn Papers.

[38]On forty-nine roll calls, the delegation voted as a bloc forty-two times. Their index of cohesion (93) was the highest for any section or party in any legislature from 1858 to 1870. See Appendix C and Appendix Table D-6 for a cluster-bloc analysis which reveals the unity within the Baltimore delegation.

Toward the end of the session, debate focused entirely on the "gross usurpation, unjust, oppressive, tyrannical acts of the President of the United States."[39] In the view of many Democrats the suspension of the writ of habeas corpus, followed by the arrest of Ross Winans, a wealthy Baltimore inventor and state legislator, and the detention of Baltimore city officials by federal troops were flagrant violations of the rights of Marylanders. In September, Secretary of War Simon Cameron and General George B. McClellan, clearly overestimating both the rumors of a conspiracy to "free Maryland" as well as the secessionist tendencies of certain Democrats, ordered the arrest of twenty-seven legislators.[40] The removal of almost one-third of the House effectively prevented that body from reaching a quorum, and thus ended the longest legislative session in state history.

For many delegates the most offensive violation of Maryland's "dignity and independence" began in May, when John Merryman, a farmer from Baltimore county was, in the words of his complaint, "compelled to rise from his bed, taken into custody and conveyed to Fort McHenry where he was imprisoned by the commanding officer without warrant from any lawful authority."[41] John Merryman's pro-southern sympathies, his position on the Baltimore county Democratic executive committee, and his commission as an officer of a militia troop that patrolled the railroad routes heading to the South assured his case the instant notoriety it received.[42]

[39]*Proceedings of the House of Delegates, Extra Session, 1861*, p. 296.

[40]*O.R.*, 1st ser., 5: 193; 2d ser., 1: 667–748; Civil War Diary of William Glenn, August 5, September 13, 1861, Glenn Papers. Federal authorities ranked the legislators on a scale from one to four, with four indicating the strongest secessionist tendencies, and arrested those with high ratings. Many legislators were released when they took an oath of allegiance, but others, who would not, languished in prison to become "graduates of the American Bastiles" and martyrs to the "politics of the trampled ballot." *Secret Correspondence Illustrating Conditions of Affairs in Maryland*, Baltimore, 1863, Chrysmer Collection, Bel Air, Maryland. A number of Marylanders are mentioned in John A. Marshall's *American Bastile: A History of the Illegal Arrests and Imprisonment of American Citizens during the Late Civil War* (Philadelphia: Thomas W. Hartley, 1870), and Frank Howard, *Fourteen Months in American Bastiles* (Baltimore: Kelly, Hedian, and Piet, 1863).

[41]Samuel Tyler, *Memoir of Roger Brooke Taney* (Baltimore: John Murphy & Co., 1872), p. 640. A few weeks earlier, federal authorities at Fort McHenry had refused to answer a writ of habeas corpus directed at the release of an underage federal soldier. *St. Mary's Beacon* (Leonardtown), May 13, 1861. Civil War Diary of William Glenn, June 2, 1861, Glenn Papers. Carl Swisher, *Roger B. Taney* (New York: Macmillan Co., 1936), p. 549.

[42]According to Severn Teackle Wallis, "Merryman was to have been discharged [from the Maryland militia] and the order for his discharge had in fact been written and overlooked by Cameron in the press of business. When Merryman applied for the writ of habeas corpus, they became offended and withdrew the order, and he has been since held and indicted for treason because of his effort to bring the Judiciary in conflict with the Executive. My

Lawyers for the tall, handsome Baltimore countian applied for a writ of habeas corpus, which Taney, the aging Supreme Court Chief Justice, heard in chambers, while on circuit duty, and immediately granted. Yet military authorities at Fort McHenry, where Merryman remained imprisoned without formal charges, refused to honor the writ, noting, in explanation, their authority from the President to suspend habeas corpus "for public safety." Angry, Taney denied both the Presidential power to suspend habeas corpus and the right of a military officer to arrest a civilian "except in and of the judicial authority and subject to its control." With little recourse from the "face of power so notoriously superior," Taney delivered to a crowded courtroom his impassioned opinion, a copy of which he sent directly to Lincoln. Despite his Maryland birth and his acknowledged position as an elder statesman whose career spanned the life of the Republic, the gimlet-eyed, stoop-shouldered Chief Justice feared, in an unusual moment of melodrama, that his actions might lead to imprisonment. "I am an old man, a very old man," Taney said to his friend Mayor Brown of Baltimore, "but perhaps I was preserved for this occasion."[43]

Taney's arguments in *Ex Parte Merryman* were extensions of his position that the President could not suspend habeas corpus. In Taney's view, and that of two giants of American jurisprudence, John Marshall and Joseph Story, this power fell incontestably to Congress. Indeed, as Taney pointed out, the provision regarding habeas corpus appeared in the part of the Constitution, Article I, that related to legislative powers. Yet for the Chief Justice the violation of habeas corpus was only a symptom of "the substitution of military government . . . administered and executed by military officers."

> . . . if the authority which the Constitution has confided to the judiciary department and judicial officers may thus upon any pretext or under any circumstances be usurped by the military power at its discretion, the people of the United States are no longer living under a government of laws, but every citizen holds life, liberty, and property at the will and pleasure of the army officer in whose military district he may happen to be found.[44]

---

authority is Merryman himself to whom Cameron stated the facts when personally at the Fort on the 4th of July." Wallis to Senator James A. Pearce, July 18, 1861, Pearce Papers, MHS.

[43]The pertinent documents in the case are published in Tyler, *Roger Brooke Taney*, p. 427; *O.R.*, 2d ser., 1: 575–86; *Ex Parte Merryman*, 17 Fed. Cases 144 (No. 9,487, Circuit Court, District of Maryland, 1861). For Taney's comment to Brown, see Brown, *Baltimore and the Nineteenth of April*, p. 90.

[44]Tyler, *Roger Brooke Taney*, p. 659. There is a review of the precedents in James G. Randall, *Constitutional Problems under Lincoln*, rev. ed. (Urbana: University of Illinois Press, 1964), pp. 123–39.

Taney's argument, long considered a courageous and important step in the development of American law, actually has played little part in the tradition, application, and development of the writ. After both Attorney General Edward Bates and Horace Binney, the legal pamphleteer, defended the President's prerogative, and after Congress in 1863 authorized the President to suspend habeas corpus "during the present rebellion whenever in his judgment the public safety may require it," subsequent suspensions have been performed "by the executive pursuant to delegated authority."[45] In the 1871 Ku Klux Klan Acts, Congress continued this precedent by giving the President the disputed power "when in his judgment the public safety shall require it to suspend the privilege of the writ of habeas corpus to the end that such rebellion may be overthrown."[46] In all subsequent cases Congress empowered the Executive to suspend the writ of habeas corpus, and hence the Merryman case, which involved authority to withdraw the writ, has become a moot point. Furthermore, while most contemporary observers agree that Congress has the power to suspend the writ, few accept Taney's reasoning that this power comes from the suspension clause, which in form is only a limitation on the power.[47] Thus *Ex Parte Merryman* has become a legal backwater, with little relation to the application or development of habeas corpus to contemporary problems of state and military proceedings, custody, and federal evidentiary hearings.

[45]A typical example of the laudatory view of Taney's argument is found in Walker Lewis, *Without Fear of Favor: A Biography of Chief Justice Roger Brooke Taney* (Boston: Houghton Mifflin, 1965). Recently a prominent Baltimore lawyer eulogistically referred to *Ex Parte Merryman* as "symbolic of the deepest aspirations of our times. . . . Just as the ordinary man may be confused by the debates of theologians' and yet be moved by the examples of the saints, so . . . he may respond in his inmost being to a great act of faith, such as the ruling of Chief Justice Taney in *Ex Parte Merryman.*" Lewis, p. 453. Both Binney and Bates argued that the President had the power to suspend the writ on two grounds: the coordinate power of the three branches of government gave the President the right of suspension as did the right to protect public safety. Horace Binney, *The Privilege of the Writ of Habeas Corpus under the Constitution* (Philadelphia: C. Sherman and Son, 1862) and Bates to Lincoln, July 5, 1861, *O.R.*, 2d ser., 2: 20–30.

[46]Randall, *Constitutional Problems under Lincoln*, p. 135. For an examination of congressional attitudes toward Lincoln's actions, see George Clark Sollery, "Lincoln's Suspension of Habeas Corpus as Viewed by Congress," *Bulletin of University of Wisconsin* 1, no. 3 (1907): 213–86, and William Wiecek, "The Great Writ and Reconstruction: The Habeas Corpus Act of 1867," *Journal of Southern History* 36 (November 1970): 530–48. Wiecek argues that the Habeas Corpus Act of 1867 was "a decisive element in tipping the federal-state balance in favor of the national government."

[47]"Federal Habeas Corpus," *Harvard Law Review* 83 (March 1970): 1265.

For Merryman, however, the intervention of Taney probably helped obtain his release—after seven weeks in prison. Subsequently, Merryman was indicted in civil court for treason and released on bond. His case, like many others, never came to trial—partially because Taney ordered U.S. District Judge William F. Giles not to try capital cases alone, thus insuring that the case would come before the unsympathetic Chief Justice himself.[48] Unchastened, Merryman continued his opposition to the war as well as his associations with "pro-Southern gentlemen," and in the fall of 1862, he was again briefly detained by federal troops.[49] After the war Merryman, his popularity enhanced by his seven-week martyrdom, served as Treasurer of Maryland, and his gratitude to his benefactor was explicit in the name of his son—Roger Brooke Taney Merryman.

Both Merryman and Taney had supplied the Democratic party with a priceless and durable political weapon. A monument to the supposed persecution exacted by Lincoln and his party, the Merryman case provided a vivid symbol of the politics of the trampled ballot, assailed freedom, and violated Constitution. "The imprisonment of Merryman," thundered one Democrat, "finds no precedent in the history of the old Bourbon monarchy of France and of the *lettres de cachet* by which the government consigned those obnoxious to it to the Bastile."[50] Even embarrassed Unionists criticized the Administration's intemperance. In a masterful evasion, Augustus W. Bradford, the Unionist gubernatorial candidate in 1861, described the case "as a source of sadness that civil authorities are subordinate to the military," but, he added, "the Constitution does provide for the suspension of habeas corpus."[51] As long as the opposition made appeals to patriotism, loyalty, and later to "the bloody shirt," Democrats countered with references to unnecessary arrests, the withdrawal of the writ, and "trampled ballots." As long as Unionists complained of treason, Democrats lamented the end of constitutional liberties, and while there were many other examples of what Democrats called violations

[48]John Merryman hardly endeared himself to federal authorities when he refused to see General Banks, who came to visit him in Fort McHenry. For Merryman's explanation of this affair, see Merryman to Banks, June 17, 1861, Banks Papers.

[49]*Cecil Democrat* (Elkton), September 6, 1862.

[50]O. Howard McHenry to Major John Barnard, June 20, 1861, Banks Papers. According to McHenry, the complaints of an angry neighbor, who held a personal grudge against Merryman, had convinced federal authorities of Merryman's disloyalty.

[51]Bradford Campaign Notes, 1861, Bradford Papers, MHS.

of Constitution and Union, none was to be so important in Maryland politics as the Merryman case.

☆ ☆ ☆

THE EFFECTS OF THE EVENTS of 1861 on the state's political parties were immediate and sharp, yet curiously transitory and superficial. The decision to remake the Know-Nothing organization preceded the election of Lincoln, and its implementation continued when Bell supporters gathered to form a party in November. In March 1861 at the direction of a group of former Know-Nothings and Constitutional Unionists in Frederick, state newspapers printed a call "to embrace Union and Constitution and to exclude those who regard secession as a possible remedy."[52] In June, Unionists nominated candidates to stand at a special congressional election. Unopposed in two of six districts, the party elected all of its candidates and won 72 percent of the state vote. For a party of questionable durability in 1860, it was a display of considerable vitality.

In large part the Unionist success was the result of the war, which removed opposition voters from the state, scared others from the polls, and permitted Unionism the luxury of becoming the party of loyal Marylanders. Inheriting the voters and organization of the Constitutional Unionists as well as the support of some former Democrats, the party played artfully on the strings of Constitution and Union. In the words of one party member, "war is not waged for subjugation or to impair the institutions of the South but rather it is fought to maintain the pillars of government, Constitution and Union."[53] The

[52]Baltimore *Clipper*, March 21, 1861. There are references to preliminary meetings among Union men in both the Bradford and Randall Papers, MHS. See Diary of Alexander Randall, November 21, 1860, and January 1861, Randall Papers and Augustus Bradford to William Fisher, December 4, 1860, Bradford Papers. In two congressional races, the second district in Baltimore county and city and the fifth district in northwest Maryland, Unionists ran without opposition, and in Baltimore's fourth district both candidates, Henry May and Henry Winter Davis, ran as Unionists. In the first, third, and sixth districts Unionists received 53 percent of the vote. Some 67,000 Marylanders voted, compared to a turnout of 87,000 in the congressional races two years earlier, but this decline was partially the result of two uncontested congressional races. As Charles Wagandt points out, "no charges of corrupt or prejudicial practices marred the results." Charles Wagandt, *The Mighty Revolution: Negro Emancipation in Maryland, 1862–1864* (Baltimore: Johns Hopkins Press, 1964), p. 17. A New York soldier stationed in Annapolis agreed. "All even to the half-traitor and rebel were permitted to exercise the free and unmolested expression of his political opinions." Diary of Philip W. Holmes, June 1861, New York Public Library.

[53]Baltimore *American*, September 6, 1861.

rhetoric of the Union party unremittingly stressed the twin verities, Constitution and Union, which were present on the lips of every candidate.[54]

Quite naturally, if unfairly, Unionists developed the corollary position that the opposition party was the party of treason. According to one Unionist, "There are only two parties. One is for secession and to kiss the hem of Jefferson Davis or Beauregard and the other is the Union Party."[55] To many Unionists any political opposition was evidence of disloyalty and secessionism. Certainly Governor Hicks—at least for campaign purposes—accepted this equation with his reference to the opposition as "the serpent's head of secessionism" and "the wolf in sheep's clothing."[56]

This representation of loyalty and its inverted image of treason enabled Unionists to present themselves as more than mere politicians, and their party as more than the traditional wire-pulling organizations so despised by Marylanders. While insisting that "the Disunion party spawned at Frederick is the progeny of a few desperate and heavily played-out wind-broke politicians," Unionists conveniently found themselves the party of "patriots in a struggle with traitors and the Devil."[57] For some, Unionism represented a return to the spontaneous patriotism of the Revolution; for others, the emphasis on one party was a response to the failures of partisan politics. "One country, one Constitution, and one people now and forever," proclaimed party banners, and Montgomery Blair agreed that "there was no other party but the American people."[58]

Some Unionists found that appeals to loyalty and patriotism served as successful masks for the embarrassments of specific policies. Thus, the issue of slavery in the territories was, in the view of one

[54]An analysis of word frequency in the "Address of the Union State Committee" in the fall of 1861 reveals that the word union was used 25 times, constitution 18 times, and Maryland 17 times in an address of 4,100 words. The address ended with a typical peroration: "They do not tear or stir us from our anchorage on the Constitution and our honored flag is still at the peak, Union up, and every star on it." Address of the Union State Central Committee, October 8, 1961. Civil War Diary of Samuel Harrison, October 9, 1861, Harrison Papers, MHS.

[55]*Cecil Whig* (Elkton), August 10, 1861.

[56]Hicks to Banks, November 2, 1861, Banks Papers; Hicks to Bradford, August 19, 1861, Bradford Papers.

[57]*Cecil Whig* (Elkton), August 31, June 29, 1861.

[58]Baltimore *Sun*, November 5, 1861; Blair's statement is quoted in a letter from Jacob Tome to John A. J. Creswell, May 16, 1861, Aldine Papers, MHS and in the Baltimore *Sun*, May 22, 1861.

prominent politician, "an abstraction."[59] When ex-Governor Francis Thomas, newly elected to Congress from western Maryland, observed that the South might as well appeal to him for support because he had horses as demand his support because he had slaves, some Unionists wished he had not mentioned the institution.[60]

Only economic issues led Unionists into explicit commitments. In a year of undeniable economic hardship, and at a time when some Marylanders struggled as much for food as for proper answers to the crisis of the Union, the party continually emphasized the economic advantages of maintaining the Union.[61] Reverdy Johnson, the prominent former U.S. Attorney General and candidate for the 1862 state legislature, noted the disparity in wealth between free and slave states and urged Maryland's allegiance to the Union. In his campaign for governor, Augustus Bradford, an effective and persuasive stump speaker, frequently described secessionists as wealthy aristocrats who, once in power, would raise taxes on the poor.[62] Not all Marylanders were persuaded that the election of Unionists would lead to better times. One angry citizen described a political procession "with martial music, mingled with hollow cheers from the empty stomachs . . . rising above the wailing cries of little ones at home for bread, bread. Is this a time to talk politics?"[63]

To instill the image of their party as a spontaneous and natural community expression, the Unionists of 1861 tried to choose candidates whose associations with political organizations of the past were either limited or lapsed. Such a man was Augustus Bradford, the prominent Baltimorean who had retired from the turbulent politics of the 1850s and who now returned "unencumbered by previous political impediments."[64] A former Harford countian, Bradford had been a

[59]Thomas Swann to Salmon P. Chase, January 28, 1861, Chase Papers.

[60]Baltimore *American*, October 30, 1861; *Mountain Valley Register* (Middletown), November 2, 1861.

[61]For evidence of economic hardship, see W. Catton, "Baltimore Business Community and the Secession Crisis"; Civil War Diary of Samuel Harrison, August 22, 1861, Harrison Papers; Baltimore *Sun*, March 25, 27, 1861; and Diary of Richard T. Townshend, 1861, Enoch Pratt Library, Baltimore, Md. One Baltimore newspaper estimated that there were 5,398 unemployed in Baltimore of an industrial work force of 16,000. Baltimore *Daily Exchange*, April 7, July 12, 1861.

[62]Baltimore *American*, May 8, 1861; Bradford Campaign Notes, 1861, Bradford Papers.

[63]L. M. Blair to Editors of the Baltimore *Daily Exchange*, 1861, State Department Records.

[64]Civil War Diary of Samuel Harrison, July 26, August 1, 1861, Harrison Papers.

Whig elector in 1844 and clerk of the Baltimore City Court until his retirement from politics.[65] Representing the patriot restored to public affairs in an hour of need, a Maryland Cincinnatus, Bradford received the gubernatorial nomination over a number of candidates whose ties to party organizations were more substantial. Bradford's success encouraged other Unionist candidates to present themselves as disinterested patriots intent on serving their country. So convinced of the change in the caliber of candidates was Allen Davis of Montgomery county that he feared the party's nominations for the fall elections "too good and elevated for the present degenerate day of American democracy."[66]

Actually most Unionists had some association with parties of the past, and in many instances this political journey had led from the Know-Nothings of the 1850s to the Constitutional Unionists of 1860 and the Unionists of 1861. While the Unionists publicized their success in creating a new coalition of all parties, only a handful of Democratic leaders, including Reverdy Johnson, Henry Goldsborough, and Samuel S. Maffitt, actually joined the party. Both the Frederick *Examiner* and the Baltimore *Daily Exchange* quite correctly described Unionists as former Know-Nothings.[67] The new faces among the party were those of men who, temporarily retired from the turbulent politics of the 1850s, now returned to public service.

Like their Know-Nothing and Constitutional Union counterparts, Unionists were more likely to be lawyers and businessmen than their opponents and less likely to be slaveholders. Yet the ownership of slaves was neither an asset nor a liability for ambitious Unionists. Charles B. Calvert, direct descendant of the colonial proprietors of the state and a Unionist congressional candidate, was one of Maryland's largest slaveholders, and at least fifteen other party leaders owned slaves.

From its beginnings the Union party kept the national Republican organization at arm's length. Such a posture led newspapers to note the reluctance of Maryland Unionists to aid Lincoln's party. Only through the medium of patronage did the two political organizations achieve even a temporary embrace. Hicks, promised more than the

[65] Augustus Bradford, "Application for Membership in the Maryland Historical Society," Dielman File, MHS.

[66] Allen Davis to Willie Davis, August 24, 1861, Allen B. Davis Papers.

[67] Frederick *Examiner*, March 27, September 18, 1861; Baltimore *Daily Exchange*, June 4, 1861. For a social profile of Unionist and States' Rights leaders, see Appendix Tables D-7, D-8, D-9, and D-10.

usual governor's voice in federal appointments if he would "stand firm" during the secession winter of 1861, shared these appointments with Henry Winter Davis, the deposed congressman, and Montgomery Blair, Lincoln's newly appointed Postmaster General.[68] While Hicks saw the patronage as a state matter, Blair and Davis, both ambitious and anxious for a national reordering of parties, sought, in Blair's words, to create "an administration party in Maryland."[69] Some out-of-state newspapers predicted that Marylanders would resist the appointment of a Republican collector, postmaster, and naval officer. Yet the only resistance that followed Lincoln's appointment of Republicans to one-half of Maryland's important patronage jobs came from unhappy Unionists who still recognized, in their state at least, important differences between the two organizations.

Partially successful in their attempts to hide division over patronage, Unionists were less successful in concealing a sharp battle over organization. Touted as a patriotic mass movement, yet functioning as a nineteenth-century political party, the organization had difficulty in serving two such divergent functions. The party began in the traditional way. One early Unionist noted: "We can only agree to attend primary meetings which will be held in different wards for the purpose of selecting delegates to a city convention, which convention will appoint delegates to a state convention which will have the selection of a candidate."[70] In the uncertain days of 1861, such local organizations also served as the nucleus for a military organization. From the beginning there was dissension between these local units and the self-appointed state central committee which represented many of the older "patriots" returned to politics. Even after a palace revolution installed a new central committee to organize the fall elections, division within the party continued. In a letter to Salmon P. Chase, Montgomery Blair complained of the jealousy between the officeholders of the party who refused to contribute to the Unionist campaign and the central committee.[71] Henry Winter Davis described the central com-

[68]John Lucas to Hicks, December 11, 1861, Hicks Papers; Harry Carman and Reinhard Luthin, *Lincoln and the Patronage* (New York: Columbia University Press, 1943), pp. 205–8; Frederick *Examiner*, April 17, 1861.

[69]Blair to an unidentified correspondent, n.d., Box 11, Blair Papers, Library of Congress.

[70]Civil War Diary of Samuel Harrison, June 15, 1861, Harrison Papers.

[71]Blair to Chase, November 2, 1861, Chase Papers; Frederick *Examiner*, July 17, 24, 1861.

mittee as worse than useless and concluded that "the party machinery is sadly out of gear."[72] Such friction revealed the Unionist failure to integrate Republicans into a patriotic movement which was, at the same time, a political party.

☆ ☆ ☆

WHILE UNIONISTS WORKED to present the image of a spontaneous patriotic organization, Democrats became victims of their own propaganda. The endless talk of administration repression, trampled ballots, and military obstruction ended in an egregious blunder—the party merged with the new States' Rights organization. By the spring of 1861, the chairman of the executive committee insisted that it was "inexpedient to organize a Democratic party ticket."[73] Even the name—Democrat—a powerful talisman for generations of Maryland voters, disappeared from voting tickets amid a welter of references to the States' Rights, Southern Rights, Peace, and Constitutional parties. "In Cambridge," joked the Unionist Easton *Gazette*, "they are called the Peace Party, in Somerset the Southern Rights, in Worcester States' Rights."[74]

Efforts to form a new organization had begun early in 1861 when Democrats tried to force Hicks to convene the legislature. William Glenn, a prominent Democrat, described the early meetings of the party:

> Half a dozen of us had a meeting in the office of John Thompson Mason, Collector of the Port. It was their determination to have a preliminary meeting of prominent ward Democrats to get an expression of the sentiment of the people. Messages were sent by Custom House clerks to about two men from each ward. Jesse Hunt, who had been Mayor, Vansant the Hatter, always a prominent ward politician, Peter Morvell, iron master, one or two members of the city council and men of that class of people having influence over men by whom they were supported or whom they employed. . . . After meeting in late January ward organizations were formed and meetings held from time to time.[75]

[72]Davis to Hiram Barney, October 31, 1861, Chase Papers.

[73]*St. Mary's Beacon* (Leonardtown), August 22, 1861.

[74]Easton *Gazette*, June 1, 1861.

[75]Civil War Diary of William Glenn, January 18, February 3, 1861, Glenn Papers. John T. Mason, a friend of President James Buchanan, was an important Democratic official during the 1850s as were Jesse Hunt, Joshua Vansant, the prominent hat manufacturer, and Peter Morvell, owner of an iron foundry.

From this meeting in January came the political organization which elected ten Baltimore delegates to the General Assembly in the spring of 1861 and which contested the state elections in the fall.

While the States' Rights party employed largely the same organization, leaders, and appeals as its parent, it was never more than a weak reflection of the Democracy of the 1850s. "Nowhere," complained one of its founders, "was there any concerted action or any well-digested plan of operation."[76] The chairman of the States' Rights organization admitted his confusion to the party's gubernatorial candidate:

> I propose having a council on Monday of our States Rights Convention Committee upon the question of having candidates in the field for a vote in this city, in full contest with the Unionists. . . . It is advisable, I think, that the names of our candidates do not come forward as States Rights Convention nominations but as nominations from the body of people designated as independent or, if more attractive, as Democrat.[77]

Such indecision led some candidates to protest that while opponents were "efficiently officered and drilled," theirs was not an organized party.[78]

Similar confusion was apparent in the party's leadership and nominations. Although a few Democratic officials had joined the Unionists, many more had left for the Confederacy. Bradley Johnson had marched a large portion of the leadership in Frederick county to Virginia, while former Governor E. Louis Lowe and Elias Griswold, a party official, worked to recruit Confederate soldiers from among their Democratic friends. War, the occupation of the young, had left the old to run the States' Rights organization. As vigorous and youthful Democrats marched off to military battle, they left behind venerable uncles, fathers, and cousins to fight political campaigns. Thus, seventy-year-old Benjamin Chew Howard replaced his cousin, the energetic thirty-five-year-old editor of the Baltimore *Daily Exchange*, Frank Howard. Fifty-six-year-old Benjamin Harris succeeded the youthful George Hughes as party leader in southern Maryland. Even William Preston, rejected in 1859 as a candidate, found few competitors for the congressional nomination which he had long sought. The average age of the States' Rights leaders, fifty-one, reversed the trend

[76] Civil War Diary of William Glenn, January 18, February 3, 1861, Glenn Papers.

[77] Charles F. Mayer to B. C. Howard, October 12, 1861, Bayard Papers.

[78] Baltimore *Sun*, June 18, 1861.

toward younger officials instituted by the Democrats in the late 1850s and put the party in the hands of the state's older gentry.[79]

Certainly the nomination of Howard, the wealthy son of a Revolutionary war hero whose own sons now served in the Confederate Army, had symbolic implications for the States' Rights party. Yet in terms of practical electioneering, the choice of a Catholic candidate for governor in a state where nativist sentiments were both obvious and pervasive and where the Catholic voting bloc was neither established nor numerically significant, reflected the party's indifferent and negligent attitude toward winning elections. Howard was also handicapped by his own indecisiveness about whether to run, but finally in late September he began his campaign.[80]

The appeals that Howard and the limping States' Rights party brought before the electorate were based on "the politics of the trampled ballot." Resolutions throughout the state protested the coercive policy of the Lincoln administration and urged a peaceful solution to the war. With numbing repetition, candidates returned to the Merryman case as an example of the repressiveness of the "war party," which had violated Constitution and Union. In the words of the popular jingle:

> John Merryman, the Marylander,
> Would not stoop to Lincoln's pander.[81]

In many counties, the States' Rights organization was known as the habeas corpus party, and while not all States' Rightists agreed with one candidate's ironic pronouncement that all Marylanders were slaves, few hesitated to sing the denunciatory new poem:

> The despot's heel is on thy shore,
> Maryland:
> His torch is at thy Temple door,
> Maryland:
> Avenge the Patriotic gore,
> That flecked the streets of Baltimore.
> And be the battle queen of yore,
> Maryland, my Maryland.[82]

[79]See Appendix Tables D-7, D-8, D-9, and D-10. Of sixty States' Rights leaders, I found only three former members of the Know-Nothing party, whereas thirty-eight had some associations with the prewar Democracy.

[80]John Crisfield to Augustus Bradford, September 29, 1861, Gratz Papers, Historical Society of Pennsylvania, Pa.

[81]Stinnecke Scrapbook, Peabody Library.

[82]Written by the Baltimore-born James Ryder Randall after the Baltimore riot in April 1861 while he was teaching at a Louisiana college, the poem was put to the music of a

Yet there was little agreement about how to remove the "despot's heel." On the Eastern Shore, Daniel M. Henry, a candidate for Congress, favored an end to the war and recognition of the Confederacy. Such a position led Henry to oppose voting money for the prosecution of the war.[83] By summer few candidates for state office held such extreme views, although many favored reconstruction and restoration of the Union. In Montgomery county, States' Rights leaders proclaimed their devotion to Constitution and Union, their opposition to military arrests and the Republican party, and their commitment to "all constitutional and legal means to bring about a speedy, amicable, and honorable settlement of the existing national difficulties."[84]

In the northern and western counties, States' Rights candidates avoided the issue of the war and simply attacked the opposition as abolitionists, Black Republicans, and "corrupt relics of the defunct Know-Nothings, christened the Union party."[85] Such name-calling was as close as the States' Rights organization ever got to the issues of slavery, free Negroes, and other local problems. One Harford countian, astonished at this neglect of slavery, gave an impassioned defense of the institution based on the Bible, a defense which never played the slightest part in the party's public appeals.[86]

On a damp, rainy day in November 1861, with the war at a standstill in nearby Virginia, Marylanders went to the polls to elect a governor, a new General Assembly, eleven state senators, and a variety of local officials. The election results surprised no one. Bradford received 68 percent of a total vote which had declined less than 10 percent from the presidential vote of 1860. Failing to carry even the county named for his father, Howard won only three southern Maryland counties and Talbot on the Eastern Shore. Exuberant, Henry Winter Davis reported to his faithful correspondent, Samuel Francis Du Pont: "We carried every county and almost every district of every

---

popular college song. With minor changes it became the state's official anthem. Later Randall complained that his career had been handicapped by "Maryland, My Maryland." "I have written better poems, but the world tags me with the more sonorous lyric." James Randall to Mr. Cleveland, January 6, 1905, Randall Papers, Southern Historical Collection, University of North Carolina. See also "James Ryder Randall," Dielman File.

[83]Easton *Gazette*, June 1, 1861; Port Tobacco *Times*, May 30, 1861.

[84]M. Veirs Bouic, William Brewer, and Isaac Young, "Description of a Political Convention," September 13, 1861, Banks Papers.

[85]"Unus" to Editors of the *Daily Exchange*, June 25, 1861, State Department Records.

[86]George A. Nitte to Kerr *et al.*, August 17, 1861, State Department Records.

county except St. Mary's, Charles, and Calvert between Patuxent and Potomac. Only six opposition men in the House of Delegates. We have Senate and Court of Appeals and Governor (Bradford) and local judges."[87] (Map 2 shows a geographic distribution of the Unionist vote.)

The Unionist majority included the votes of some 7,000 Marylanders who had not voted for Bell, Douglas, or Lincoln in 1860. Yet the bulk of the party's support still came from the Unionist-Know-Nothing organization. For all the appeals to a new coalition of patriots, Unionism received its votes primarily from those Marylanders who had voted against the Democrats in the late 1850s.[88]

To the States' Rights organization, such an overwhelming defeat clearly demonstrated the military intimidation and coercion which prevented a free election. In fact, by heeding their own appeals and staying away from the polls, Democrats fulfilled the prophecy of the "politics of the trampled ballot." Certainly the presence of federal troops in the area of the polls and the arrests of returning Confederate soldiers inhibited some voters, although not as many as either the losers or the historians have suggested.[89]

Actually, the activities of the army were remarkably restrained and curiously disassociated from partisan politics. Apparently oblivious to the coming election, in the fall the army released some political leaders, the so-called "graduates of Fort McHenry."[90] During the campaign, soldiers rarely interfered with political meetings or arrested candidates. Following Lincoln's announcement that arrests could be made only "on substantial and unmistakable complicity with those in armed rebellion against the government of the United States,"[91] army

[87]Davis to Du Pont, November 15, 1861, Du Pont Papers. Davis overlooked Talbot, which Howard won by one vote.

[88]The coefficient of correlation between the vote for Bradford on a county-by-county basis, and that of the Know-Nothing party in 1859 is +.8576; that of the Bell party in 1860 and the Bradford vote, +.9337. Approximately 83,572 Marylanders voted in the gubernatorial election compared to 92,502 in the presidential election of 1860. The Unionist vote of 57,502 is 7,000 more than the combined vote of Bell, Douglas, and Lincoln in 1860 which was 50,020. Thus at least 7,000 Marylanders who either had not voted in 1860 or who voted for Breckinridge voted Unionist in 1861.

[89]See, for example, Charles Clark, *Maryland Politics during the Civil War* (Chestertown, Md., 1952), p. 25. Actually few soldiers even approached the polls except to vote themselves. In most election districts there were no troops even in the area. See *O.R.*, 1st ser., 5: 386, 646, 561; 2d ser., 1: 609.

[90]The phrase is used in a letter from S. T. Wallis to W. W. Glenn, June 3, 1861, Glenn Papers.

[91]Basler, *Collected Works of Abraham Lincoln*, 4: 523.

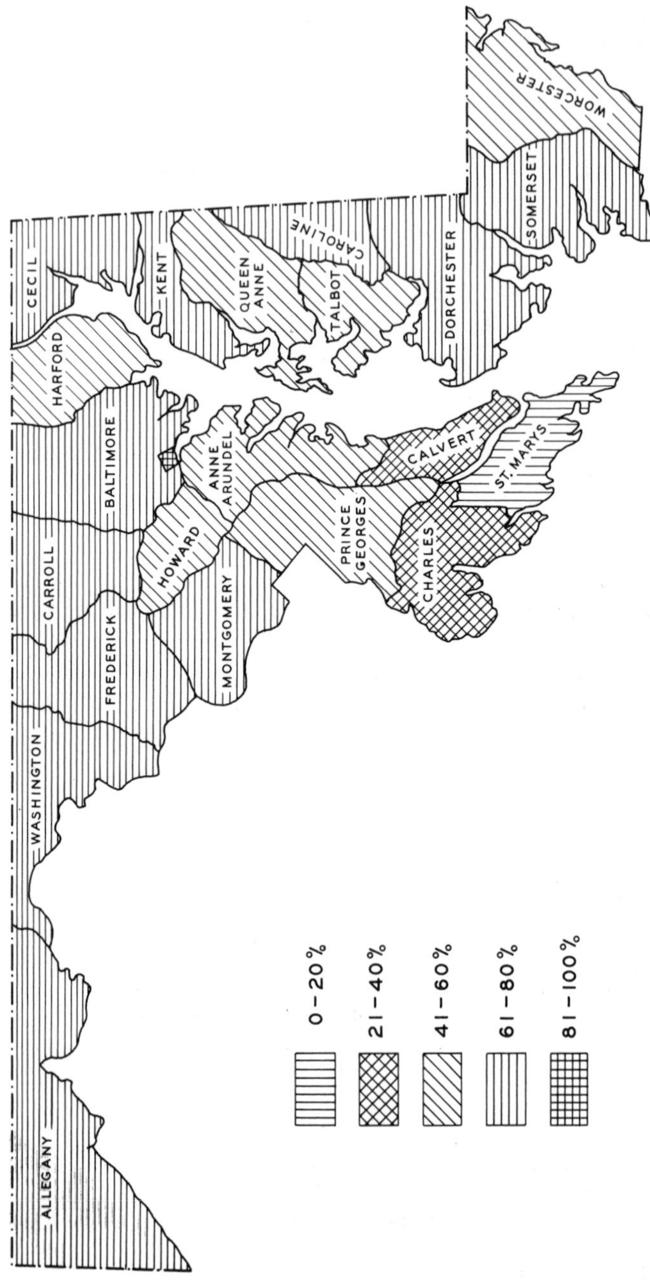

Map 2. *Geographic Distribution of the Unionist Vote for Governor in 1861*

commanders usually showed their recognition of the crucial difference between disloyalty and opposition politics.

Certainly John A. Dix, Commander of the Middle District, defined his prerogatives narrowly. In a letter to two Harford county election judges who had requested that a loyalty oath be administered to all prospective voters, Dix denied his power to introduce such a restriction. Dix argued that "... the Constitution and laws of Maryland provide for the exercise of the elective franchise by regulations with which I have no right to interfere."[92] Insisting that there should be no obstruction to a fair election, Dix refused numerous requests for the protection of Unionists who feared that the States' Rights organization would prevent voting in isolated districts of the state. Dix did agree that Maryland's federal troops, numbering approximately 8,000 in the fall of 1861,[93] should be furloughed to vote, and many regiments quickly made such arrangements. As one soldier wrote to his wife, "Don't look for me before the election."[94] There was nothing illegal about such a procedure, although opponents finding no precedent used military voting as another example of the "politics of the trampled ballot." On the other hand, the army did try to prevent members of the Confederate Army, some of whom mysteriously appeared in the state just before the election, from voting.

The best evidence that the Unionist victory was not a product of federal intervention came from States' Rights sympathizers who described the election as "quiet" and "free from molestation." "In my little district in this county where we poll but 420 votes we gave 100 majority for States Rights candidates," explained Ramsay McHenry of the area he knew firsthand.[95] Yet McHenry insisted that other areas, of which he had no firsthand knowledge, had fallen victim to federal interference.

Actually the decline in the Democratic vote came not from military interference but from a poorly organized campaign, the party's failure to appeal to Democrats, the departure of many States' Rights voters to Virginia, and the defection of others to the Unionists. As one dedicated party leader admitted in a letter to the defeated gubernatorial candidate: "While you were ready to sacrifice yourself if

[92]Dix to Daniel Engel and William Ecker, November 1, 1861, Bradford Papers.

[93]Millard Les Callette, "A Study of the Recruitment of the Union Army in Maryland" (master's thesis, Johns Hopkins University, 1954), pp. 44, 53, 114; *O.R.*, 1st ser., 5: 628.

[94]William J. Sherwood to his wife, October 23, 1861, vertical file, MHS.

[95]McHenry to Colonel George Gale, December 9, 1861, Gale Papers, MHS. See also Diary of Mrs. Benjamin G. Harris, November 7, 1861, Harris Papers.

necessary, your friends were not equally ready to support you."[96] Howard also suffered from the failure of some States' Rights voters, frightened by that party's harangues about military interference, to support a new political organization which did not even use the Democratic label.[97] Other potential States' Rights voters had left the state to take up residence in the Confederacy or to join the Confederate army in northern Virginia. After the congressional elections in June, a perceptive party member found that in almost every case the difference in the vote between the States' Rights candidates in 1861 and the Breckinridge vote in 1860 was "accounted for by those in the army or elsewhere and States Rights men not voting."[98] By fall even more Marylanders had joined the Confederacy, and it was this removal of able-bodied males who were coincidentally voters which helped to explain the low States' Rights vote.[99]

Thus, by the fall of 1861, two apparently new political organizations controlled Maryland politics. Both had emerged during the confused and turbulent secession crisis, and both insisted that they were new political organizations. Yet, in fact, the States' Rights and Unionist parties owed much to the past. Unionism, in terms of its structure, constituency, leaders, and appeals was a replica of the prewar Constitutional Unionist movement, which, in turn, had grown out of the American party. And like the old Know-Nothings, Unionists of 1861 played on the themes of patriotism, loyalty to Constitution, and devotion to Union. Although these themes took on a new urgency when the war began, they had been essential parts of political platforms in the past. The constituency which responded to these appeals, with a few new recruits, was the same one which contested Democratic control of the state in the late 1850s. The States' Rights organization, formed by older Democrats, also failed to achieve its promised new direction in Maryland politics. Employing the familiar accusation used

[96]"Gouv" Kemble to B. C. Howard, November 10, 1861, Bayard Papers.

[97]Very late in the campaign some Democrats tried to remedy this error by printing voting tickets under the heading of the Democratic party. Decorated with etchings of Jefferson and Jackson, these tickets were distributed in Baltimore. Baltimore *Sun*, November 6, 1861; Civil War Diary of Samuel Harrison, November 6, 1861, Harrison Papers.

[98]Memorandum on Voting, June 1861, State Department Records. Coefficients of correlation reveal that those who did support the States' Rights organizations lived in areas of former Democratic strength. Coefficients of correlation on a county-by-county basis between the vote for Howard in 1861 and that for Breckinridge in 1860 are +.9151, for the Democratic candidate for Comptroller in 1859 and for Howard, +.7830.

[99]According to Les Callette, "many had left for Canada and other British possessions." Les Callette, "Recruitment of the Union Army," p. 52; Baltimore *Sun*, August 9, 1861.

by Democrats in the 1850s that their opponents interfered with free elections, States' Rights leaders developed the "politics of the trampled ballot." In place of partisan police and unruly mobs, party members substituted the interference of the soldiers in blue. Even as neighboring Virginia towns became the names for bloody military engagements, both political organizations continued to find their most important symbols in nostalgic appeals to Constitution and Union. Popular predictions in the spring of 1861 that the crisis of secession and war had transformed Maryland's political parties, were not valid.[100] Neither the politics of patriotism nor those of the "trampled ballot" had disturbed the traditional patterns of Maryland parties.

[100] For an example, see Bradford's "Address at Snow Hill, Maryland, 1861," Bradford Papers.

IV. "THE ODIUM OF FACTION": DIVISION WITHIN THE UNIONIST PARTY, 1862-1864

IN JUNE 1863, while Union forces maneuvered near Gettysburg, the Union party in Maryland prepared to fight an equally bitter, if less sanguinary, struggle against the perennial infirmity of political parties—faction. The successes of the army however, were not repeated among Maryland Unionists, and by July, as veterans of the fighting in Pennsylvania straggled through the state, two central committees directed the party, two conventions nominated candidates, and two sets of Unionist candidates sought office. The Unionist organization did not recover from this division, and while the party continued to direct the political fortunes of the state for three more years, these wounds of faction never healed.[1]

The division among Unionists surprised some Marylanders who, convinced that the party was a patriotic expression rather than a political organization, anticipated no dissension within the self-named "party of loyalty." Certainly campaign appeals to Constitution and Union gave no indication of differences within the party, and without statewide elections in 1862, there was no platform on which to display disagreements.

Unionist delegates in the 1862 legislature, who controlled sixty-eight of the Assembly's seventy-four seats, gave little evidence of factionalism.[2] On most issues they voted together with remarkable consistency. Avoiding the possible lures of division over war measures, Unionists quickly established their support of the administration by voting increased taxes, rewriting a militia bill, and passing a treason

[1]The Unionist party from 1862 to 1864 represented what political scientists call a modified one-party system. In 1862 the party controlled 82 percent of the legislature, in 1864, 76 percent, while 81 percent of Maryland's delegation to both the Thirty-seventh and Thirty-eighth Congresses was Unionist. In 1864, 54 percent of the Maryland electorate voted for a Union governor, 54 percent for the party's presidential candidate, Lincoln. Political scientists have used numerous ways to measure the degree of party control by measuring the proportion of success, duration of success, and frequency of divided control. I devised an index of competitiveness based on the average percentage of popular vote in state and national elections and the average percentage of seats controlled in the state legislature. According to this index, the Maryland Union party registered .723 on the scale of competitiveness. This compares with .615 for the Democrats in 1859-60, and .850 for Democrats in 1867-70. Any average of more than .900 or less than .100 defines a one-party system; .700-.900 or .100-.299, a modified one-party system; .300-.699, a two-party system. See Richard Hofferbert, "Classification of American Party Systems," *Journal of Politics* 26 (August 1964): 550-68, and Herbert Jacob and Kenneth Vines, *Politics in the American States* (Boston: Little, Brown & Co., 1965), p. 64.

[2]The index of party cohesion on forty-eight roll calls chosen according to procedures outlined in Chapter 1 was 72, only slightly below average for a majority party in the period 1858-70. This index of cohesion does not include roll calls from the special session convened by Governor Bradford in December 1861.

bill that prescribed penalties for "acts which promoted rebellion." Despite earlier hesitation about Lincoln, leaders even checked with the President, so that "assembly resolutions would not conflict with the policy you have adopted."[3]

In keeping with the traditions of Maryland parties, Unionists took a careful look at national policy, and in 1862 they had special reason to do so, for Simon Cameron, Lincoln's Secretary of War, had proposed that Maryland's western counties be transferred to Virginia, that the Eastern Shore become part of Delaware, and that portions of Virginia be joined to Maryland.[4] Not only did the Assembly condemn this intemperate plan, but legislators also considered Lincoln's war strategy, the tariff, and even foreign policy to be proper subjects for their review. Whatever the differences between party members in debate, pronouncements on national policy produced great unanimity among Unionists, whose top-heavy voting majority could have led, without embarrassment or risk, to disagreement.

Wartime concerns did not completely replace the more parochial interests of Maryland legislators. The usual complaints that the legislature did not "live up to the expectations of the people" included accusations that the Assembly was "trifling with private bills and federal resolves."[5] A party which had come to office with few specific policies had little difficulty in translating the abstractions of Constitution and Union into explicit proposals redistricting the state, defining riparian rights, organizing a state-funded public-school system, and extending stay laws.[6] Unionist policy aided no discernible economic groups, although the party did reward faithful supporters with incorporations and patronage.[7]

Amidst this display of voting unity on general roll calls, there was one issue which consistently divided Unionists—the future of slavery and free Negroes. In the early meetings of the legislature, party members insisted that any reference to slavery distracted from the issue at hand—the restoration of the Union. Delegate after delegate urged the

[3]Reverdy Johnson to Lincoln, January 16, 1862, Lincoln Papers, Library of Congress.

[4]*O.R.*, 3d ser., 1: 698, 708; Baltimore *Sun*, December 6, 1861.

[5]*Cecil Whig* (Elkton), January 18, 1862.

[6]The stay law, a legacy of the 1860 legislature, was a boon to hard-pressed debtors, as it "stayed" or prevented execution of some mortgage loans. *Journal of the Proceedings of the House of Delegates* (Annapolis: Thomas J. Wilson, 1862), p. 855.

[7]Walter Sanderlin, "A House Divided—The Conflict of Loyalties on the Chesapeake and Ohio Canal, 1861-1865," *Maryland Historical Magazine* 42 (September 1947):207. See also Proceedings of the President and Directors of the Chesapeake and Ohio, 1862, Record Group 79, Records of the Department of the Interior, National Archives.

postponement of topics calculated "to stir up trouble."[8] Yet the issue of Maryland's black population and the relationship of the Union party to slavery kept intruding. While members unanimously passed the anachronistic constitutional amendment prohibiting congressional interference with "the domestic institutions of any state" as well as a proposal condemning the emancipation of slaves in the nearby District of Columbia, problems of fugitive slaves and special manumissions produced significant disagreement. When George Smith of Worcester county introduced a bill "to allow an estimable old gentleman to manumit a number of faithful servants," debate ensued over Maryland's free Negroes. According to Reverdy Johnson, soon to be elected to the U.S. Senate by the legislature, Maryland already had enough free Negroes who had nowhere to go, for the "North would not have them." Other delegates, some from western Maryland, agreed that free blacks were a "curse to the state."[9] Even the party's plan to call a new Constitutional Convention produced anguished discussion about whether slavery should be a proper topic of convention debate. Alert newspaper reporters noted increasing acrimony within the Unionist caucus meetings, particularly on racial issues.

Such disagreements were not played entirely on the local stage. In March 1862, Lincoln presented a plan for compensated emancipation, based on a congressional appropriation to state governments for the purchase of slaves from loyal owners. Even the added fillip of possible colonization for emancipated slaves failed to make the Lincoln proposals palatable to most Maryland Unionists. While newspapers grumbled that "Maryland never would have ceded the District of Columbia if she had known the government would abolish slavery," the state's congressional delegation opposed the bill to emancipate slaves in the District of Columbia. These Unionist congressmen said little during the debates in Congress, although all supported a report opposing Lincoln's plan and urging the President to wage war solely "for the restoration of the Constitution."[10] Constituents at home were more explicit. Calling the President's proposals "ungracious at this time to the Union men of border states," Unionist Samuel Harrison pointed to their possible effects: "The undermining of the con-

[8] Baltimore *American*, April 4, 1862.

[9] *Proceedings of the House of Delegates, 1862*, pp. 93, 164; Baltimore *American*, February 27, 1862; Baltimore *Sun*, January 24, 1862.

[10] *Maryland Union* (Frederick), April 17, 1862; *Congressional Globe*, 37th Cong., 2d sess., 1862, 32, pt. 2, pp. 1179, 1197, 1649; Charles Wagandt, *The Mighty Revolution: Negro Emancipation in Maryland, 1862–1864* (Baltimore: Johns Hopkins Press, 1964), pp. 55–70.

fidence in government of the millions of white men who make up its chief support . . . and the resuscitation of the Democratic party."[11]

For the first time in state history, however, emancipation became a public issue. Samuel Harrison noted that "the policy of gradual emancipation is publicly discussed and the economy of free labor in opposition to the slave is defended."[12] The Maryland correspondent of the New York *World* agreed: "The rebellion has at least secured people of the border states what they never had before: The power to discuss the subject of slavery and emancipation in their public journals and on the hustings."[13]

Gradually, most Unionists came to accept the principle of emancipation, while condemning what was still described as the fanaticism of abolitionists. Even Thomas Hicks, a slaveholder and by 1862 a candidate for an important federal patronage job, gave his support to emancipation, calling it as much a blow "against ultraists of the North as at Southern fanatics."[14] The important Unionist daily, the Baltimore *American*, supported emancipation in the spring of 1862, and by July the paper found a welter of arguments to support its contention that slavery crippled Maryland's economy. In the fall, when Lincoln announced his preliminary Emancipation Proclamation, promising to free slaves "in rebellious states" after January 1, 1863, the *American* used the President's own arguments to justify freedom as a war measure.[15]

While some Unionists assumed that public debate insured support of emancipation,[16] this was not the case. To an important segment of the Union party, plans for gradual emancipation served as distractions from the war; the Emancipation Proclamation was an infringement on state powers; and discussion of either would only increase southern resistance. When the Baltimore city convention passed resolutions favoring gradual emancipation, Unionists who feared any association with a movement to abolish slavery challenged the convention's right

[11]Civil War Diary of Samuel Harrison, April 17, 26, 1862, Harrison Papers, MHS.

[12]*Ibid.*, March 22, 27, 1862.

[13]New York *World*, April 15, 1862.

[14]Hicks to Lincoln, March 18, 1862, Lincoln Papers.

[15]Baltimore *American*, May 10, 15, July 31, September 1, 29, 1862; January 3, 1863. Cynics suggested that the change in the *American's* attitude emanated in part from the fact that the paper's editor, C. C. Fulton, was now an official war correspondent. As Lincoln wrote Seward, "Fulton is now with us." Lincoln to William Henry Seward, June 29, 1862, Roy P. Basler, ed., *Collected Works of Abraham Lincoln* (New Brunswick, N.J.: Rutgers University Press, 1953), 5:292.

[16]Francis Corkran to Montgomery Blair, May 20, 1862, Lincoln Papers.

to make such a pronouncement.[17] Yet behind such strictures and complaints waited few defenders of slavery. From the Eastern Shore to Allegany county, there were no Unionist apologies for the peculiar institution. One county paper, without a mention of slavery, complained instead of "the suicidal policy of the Baltimore Convention" and urged that the state central committee prohibit local conventions from passing resolutions influencing party policy.[18]

Anxiety over the political effects of emancipation fostered such disagreements among Unionists. Apprehensive of parties which would "shriek Union as loud as any" yet encourage "ultraists,"[19] some Unionists declined to challenge slavery, not because of their reverence for the institution, but because its destruction would immediately double Maryland's free black population. In their view, any party identified with such a policy would inevitably fail in Maryland. It was this point which Hicks made somewhat repetitiously in a letter to Lincoln:

> Now my dear . . . , while I care not for myself or my slaves, I beg you to prevent as far as you can the mad doings of Sumner, Willson [sic], Lovejoy until [the] Rebellion shall be put down. . . . That done, then I care but little what shall follow provided all shall look to a proper restoration of the Union, one thing at a time, let us put down the Rebellion. Then I care nothing for slavery, but see My dear sir, the effort being made to resurrect the Democratic Party. That infernal party that has ruined the Country and if we do not manage things well, it is bound again to get control and then the country is cursed.[20]

Governor Bradford, a slaveholder and by 1862 the father of a Confederate officer, did little to quiet such fears. In part, Bradford's difficulties emanated from his lack of control over the Unionist party. Without the tools of power such as a veto, significant patronage, and even good health and a forceful personality, Bradford gradually became an administrator, busily attending to the increased gubernatorial duties caused by the war.[21] In part, Bradford's failure to resolve dif-

[17] *Maryland Union* (Frederick), Mary 29, 1862.

[18] Easton *Gazette*, June 21, 1862.

[19] *Montgomery County Sentinel* (Rockville), June 13, 27, 1862.

[20] For a copy of this letter, see Hicks to Lincoln, May 26, 1862, Hicks Papers, MHS. The references are to Charles Sumner, Henry Wilson, and Owen Lovejoy, all Republicans identified with the "radical" bloc.

[21] A number of Marylanders commented unfavorably on Bradford's leadership. While there were personal reasons for his ineptitude, the Governor certainly suffered from the weakness of his position. One study of the powers of Maryland governors concludes that the mid-nineteenth century was the nadir of executive power, and even under the new Constitu-

ferences within the Unionist party stemmed from his personal confusion over emancipation. Early in his administration, Bradford had praised Lincoln's refusal to interfere with slavery and criticized those who wanted to complicate the cause of Union with that of freeing the slaves. As chairman of a conference of northern governors gathered at Altoona, Pennsylvania in the late summer of 1862, Bradford refused to sign resolutions supporting the Emancipation Proclamation. Later he explained his position to Hicks who, according to Bradford, understood the "true grounds of that non-approval": "[The Emancipation Proclamation] might in all probability prolong [the rebellion] by uniting and concentrating its various elements and even bringing to its support many who had hitherto held aloof from it."[22] By 1863, however, Bradford shifted ground and supported gradual emancipation. Modifying his fears that emancipation would disrupt the party, Bradford now found another cause for worry: "If such practices [slave kidnapping and recruiting] are not speedily arrested we are given over in spite of all we can do once more to Democratic rule."[23]

Throughout 1862 and early 1863, Unionists tried to camouflage division on the vexed question of emancipation with the same appeals that had brought their party together in the troubled days of 1860 and 1861. "There should be but one party now, the party of Union, and aspirants to office should be voted on solely on account of their patriotism and competency."[24] Insistent that Unionism meant far more than simply supporting particular candidates and policies, enthusiasts joined militia companies, reading societies, and ward organizations designed to raise commutation fees so that citizens would not be drafted. The term "Union" soon became a popular title for clubs, relief associations, hotels, and even corporations.

---

tion of 1864 the executive was not given a suspensive veto. For comments on the weakness of the governor, see Henry Winter Davis to Samuel F. Du Pont, March 10, November 20, 1862; August 10, 1864, Samuel Francis Du Pont Papers, Eleutherian Mills Historical Library, Wilmington, Del. See also Charles Rohr, *The Governor of Maryland: A Constitutional Study*, Johns Hopkins University Studies in Historical and Political Science, ser. 50 (Baltimore: Johns Hopkins Press, 1932). For comments on Bradford's lack of leadership and ill-health, see Baltimore *American*, October 3, 1864; Easton *Gazette*, October 8, 1864; William Brewer to Lincoln, November 13, 1863, Lincoln Papers; Civil War Diary of Samuel Harrison, February 17, 1864, Harrison Papers.

[22] Bradford to Hicks, December 29, 1862, Bradford Papers, MHS. See also Augustus Bradford, *Address to the Legislature of 1862* (Annapolis: Schley & Cole, 1862); and William B. Hesseltine, *Lincoln and the War Governors* (New York: Alfred A. Knopf, 1948), pp. 251-59.

[23] Bradford to Montgomery Blair, September 11, 1863 [copy], Bradford Papers.

[24] Frederick *Examiner*, October 29, 1862.

As Unionism attempted to substitute a spiritual experience for a political allegiance, party members insistently denied that theirs was, in fact, a partisan organization. Union purposes became higher intentions than those of mere party. This connection between religion and party occasionally became explicit in newspaper reports that party meetings were religious experiences. Such feelings were frequently reciprocated when churches made clear their support, and sympathetic press accounts noted approvingly that synods and presbyteries endorsed the party.[25] Soon the comparison of Unionists to religious leaders of the past became ineluctable: "Bradford's hands will be upheld by the true men of Maryland, as were those of Moses, whilst our Joshua goes forth to strike in God's name and the country's against the sinner, the Amalekites of the day."[26]

Thus an invitation to join a new association called the Union League, extended in 1861 "to all men who pledge unconditional loyalty to the government of the United States," seemed merely an extension of such fervent Unionism. Certainly the military need for such an organization was obvious in a state invaded almost at will by the Confederates, and the fraternal aspects of the League—the passwords, handshakes, and secret grips—pleased many Marylanders familiar with such procedures from their activities in ante-bellum lodges and nativist societies. By 1863, 15,000 Marylanders were members of local leagues dedicated to "the preservation of our Union, our Constitution and our laws."[27] Besides providing security to the civilian population, Union Leagues raised money for the destitute families of federal soldiers and provided support for the unpopular draft.

Such philanthropic and military functions masked, for a time, the growing political ambitions of this organized and disciplined statewide force. Increasingly dissatisfied with"the old Bell and Everett" Union state central committee, the Grand Union League of Maryland issued a call, in the spring of 1863, for a new convention of those who "unconditionally" supported the Union, and by the fall there were two Unionist candidates for many state and national offices. In part, this division reflected personal and political differences between two

[25]Baltimore *Clipper*, March 12, 1862; Baltimore *American*, November 8, 1864; and *An Address to the Moral and Religious People of the United States* (Baltimore: Levi Perry & Co., 1864).

[26]Baltimore *Clipper*, January 11, 1862.

[27]*Cecil Whig* (Elkton), March 21, 1863; Baltimore *Clipper*, June 19, 1863. See also the *Opening, Initiatory and Closing Ceremonies for Union Leagues, August, 1862* (Baltimore: James Young, 1862). For a description of the Leagues in 1861, see Thomas R. Rich to Governor Bradford, December 28, 1861, Executive Papers, Hall of Records, Annapolis, Md.

Maryland leaders, Henry Winter Davis and Montgomery Blair. Most of the old Know-Nothing organization joined Davis's Unconditional or League Unionists, while former Whigs, Republicans, and many of those not identified with any party in the 1850s supported the Blair or Conservative Unionists. Committed to immediate emancipation without compensation to slave-owners, the Unconditionals initially disagreed with the Conservative Unionists on the importance and timing of emancipation as well as the need for compensation.

By dint of both careful organization and superior numbers, the insurgent League or Unconditional Unionists controlled many local meetings. On the Eastern Shore, Conservative Unionists, loyal to the old central committee, complained that "the radical group" had succeeded in controlling their nominating conventions and had chosen John A. J. Creswell to challenge the incumbent Unionist Congressman John W. Crisfield. Similar Union League support in Baltimore enabled Henry Winter Davis to defeat Thomas Swann for a Unionist congressional nomination from Baltimore.[28] In Frederick one disgruntled Unionist described the League's tactics during a local nominating convention:

> The abolitionists were disposed if possible to carry their ends. They started from a store in a body, entered the school before one-half of the voters could get in, called a certain government official . . . then announced a meeting of Unconditional Union men . . . and then peremptorily ordered all others to leave the room.[29]

Angered by such success, the Union state central committee organized its own competing hierarchy of conventions and made frantic, if unsuccessful, attempts at adjustment between the two groups. Insisting quite correctly on its legitimacy as a party organ, the central committee pledged its undivided, but not unconditional, support to the government, and demanded that Union, not such distractions as slavery, be the paramount issue in the elections of 1863.

On face value, there was little to compromise between the principles of the two factions. By 1863, both the Unconditional and Conservative Unionists accepted the inevitability of emancipation. The Conservative Thomas Swann, long convinced that "abolition without deportation will lead to amalgamation," now agreed with Uncondi-

[28] Samuel S. Masters to Bradford, October 20, 1863, Bradford Papers; Thomas Swann to Salmon Chase, June 5, 1863; Hugh Bond to Chase, August 18, 1863, Chase Papers, Historical Society of Pennsylvania, Philadelphia, Pa.

[29] *Maryland Union* (Frederick), September 10, 1863.

tionals that "we are in the midst of a revolution. We could not bring back slavery in Maryland if we desired it."[30] Bradford, Hicks, and Samuel Maffitt, all slaveholders and aligned with the Conservative faction, agreed with their opponents on the need for a constitutional convention to end slavery. "Slavery is doomed," admitted the Easton *Gazette*, "the question is how it should be eliminated."[31]

Behind these agreements in principle lay considerable differences in political strategy. Unconditional Unionists favored immediate and uncompensated emancipation, and wanted to make this program the central issue in Maryland politics. In 1863, Henry Hoffman, Henry Winter Davis's political lieutenant and a former Sergeant-at-Arms in the House of Representatives, argued that emancipation and the use of Negro soldiers should be "the leading issues of the approaching canvass."[32] While Conservatives gradually adopted the same position on slavery, few wanted the elections to become a referendum on issues relating to blacks, and few accepted the need for encouraging Negro enlistments in the Union army. At an important meeting in Baltimore county, one Conservative avowed his desire to see "the institution of slavery abrogated but doubted the policy of making it a political question" in 1863.[33] Sentiments like those of Hoffman and his allies struck Conservatives as "toadying to the present administration" and "the work of prisoners on duty for the cause of abolitionism."[34] Agreeing with Thomas Swann that differences grew out of making the slavery question "the prominent and leading issue in the canvass," Conservatives found their opponents guilty of the sins of abolitionism, Black Republicanism, and political self-destruction.[35] John Pendleton Kennedy angrily explained:

> One would suppose that it was [Henry Winter Davis's] premeditated purpose to reduce the supporters of the Administration in Maryland to the smallest number and to drive off every man from the effort to suppress the

[30]In the 1840s Swann wrote a long memorandum on slavery. This memorandum can be found in his private papers, currently in the possession of Mrs. George Gillet, Glyndon, Maryland. The first quotation is from "Slavery," the second from *Immediate Emancipation in Maryland: Proceedings of the Union State Central Committee* (Baltimore: Bull and Tuttle, 1863), p. 6.

[31]Easton *Gazette*, March 28, 1863.

[32]Peter Sauerwein to James Ridgely, December 19, 1863, Lincoln Papers.

[33]William Price to James Ridgely, December 18, 1863, *ibid.*

[34]James Touchstone to Bradford, September 29, 1863, Bradford Papers.

[35]George Vickers to Bradford, September 14, October 30, 1863, Bradford Papers; *Immediate Emancipation in Maryland*, p. 5.

> rebellion except those who are willing to coerce the immediate abolition of slavery in the state, and this when Davis himself says that slavery itself has received its death blow and is rapidly falling into inevitable extinction.[36]

Yet, as the condition of slavery disappeared, the victim of circumstances and convictions, the label "abolitionist" remained a powerful curse with which to damn opponents. For Conservative Unionists, there was no need to define the accusation "abolitionist," although by 1863, Conservatives themselves were technically abolitionists. Typical of such vague, but damaging, political charges were those of a Frederick paper: "The abolitionists crept into bed with the Union party when rebellion broke out and hiding themselves away like bed bugs between the sheets and in cracks and corners, there they will stick until they are kicked or scalded out."[37] Gradually the term "abolition," an epithet which survived both the war and emancipation, came to mean support of Negro equality.

Fearful of any political mixture that included specific commitments to emancipation or the recruitment of slaves into the Union army, Conservatives emphasized a different, but familiar, set of priorities—the need to support Constitution and Union. With the Republic in two and the Constitution in fragments, such appeals still suffused the rhetoric of the party. Charles Calvert, in his campaign for Congress in 1863, announced his "opposition to those who opposed the Union as it was and the Constitution as it is."[38] Another incumbent congressman, John Crisfield, agreed that "the war should be finished before social questions are introduced."[39] In the same vein, the Unionist state convention resolved "to ignore all issues, but those of war until Treason shall succumb."[40]

Union League Unconditionals found such attitudes reactionary. Employing the hyperbole of angry partisans, Unconditionals found their opponents guilty of an attempt to place the Union party on the same platform as peace Democrats who favored an end to the war and the continuation of slavery. While Conservatives called their opponents abolitionists, radicals, and "nigger" lovers, the Union League faction traded political billingsgate and retaliated with charges of "copperheads," "rebel sympathizers," and Democrats.

[36]John P. Kennedy, "Journals," October 12, 1863, Kennedy Papers, Peabody Library, Baltimore, Md.

[37]*Maryland Union* (Frederick), August 13, 1863.

[38]Charles Calvert, "To the Voters of the 5th District," Broadside, 1863, MHS.

[39]Easton *Gazette*, August 29, 1863.

[40]Baltimore *Clipper*, June 19, 1863.

To men like Davis, Hoffman, and the Baltimorean Judge Hugh Bond, freeing Maryland's slaves and recruiting Negro soldiers were weapons that could shorten the war. Carefully delineating the advantages of emancipation to Maryland's white laborers, the Unconditionals denied any interest in Negro equality. "The veriest fool in a lunatic asylum knows the two will not be placed on an equality by emancipation," concluded an Unconditional paper, the *Cecil Whig.*[41]

Although leaders of both factions of the party were similar in age and wealth, they differed greatly on political strategy.[42] Conservative Unionists appealed to all Marylanders, regardless of previous political affiliation, to join their party. Former Democrats like Samuel Maffitt found themselves prominently displayed as candidates for office on the Union ticket. On the other hand, Unconditionals, intent on forming a different political constituency, wished to create a majority party based on Maryland voters who were united by a traditional hostility toward the Democratic party.

The elections in November 1863 clearly revealed the strength of the Unconditionals, for that faction won a decisive victory among the 52,000 Marylanders who voted. In the Comptroller's contest between Samuel Maffitt, the Conservative candidate, and Henry Goldsborough, the Unconditional—the only statewide race in 1863—Goldsborough received 69 percent of the total vote. The Unconditionals also won four of Maryland's five congressional seats as well as fifty-two of the Assembly's seventy-four seats.[43] Enthusiastic members of the Union Leagues received an added dividend when Henry Winter Davis regained the congressional seat he had lost in 1861.

As was so often the case in Maryland's political history, postmortems on the election led to charges of fraud and mishandling. Again the military served as a convenient target for such complaints, and in some isolated cases, Union soldiers did influence state voting. In fact, the orders of the Military Commander of the Middle District, Major General Robert C. Schenck, gave federal troops "the right to support judges of election in requiring an oath of allegiance to the United States as the test of citizenship of anyone whose vote may be challenged." Furthermore, the military had the power to report any election judge who refused to compel a challenged voter to take the

[41] *Cecil Whig* (Elkton), March 14, 1863.

[42] See Appendix Tables D-11, D-12, and D-13 for a social profile of the members of the Conservative and Unionist central committees in 1863.

[43] The Baltimore *American*, November 12, 1863, lists four "Unionists," forty-seven "Emancipationists," five pledged to a Constitutional Convention, and eighteen Democrats.

oath of allegiance. To carry out such orders, soldiers were sent to many polling places.[44]

The presence of these troops led to anguished outcries by disconcerted losers that the election was determined "by sword." Crisfield complained that his followers, including his son, had not been permitted to vote.[45] In Baltimore county, William Preston vividly described the role of troops in his district:

> We had not proceeded far before we met a couple of our neighbors who, dispirited, disapproving, and alarmed, were returning from the polls and said the polls were in possession of the military. . . . The polls were surrounded by armed men, soldiers with weapons and miserable low backgrounds wearing badges designated as U.S. marshals. I at once concluded that to put my name on the poll books under such circumstances would be to sanction the most flagrant and infamous outrage.[46]

Yet many of these protests, which never have been examined critically by historians, reflected the anguish of incumbents, who had expected easy victory and not defeat at the hands of a detested faction. "Their clamor," according to Michigan's Republican Senator Jacob M. Howard, was that "of diappointed partisans, not the outcry of the oppressed."[47] Certainly the complaints of Crisfield represented, in part, an incumbent's chagrin at losing a "safe" congressional seat. The former congressman never did gather enough evidence to contest the election, and his endless laments that his son was not permitted to vote should be analyzed in the political climate of a border state where many Union families, including the governor's, held disloyal sons. Challenges, even to the sons of congressmen, were not out of

[44]A copy of Schenck's General Orders Number 53 can be found in the Bradford Executive Papers, Hall of Records. See also James B. Fry, Provost Marshal General, to Major Jeffries, October 31, 1863, Bradford Papers; and Basler, *Collected Works of Abraham Lincoln*, 6:555-57.

[45]Most historians accept the argument that there was massive interference in Maryland's wartime elections. See particularly J. Thomas Scharf, *History of Maryland from the Earliest Period to the Present Day*, 3 vols. (1879; reprint ed., Hatboro, Pa.: (Tradition Press, 1967), 3:560-93. Even recent histories of the Civil War period stress the part played by the military. See Wagandt, *Mighty Revolution*, p. 157; Margaret Callcott, *The Negro in Maryland Politics, 1870-1912* (Baltimore: Johns Hopkins Press, 1969), pp. 7-11; and Charles Wagandt, "Election by Sword and Ballot," *Maryland Historical Magazine* 59 (June 1964): 143-64. For contemporary judgments, see John Crisfield to Bradford, November 14, 1863, Bradford Papers and House of Delegates, *Documents of the State Legislature, 1864*, "Reports of the Committee on Elections in Somerset County," Document J (Annapolis: Richard P. Bayley, 1864).

[46]William Preston to Madge Preston, n.d. [1863], Preston Papers, MHS.

[47]*Report of Honorable Mr. Howard in the United States Senate on Interference in Elections by Military and Naval Officers* (Philadelphia, 1864), p. 13.

order, unless the assumption that Maryland Confederates should vote is granted.

The complaints of William Preston, a loyal Democrat and vociferous Union party critic, should be viewed in the same light. Preston had been lamenting unfair interference in elections since 1850, when he lost to "the Know Nothing clubs."[48] In 1863 this unhappy Democrat did not try to vote himself and therefore was not kept away from the polls. His testimony rested entirely on hearsay evidence which clearly reinforced his own long-held contention that force determined Maryland elections.

In those instances where there was significant military interference, such meddling represented the political ambitions of local military personnel, rather than the tyranny of Lincoln. Many Maryland officers were candidates for office, and the stationing of their army cohorts as poll-watchers became a temptation that ambitious Unionists could not resist. Certainly the Provost Marshal, John Frazier, a candidate for the politically sensitive job of Clerk of the Circuit Court in Kent county, exceeded his authority by arresting several Conservative Unionists just before the election. Yet his superior in Baltimore, Lieutenant Colonel Donn Piatt, quickly intervened and rushed the prisoners back to Chestertown in time for the election. In fairness to Frazier, there were rumors that the Conservatives taken in custody had planned to arrest Unconditional Unionists for violating the slave code.[49]

In other instances, the stationing of troops near the polls was a direct response to fears that Unionists could not vote unless they were protected. One party supporter from Prince Georges wrote the central committee that "another citizen has threatened to cut the heart out of my son, if he votes."[50] To forestall this and other possible violations, soldiers patrolled near some voting windows, but in more than one instance, armed citizens drove such protective forces from the polls.[51]

[48]William Preston to Madge Preston, November 1857, Preston Papers.

[49]For documentation of this incident, see C. Carroll Tevis to Donn Piatt, November 6, 1863 [copy], Letters Received, Middle Department, 1863, Record Group 94, U.S. Army Commands, National Archives; Tevis to Piatt, November 2, 1863, Letters Received, Middle Department, 1863, Record Group 98, U.S. Army Commands, National Archives.

[50]T. H. Robey to J. H. Bayne, April 25, 1864, Bayne Papers, owned by Mrs. Guy Castle, Oxon Hill, Maryland.

[51]House of Delegates, *Documents, 1864*, "Elections in Somerset County"; "Proceedings of a Military Commission to Investigate Captain Moore's Role, November 1863," Record Group 94, Judge Advocate General's Papers, National Archives; U.S. Congress, *Report on*

Certainly Lincoln and Secretary of War Edwin M. Stanton made little effort to meddle in Maryland's elections. Lincoln, consistent with his own temperate handling of such sensitive issues, revoked that part of Schenck's orders that gave the military exclusive jurisdiction over the arrests. Yet without some regulations, the President wryly noted, "the Confederate General Isaac Ridgeway Tremble [*sic*] captured fighting us at Gettysburg [is] without recanting his treason a legal voter by the laws of Maryland."[52] By leaving unchanged the military orders that instituted an oath of future allegiance for voters whose loyalty was challenged, Lincoln tried to prevent Maryland Confederates, like General Trimble, from voting. In part, the angry reactions of some Marylanders, including Governor Bradford, represented a response to the unfamiliar practices of oath-taking and of voting challenges among a constituency accustomed to the electoral permissiveness of the past.

Certainly the most obvious example of restraint by the military occurred in southern Maryland where, in a three-way congressional race, the influence of the military could have assured the election of an Unconditional Unionist. Yet even with a Union Provost Marshal, John C. Holland, running for Congress, there was no interference in the voting choices of Maryland's political "Little Egypt"—the fifth congressional district made up of St. Mary's, Calvert, Charles, Prince Georges, Howard, Montgomery, Anne Arundel, and part of Baltimore counties. Indeed, throughout the war, Democrats, occasionally of questionable loyalty, represented this district.

In part, the exaggerated reports of military interference stemmed from the need to explain the tremendous decreases in voting turnout, decreases which in fact represented the departure of many Marylanders from the state. Thirty-five thousand fewer Marylanders voted than in the 1859 Comptroller's race—a drop of 40 percent—and Marylanders have used the presence of federal troops to explain this decline.

Actually such decreases are better explained by the departure of many Marylanders to the army. By November 1863, there were nearly 15,000 Marylanders in the Confederate army, while another 15,000 served with Union forces. Lacking any official procedure for voting in the field, Union soldiers could not vote unless they were granted leave.

Military Interference at Elections, 38th Cong., 1st sess., 1864, Senate Executive Document 14, Serial No. 1176, pp. 4-5.

[52] Basler, *Collected Works of Lincoln*, 6:557.

Furthermore, uncounted thousands of Marylanders had left the state to avoid the draft, to live in the Confederacy, to find better jobs in the North, and to leave a state where the war was more than a matter of reading weekly dispatches from the front. Certainly the greatest loss of population, and as a result the greatest decline in voting, occurred in Baltimore; Samuel Harrison estimated that 30,000 Baltimoreans—a figure which included his own family—had left the city, and this migration helped to explain the decreases in Maryland's wartime voting.[53]

Undeniably, there was some military interference with the wartime election of 1863, just as there was some use of force by Democrats. Such tactics had long marred Maryland elections. Usually the work of local politicians who happened to be federal soldiers, such intervention was not the result of a tyrannical President or a political conspiracy against the Conservative Union party. As a correspondent of Governor Bradford explained: "Petty authorities transcend their orders."[54] For too long the jeremiads of partisan losers have been mistaken for the 'controls of the military, and "the politics of the trampled ballot" has tarnished the victory of the Unconditionals.

☆ ☆ ☆

BEHIND THE UNIONIST SPLIT in 1863 lay the conflicting ambitions, personalities, and past political choices of two state leaders—Henry Winter Davis, Maryland's quondam congressman who regained his seat in 1863, and Montgomery Blair, Lincoln's Postmaster General. As part of a larger design to realign American political parties, both men wished to direct Maryland's Unionist organization, and such a contest helped to create, and then to continue, the split between Conservatives and Unconditionals. The failure of Governor

[53]For evidence that Marylanders left the state for the Confederacy, see Mary E. Massey, *Refugee Life in the Confederacy* (Baton Rouge: Louisiana State University Press, 1964), pp. 43-45, 72, and 84. On Marylanders in the North, see Civil War Diary of Samuel Harrison, June 9, 1862, Harrison Papers; Baltimore *American*, March 10, 1866. The Baltimore *Sun*, August 9, 1862, reported that 1,000 persons had left the President Street Depot and Calvert Street Station for Canada. It is impossible to determine the exact number of Marylanders in the Union forces at any given date, but by October 1862, 13,343 Marylanders had volunteered and the institution of the draft calls in 1862 and 1863 increased the number of Marylanders serving in the army. A total of 33,995 white Marylanders fought in the Union army. See Millard Les Callette, "A Study of the Recruitment of the Union Army in Maryland" (master's thesis, Johns Hopkins University, 1954).

[54]J. B. Hopper to Bradford, November 17, 1863, Bradford Executive Papers, Hall of Records.

Bradford and other state leaders to control the party gave Davis and Blair an opportunity that neither hesitated to take and which led to deep mutual hatred.

Montgomery Blair, leader of the Conservative wing of the state party, came naturally to his political role.[55] The son of Francis Preston Blair, a member of Jackson's kitchen cabinet and editor of the *Globe*, Montgomery Blair was born in the border state of Kentucky, and graduated from West Point in 1836. After a stint fighting the Seminoles, he studied law at Transylvania University. Trained in Senator Thomas Hart Benton's Missouri law office, Blair became in quick succession a U.S. Attorney for Missouri, mayor of St. Louis, Judge of the Court of Common Pleas, and an unsuccessful candidate for a cabinet post under Franklin Pierce. Like his antagonist Davis, Blair moved to Maryland after the death of his first wife, and soon he maintained a residence on his father's estate in Montgomery county, Silver Spring, as well as the well-known townhouse across from the White House. Only a voice impediment kept the thin, sharp-faced judge from the more active political involvement of his brother, Frank, a Missouri congressman. But Montgomery made his own mark in frequent appearances before the Supreme Court, as in 1856, when he unsuccessfully argued for the freedom of the slave Dred Scott.

The politics of the ambitious Blair family had been consistently Democratic until the 1850s,[56] when Montgomery's dismissal from the office of Solicitor of the Court of Claims by Buchanan encouraged him to desert to the Republican party—a political institution the Blairs expected to make as strong in the South as in the North. Francis Preston Blair, Montgomery's father, had decided to accomplish the reorganization of American political parties on the basis of Jeffersonian-Jacksonian principles, and his chosen medium for this task was the Republican organization.[57] While such expectations for the party in Maryland were sadly inflated, Montgomery's leadership of the state

[55]The following biographical sketch is based on William E. Smith, *The Francis Preston Blair Family in Politics*, 2 vols. (New York: Macmillan Co., 1933); *The Dictionary of American Biography*, s.v. "Montgomery Blair" (New York: Charles Scribner and Sons, 1927), 1:339–40; Reinhard Luthin, "A Discordant Chapter in Lincoln's Administration: The Davis-Blair Controversy," *Maryland Historical Magazine* 39 (March 1944):25–47; and the Blair Papers in the Library of Congress and Princeton University Library.

[56]The Blairs supported Free Soil candidates in 1848, and two authorities have asserted that Montgomery Blair was a Know-Nothing. See J. Frederick Essary, *Maryland in National Politics* (Baltimore: John Murphy Co., 1915), p. 227; and Smith, *Blair Family*, 1:515.

[57]*Letter of Francis Preston Blair to the Republican Association* (Washington, D.C., 1858); F. P. Blair to Salmon Chase, March 26, 1861, Chase Papers.

Republican party, his residence in a border state, and his family's ceaseless political maneuvering made him an attractive and successful candidate for a cabinet post.

As Postmaster General, the efficient Blair managed a vast network of 27,000 officeholders. The 500 postal employees who ran Maryland's postal service gave Blair control over the largest group of federal or state appointments in the state.[58] This federal patronage served as the fulcrum for Blair's attempts to direct the Union party of Maryland.

Not satisfied with this supply of officeholders, Blair tried to dominate other Lincoln appointments. In this, the postmaster was not entirely successful, and he ended in sharing these positions with the supporters of Henry Winter Davis. Yet Blair did preside over the installation of a number of Republicans to important Maryland positions. Soon citizens from every part of the state and every political complexion petitioned the Postmaster General for favors ranging from Benjamin Howard's demand for rent after the federal occupation of Federal Hill to a request by prominent Marylanders that ex-Governor Pratt be released from federal prison. Even the ambitious Secretary of the Treasury, Salmon Chase, with his own need for a political machine, reluctantly chose Blair men to the new posts of district internal revenue collector.[59]

Blair was less successful in his attempts to control Maryland newspapers. Lacking the daily voice that Davis had in the Baltimore *Patriot*, Blair tried to "buy" the *Clipper's* editorial page for $5,000. Embarrassed when word of this leaked to other newspapers, Blair claimed that he simply sought a paper to "press emancipation," not his partisan ends. But the independent editors of the *Clipper* turned down Blair's offer, and he thus remained without control of a daily.[60]

Behind such political maneuvers rested Blair's hopes for a new conservative coalition. As a member of the Blair family, Montgomery shared his father's vision of a new political party, based on Jeffersonian-Jacksonian principles and counseled by one of Andrew Jackson's

[58] U.S. Department of the Interior, *Register of Officers and Agents* (Washington, D.C.: Government Printing Office, 1862); Smith, *Blair Family*, 2:92.

[59] Blair to B. C. Howard, February 13, 1866, Howard Papers, MHS; Blair to Lincoln, December 18, 26, 1863; Salmon Chase to Lincoln, August 27, 1862, Lincoln Papers. See also the Registry Books, Box 29, Blair Papers. These lists of the political preferences of Marylanders were furnished by postmasters of Maryland districts.

[60] Baltimore *Daily Gazette*, March 18, 1864; Baltimore *American*, March 18, 1864; Blair to William Lloyd Garrison, June 22, 1864 [copy], Blair Papers.

closest lieutenants—Francis Preston Blair, Sr. In Montgomery's view, Democrats, Unionists, former Whigs, and Know-Nothings could all meet on a platform of Constitution and Union. Such a strategy rested on the conviction that Southerners would rally behind a Unionist party which effectively isolated extremists of both sections. "You assume that good and true men in the South are not more numerous than the voters of old Sarum," wrote the border state politician to that most radical of U.S. Senators, Charles Sumner. "I deny your premises, I say the great body of our people are as good and loyal as yours."[61]

Although emancipation clearly would strain this alliance, Blair felt that it was necessary for Conservative Unionists to advocate the freeing of Maryland's slaves. Since Radicals were trying to depict the Conservatives as "incorrigible pro-slavery men" and since "pro-slavery sentiments are now almost universally regarded as hostility to the Union,"[62] Blair wanted his faction to take the lead in efforts for emancipation. "We must not put it into the power of the adversary to confound us with the secessionists or their sympathizers," he wrote Thomas Swann. "We can only succeed in defeating the abolitionists by clearing our skirts of all taint of slavery and by forcing them to come to the real issue which involves the relations of the freed Negroes to the whites."[63] In November 1863, Blair urged Governor Bradford to call the legislature back into session in order to pass an act of emancipation. Failure to do so would only redound to the advantage of those "who are seeking to get up a small party with no prospect of popular favor."[64]

Committed to emancipation as a political necessity, Blair favored compensation for slave-owners. To those who "sneered" at his plan, the postmaster compared his sensitivity to "slave state traditions" to that of "the tenderness of a mother which makes her foolish when the life of her children is concerned."[65] Impelled by his hopes for a new Conservative coalition with its strength in the border states of Missouri, where his brother Frank held political influence, and Maryland,

[61]Blair to Charles Sumner, October 24, 1863 [copy], Blair Papers. The reference "old Sarum" is to a notorious rotten borough in England which, although it returned a Member of Parliament, had only a handful of voters.

[62]Blair to Bradford, November 11, 1863, Bradford Papers.

[63]Blair to Thomas Swann, October 17, 1863, Blair Papers.

[64]Blair to William Hall, September 5, 1863, *ibid.*

[65]*Ibid.*

where Blair himself hoped for office, Blair's instincts were those of a practical politician, not a moral crusader.

If, largely due to Blair's urging, emancipation did not separate Maryland's two factions, Reconstruction and what the postmaster called "the relations of freed Negroes to whites" did. For many years the Blair family had supported the principle of colonization, and as early as the 1850s, Blair had recognized the political importance of the free Negro question in his adopted state of Maryland. Throughout the war, Blair, who denied that the two races could live together peacefully, argued for federally subsidized colonization of blacks in Chiriqui and Haiti, or, alternatively, emancipation with some form of Negro apprenticeship. "It is negro equality, not slavery they [the South] are fighting about."[66]

Fearful that any efforts toward Negro equality would cause Maryland Conservatives to desert to the Democratic party, Blair opposed "the Abolition party [who] seek to make a caste of another color by amalgamating the black element with the free white labor of our land." Constantly referring to the dangers of "amalgamation" and "a hybrid race," the postmaster tried to connect Davis and his Unconditional Unionists to such extremist politics. At the same time Blair reiterated his own intention to keep Maryland "white men's country."[67]

Shortly before the elections in November 1863, Blair defined his position on Reconstruction. Emphatically denying the theory of Charles Sumner that seceded states had committed state suicide and therefore had abdicated their rights, Blair praised the "safe and healing policy of Presidential reconstruction" which was based, according to Blair, on the conviction that the national government could be a "partner" with Southerners who took an oath of future allegiance to the United States. Blair strongly supported Lincoln's restoration policies in Tennessee, Kentucky, Louisiana, and West Virginia, and he

[66]Blair to J. R. Doolittle, November 11, 1859, "Letters of Bates and the Blairs," *Missouri Historical Review* II (January 1917): 136. See also Blair to Lincoln, November 21, 1861 and a copy of a memorandum on emancipation, 1862, Blair Papers; Smith, *Blair Family*, 2:193–99. The Chiriqui Real Estate Company had been chartered in 1856 by the Maryland legislature and a number of Marylanders had invested, but there is no evidence that Blair was a stockholder. W. Gosnell to Lincoln, August 16, 1862, Lincoln Papers; Blair to S. L. M. Barlow, May 11, 1864, Samuel L. M. Barlow Papers, Henry E. Huntington Library, San Marino, Calif.

[67]Montgomery Blair, *Speech of the Honorable Montgomery Blair on the Revolutionary Schemes of Ultra Abolitionists* (New York: D. W. Lee, 1863), p. 4; Baltimore *Clipper*, April 23, 1863.

insisted that loyal citizens within each state could reinstitute their own civil government.[68] Such a program grew quite naturally from Blair's hopes for a new Unionist party and rested firmly on his view that slavery must go, southern rebels must admit defeat, and the Union party must avoid any commitment to the twin extremes of disfranchising white Southerners and promising the freedmen equality. Yet wherever Blair turned to gain support for his policy or accomplish his partisan aims, the presence of his tall Byronic antagonist, Henry Winter Davis, blocked the path toward a new political coalition.

Henry Winter Davis, the leader of Maryland's Unconditional Unionists, was a politician neither by family training nor by personality.[69] The son of a slaveholding minister and college president and briefly a reluctant slave-owner himself, Davis graduated from Kenyon College and the University of Virginia Law Department. He began his law practice in Alexandria, Virginia, but moved to Baltimore when, following the death of his first wife, he married Nancy Morris, daughter of a prominent Baltimore banker and former Whig state senator.

Soon the handsome, articulate Davis became involved in local Whig and Know-Nothing politics. By 1855 his prominence as an author and speaker led to a congressional nomination from the city's Fourth District, comprised of twelve economically diverse wards in Baltimore. Except for two years during the war, Davis represented this district as a Know-Nothing and Unionist congressman for the next nine years, although at the time of his premature death in 1865, he had failed to be renominated.

Davis's congressional career earned him national prominence, but not the adulation of his fellow Marylanders, many of whom disliked his "extremist" stands. In 1860 Davis's support of William Pennington for Speaker led to his censure by the Maryland legislature, and in 1864 Davis further alienated Marylanders by his sponsorship of the Wade-Davis Bill, which gave Congress control of the process of Reconstruction and made more difficult the return of seceded states to the

[68] Blair, *Speech on Revolutionary Schemes of Ultra Abolitionists*, p. 5.

[69] The following biographical information is based on Davis's uncompleted biography which is included in Bernard Steiner, *The Life of Henry Winter Davis* (Baltimore: John Murphy, 1916); *The Dictionary of American Biography*, s.v. "Henry Winter Davis," 3:119-21; J. A. J. Creswell's *Oration on the Life and Character of Henry Winter Davis* (Washington, D.C.: Government Printing Office, 1866); the correspondence of Davis and his wife Nancy to the Du Ponts in the Samuel Francis Du Pont Papers.

Union.[70] Later Davis contributed to a manifesto attacking Lincoln, who had pocket-vetoed the bill. It was small wonder that Conservative Unionists came to view their congressman as a "radical," "demagogue," "traitor," "paltry coward," and "white negro."[71]

Even before the war, many Marylanders had viewed Davis's nativism and his occasional verbal excesses on the dangers of immigration and Roman Catholicism as indicative of his extremism. Certainly those who, like John Pendleton Kennedy, had read Davis's *The War of Ormuzd and Ahriman in the Nineteenth Century* were convinced of Davis's "ultraism" long before the war. In this book Davis preached the necessity of American involvement in European affairs. Concerned by the replacement of republics by monarchies, Davis accepted the principle of active American intervention in European domestic affairs, and using an argument that was to become more familiar in the twentieth century, he argued that "to stand still and see despots root out freedom from Europe is not to avoid war, but only to wait till our allies fall that we may be an easy prey. I do not value greatly the Ulyssean privilege of being last devoured."[72]

The reactions of fellow Marylanders to such ideas made little difference to Davis. Convinced of the rectitude of his own positions, he displayed characteristic arrogance toward those who disagreed with him. Opponents were "fools," "chattering, whining, and timorous merchants," "mutton heads," and even "rattlesnakes."[73] According to Peter Sauerwein, a Baltimore flour merchant and a Davis admirer: "But he [Davis] never lets up on Hicks or Swann. . . . They differed from him, ergo they are fools. Perverse and hard-headed as he is, he

[70]Herman Belz, *Reconstructing the Union: Theory and Policy during the Civil War* (Ithaca: Cornell University Press, 1969), pp. 198-243. See also the same author's "Henry Winter Davis and the Origins of Congressional Reconstruction," *Maryland Historical Magazine* 67 (Summer 1972):129-43. Belz sees the Wade-Davis bill as a reflection of congressional interest in reconstruction as well as an antiadministration measure. Yet Belz notes the conservative aspects of this so-called radical measure: its emphasis on preexisting state forms, its dependence on a civil rather than a military governor, its limitation of voting enrollments to all white citizens, and its recognition of the continued existence of the state. The bill passed Congress; Lincoln subsequently pocket-vetoed it.

[71]Baltimore *Daily Gazette*, August 23, 1864; Baltimore *Clipper*, June 13, August 25, 1864; S. T. Wallis to Glenn, October 25, 1862, Glenn Papers, MHS; George Showacre to Swann, n.d., 1868, Swann Papers, Hall of Records, Annapolis Md.; and A. Chip to editors of Baltimore *Daily Exchange*, February 11, 1861, State Department Records.

[72]Henry Winter Davis, *The War of Ormuzd and Ahriman in the Nineteenth Century* (Baltimore: James Waters, 1852), p. 376.

[73]Davis to Samuel F. Du Pont, December 20, 1859; April 26, 1863; n.d., 1860; June 1862; November 11, 1859, Du Pont Papers.

has wonderful power with the people. They admire him for his very insolence."[74]

Like Charles Sumner, whose name was often linked with his in Maryland, Davis garnered some support precisely because he eschewed the usual political roles of compromise and accommodation. Armed with an inner confidence given to few men, Davis insisted on the importance of "doing what is right."[75] With magnificent contempt, he excoriated political compromisers and trimmers:

> I will not sink to an officeholding politician, but I will pursue the interests of the country alone and that over every interest personal & party & it is my resolution to do that heretofore which has made me suspicious and dangerous to persons who merely wish place and success.[76]

Many Marylanders, disenchanted with the supposed corruptness and scheming of party politicians, applauded such attitudes and found Davis "an ornament to the state," "a bright spring welling up in a muddy marsh," "a logician," and even a "genius."[77]

Davis did not hesitate to delineate his positions on national issues. While Blair supported a policy of presidential Reconstruction based on Southern Unionists, Davis insisted that Congress held significant powers over the seceded states. When Blair pleaded for Negro apprenticeship or colonization, Davis urged that "Negroes be given the rights of free laborers, protected by the laws recognized by the United States." In his view, "the government could not call Negroes into the field and then abandon them afterward to slavery." The colonization of freedmen was, in Davis's view, "simple craziness–Expel four millions of people? Where are the ships? Where is the land that will receive them? Where are the people that will pay taxes to remove them? Who will cultivate the deserted regions that they leave?" And as he argued earlier in the same speech:

> If anybody is afraid of negro equality, he is not far from it already, . . . if God has made him [the Negro] equal and only accidental circumstances have made him unequal you cannot help it; and if He has made him unequal by [the] laws of nature, and independently of accidental circumstances, then no amount of demagoguerism, no amount of abolition

[74]Sauerwein to Edward McPherson, October 8, 1864, McPherson Papers, Library of Congress.

[75]Davis to Samuel F. Du Pont, December 20, 1859, Du Pont Papers.

[76]Davis to Creswell, April 1865, Vertical File of Cecil County Historical Society, Elkton, Maryland.

[77]Baltimore *Clipper*, October 7, 1863; Cambridge *Herald*, January 15, 1862; Peter Sauerwein to Edward McPherson, October 22, 1864, McPherson Papers.

> enthusiasm can make one hair black or white or add an inch to his stature, intellectual or moral.[78]

Despite the bold sound of such pronouncements and their inevitable misconstruction in a slave state, the struggle for Negro rights was, at times, a secondary consideration for Davis who cared deeply for the separation of powers and the authority of the legislature. Armed with a Whig political philosophy, which feared the power of the executive, and convinced of the growing dangers of presidential usurpation, Davis had begun his political career by attacking Andrew Jackson's veto of the Maysville Road Bill.[79] In the 1850s Davis saw a challenge to his beloved American republic from despotic European regimes led by tyrants. In the 1860s the challenge, now more proximate, came from Jefferson Davis's regime in Richmond and from Lincoln's usurpations of power in Washington. As early as 1861, Henry Winter Davis complained of martial law, unnecessary arrests, and the denial of free speech.[80] Convinced that even the exigencies of wartime did not justify such "extraordinary methods," Davis questioned his friend Sophie Du Pont:

> Is it not of sinister import that a simple defense of the principles of American free government on the basis of Webster and John Marshall sounds like an attack on the administration? Is not that alone the condemnation of the administration and of the people who in their haste to victory have forgotten the battle of freedom?[81]

Throughout the war Davis feared that his country would abandon its constitution and written law for the despotism, lack of restraint, and "law of necessity" which characterized the nations of Europe.[82] Ironically the racial myopia of most Marylanders blinded them to the fact that their great "radical abolitionist" was at heart a Constitutional Whig dedicated to preservation, not revolution.

Certainly Davis, like Blair, found slavery indefensible, but he felt it must be dealt with "as a cancer which it is fatal to allow to remain, yet equally fatal rashly to tear out, and this danger may excuse, per-

[78] *Speech of the Honorable Henry Winter Davis at Concert Hall*, September 24, 1863 (Philadelphia, 1863).

[79] Milton Henry, "Henry Winter Davis" (Ph.D. diss., Louisiana State University, 1972), pp. 130–55. The Maysville veto refers to Andrew Jackson's veto in 1830 of a bill authorizing federal aid to a Kentucky road company.

[80] Henry Winter Davis, *Speeches and Addresses* (New York: Harper Brothers, 1867), pp. 263–91.

[81] Davis to Sophie Du Pont, December 4, 1861, Du Pont Papers.

[82] Davis, *Speeches and Addresses*, p. 290.

haps justify, the toleration of the evil till time and circumstances permit its eradication."[83] Because "only the law of the land stands between us and anarchy," Davis opposed the Emancipation Proclamation, observing that by such proclamations "Lincoln could take my house and imprison me." In Davis's view, "loyal states were obligated to observe the slavery clauses of the Constitution." Always fearful of "extreme people who run ahead of events into dream land or utopia," Davis opposed "sudden abolitionists" as strongly as men like Blair who manipulated the black issue. Yet Davis's hope that "people would remember other interests besides the Negro,"[84] remained just that, and by 1864, he led the fight to call a state convention aimed at the emancipation of Maryland's slaves.

The great constant of Davis's career—the burr in his psyche which often led to verbal intemperance—was a fierce hatred of the Democrats, or "loco-focos," as he preferred to call them. What Blair's Negrophobia was to his Union party, Davis's hatred of the Democrats was to his politics. Never forgetting his father's injunction to "beware the follies of Jacksonism," and ever "tilting against the Democracy," Davis constantly battled the devil as it appeared in Democratic form.[85] In 1859 Davis insisted that "no Democrat shall go into the Speaker's chair if my vote can prevent it." In 1860 he tried to create a new political party by uniting Know-Nothings, Republicans, and Constitutional Unionists under the banner of Edward Bates, "the only practicable point of Union." After Lincoln won the nomination, Davis complained that he would vote for Bell, "to exclude the Democrats from power in Maryland." When Davis failed to win an anticipated Senate seat in 1862, he excoriated the traitorous Douglas Democrats who had worked for Reverdy Johnson.[86] By 1863 Davis refused to make any distinction between those Democrats who were loyal to the war and those who wanted peace with the Confederacy; in his mind all

[83]Davis to Sophie Du Pont, May 20, 1862, Du Pont Papers. Both Blair and Davis initially opposed the Emancipation Proclamation—Davis because of the power it gave the President and because of the twisted interpretation it gave the Constitution; Blair because "it would be likely to carry over those [border] states to the secessionists." Howard K. Beale, ed., *Diary of Gideon Welles* (New York: W. W. Norton & Co., 1960), 1:143; Montgomery Blair, "Memo on Emancipation Proclamation," July 23, 1862, Blair Papers.

[84]Davis to Samuel F. Du Pont, July 11, 1862; July, 1862; March 20, 1861, Du Pont Papers.

[85]"Autobiography of Henry Winter Davis," Davis Papers, MHS; Baltimore *American*, October 1, 1860.

[86]Davis to Samuel F. Du Pont, December 20, 27, 1859; July 1860; December 1861; February 8, March 10, 1862, Du Pont Papers. See also Gerald Henig, "Henry Winter Davis and the Speakership Contest of 1859-1860," *Maryland Historical Magazine* (in press).

Democrats were "mere refuse that remained behind when patriotic elements withdrew for the defense of the Union."[87]

Davis never forgot—nor forgave—a Democrat. Even Francis Blair, Sr., was, in Davis's view, "an old loco-foco covered with a slight black varnish which will soon break through." Such sentiments extended to Blair's son, Montgomery, who was variously "a little creeper" and a "fool," but always a "former loco."[88]

Opposed in style, personality, ideology, and purpose, Blair and Davis fought an extended battle to form a new national coalition—with the Maryland Unionist party as part of the stakes. The competition between the two men was not new; it had apparently begun in the 1850s when Blair had left the Know-Nothing party to organize the Republicans. Later, in 1861, the two men competed for a cabinet job as well as control over the Maryland appointments. While Blair struggled to form a Unionist party based on the proposition that "we are all Republicans, [we are] all Democrats,"[89] Davis appealed to traditional anti-Democratic prejudices. When Blair played on established fears of free Negroes, Davis emphasized the importance of maintaining the Constitution—an equally venerable tradition in the border state of Maryland.

By 1863 disagreements between the two men erupted into open hostility. Blair felt that Davis had taken "the same ground as the radical Charles Sumner," and he therefore urged his friend Thomas Swann to contest the congressional nomination on the basis of differences with Davis over Reconstruction and the Negro.[90] Davis, however, easily defeated the former Baltimore mayor, but two years later, he lost the nomination to another Blair ally, Charles Phelps. Yet Blair himself, to Davis's delight, soon fell victim to Lincoln's need to placate more radical Republican opponents in an election year. In September 1864, as part of an arrangement to force Lincoln's opponent, John C. Frémont, to retire from the presidential race, Blair resigned as Postmaster General.[91] Both Davis and Blair happily saluted each other's declining political fortunes.

[87]*Speech of the Honorable Henry Winter Davis at Concert Hall*, p. 4.

[88]Davis to Du Pont, n.d., 1861; August 14, May 29, 1862; November 4, 1863; January 16, 1864, Du Pont Papers.

[89]Montgomery Blair, *Speech of the Honorable Montgomery Blair to the Maryland Legislature* (Baltimore: Sherwood & Co., 1864), p. 21.

[90]Blair to Swann, October 17, 1863 [copy], Blair Papers.

[91]There is evidence that Frémont withdrew as a presidential candidate as part of a deal, whereby Lincoln gained the support of Benjamin F. Wade and Henry Winter Davis in exchange for Blair's resignation from the cabinet. See Winfred Harbison, "Zachariah Chan-

The need for a new national political party, which might have eased the tortured process of Reconstruction, floundered amidst these squabbles of Blair and Davis. The split within the Maryland Union party continued, reinforced by the antagonistic positions of Blair and Davis. The "odium of faction"[92] irrevocably permeated Maryland's Unionist party.

☆ ☆ ☆

SHORTLY AFTER NEW YEAR'S DAY, the 1864 session of the Maryland legislature convened, and in February, the Assembly passed a bill setting up the machinery for a Constitutional Convention. So began a year of continuous political activity that ended only in November with the reelection of Lincoln and the election of a new Vice President, Andrew Johnson. Between January and November, Marylanders voted to hold a Constitutional Convention, elected convention delegates, ratified the new Constitution, elected delegates to state and national conventions, organized the Union National Convention that nominated Lincoln in Baltimore, and elected a state legislature, governor, congressional delegation, and President.

Throughout the year, the internal divisions of the Union party persisted. Eloquent pleas for harmony and for "burying all past asperities, all smouldering heart burnings, and all personal preferences"[93] fell unnoticed as Unconditional and Conservative Unionists continued to vie for party control. Lincoln warned Marylanders of "jealousies, rivalries, and consequent ill-blood, and driving one another out of meetings and conventions,"[94] but in April, two sets of Unionist delegates contested election to the Constitutional Convention, and in May, two central committees spoke for the party. By June, Unconditionals generally supported Lincoln's opponents for the Presidency, John C. Frémont and Salmon P. Chase, while Conservatives under the stern direction of Montgomery Blair resolved for "Old Abe." When queried by several New York editors about Lincoln's popularity in Maryland, Governor Bradford replied that "if Mr. Lincoln can not be elected, no other Candidate presented at this period of the Canvass in his place

dler's Part in the Reelection of Abraham Lincoln," *Mississippi Valley Historical Review* 22 (September 1935): 267–76; James Ford Rhodes, *History of the United States from the Compromise of 1850*, 8 vols. (New York: Macmillan Co., 1913), 4:529. For a somewhat different view of Frémont's intentions, see Charles Wilson, "The Lincoln-Blair-Frémont 'Bargain,' " *American Historical Review* 13 (October 1936):71–78.

92 Easton *Gazette*, July 4, 1863.

93 Baltimore *American*, February 25, 1864.

94 Basler, *Collected Works of Abraham Lincoln*, 7:226.

can."[95] Henry Winter Davis disagreed, and even rented Baltimore's convention hall,[96] but such tactics did not delay the President's nomination by the national Union party. Maryland Unionists were further embarrassed when two party members sought to be mayor of Baltimore, and on the eve of the November elections, a fight for control of the party found two executive committees complaining of mutual usurpation and interference.[97]

Yet these factions did not damage Unionist voting unity in either the legislature or the Constitutional Convention. Removed from party stump and partisan meeting, Unionists displayed the same consistency that most Maryland majority parties had previously shown on roll calls—and that they had demonstrated themselves in 1862. Economic issues, which rarely separated Maryland parties, failed to divide the two factions, and on political issues, Conservatives dutifully joined the Unconditionals. Consistent with the behavior of past legislatures, party was more powerful than section as a cue for voting behavior. Only roll calls relating to slaves and free Negroes revealed the split in the party, for Conservatives frequently voted with Democrats.[98] Such behavior led Democrats to hope that the Negro issue could serve as a bridge which dissident Conservatives could travel into the Democratic party. But the factionalism of Unionist delegates remained stronger outside the legislature—and Constitutional Convention—where words did not have to be translated into votes, nor resolutions into consistent support of the Democratic caucus.

Political battles were not the only preoccupation of Marylanders during the year. Nervously, the state watched as the Confederate Gen-

[95] Augustus Bradford to Horace Greeley, Parke Godwin, and Theodore Tilton, September 6, 1864 [copy], Bradford Papers. John C. Frémont, explorer, politician, and in 1862 a Union general, was nominated in Cleveland by the "radical Democracy"—a Republican faction. Salmon Chase, a former Ohio senator, was a dissident member of Lincoln's cabinet who never formally announced his candidacy but whose maneuvers made him a potential presidential aspirant. William Frank Zornow, *Lincoln and the Party Divided* (Norman: University of Oklahoma Press, 1954). For the differences among Unionists on their presidential choice, see W. Thomson to Governor Hicks, August 17, 1864; William Price to Lincoln, July 30, 1864; W. Philips to Lincoln, August 20, 1864, Lincoln Papers; and S. T. Wallis to William Glenn, July 23, 1864, Glenn Papers.

[96] Zornow, *Lincoln and the Party Divided*, p. 91.

[97] Baltimore *Clipper*, October 17, 31, 1864.

[98] The average index of cohesion for the Unionist party on 48 roll calls was 70; in the Constitutional Convention the index of party cohesion was 72. The average index of cohesion for Maryland's four regions ranged from the Eastern Shore's 64 to southern Maryland's 74, one of the few times that a section achieved a higher index of cohesion than a party. I studied twenty roll calls relating to blacks in the legislature and Constitutional Convention of 1864. The average index of cohesion for Unionists was 48; the index of party likeness, 62.

eral Jubal A. Early moved across the Potomac to raid Washington. In July, Early's corps, which included Maryland cavalry units, occupied Hagerstown and Frederick. The Union forces of General Lew Wallace, intent on saving Washington from a raid, engaged the Confederates at Monocacy Junction in western Maryland, but this action only delayed the Confederate advance across the state. Skirmishes in Baltimore county, the destruction of the estates of Montgomery Blair and Governor Bradford, raids in Montgomery county–all led to a call to Maryland's feeble Home Guard. Hasty fortifications were built near Baltimore and Annapolis, where delegates of the Constitutional Convention interrupted debate in order to erect earthworks. Soon the danger was over, and Early returned to Virginia. If his raid had failed to relieve Richmond, it had nonetheless succeeded in frightening Marylanders.

Despite such distractions, the ninety-six convention delegates completed their draft of the new Constitution in September. A milestone in Maryland history, the Constitution of 1864 freed Maryland's slaves, reapportioned the legislature by basing representation on white, not total population, set up a system of test oaths and registration for voters, and called for "the paramount" allegiance of Marylanders to the Constitution and government of the United States. To thirty-five Democrats, who represented more than one-third of the convention, such provisions were unacceptable, and accordingly they voted against the final version of the Constitution.

Democratic objections were not based primarily on opposition to emancipation, since by 1864 slavery was dying in Maryland. After 1810, the state's slave population had decreased approximately 5 percent each decade, until in 1860, the number of slaves had declined some 24,000 over a half-century, while the white and free Negro populations in the same period had more than doubled.[99] The war expedited this attrition, as slaves freed themselves by joining the army or disappearing into the nearby District of Columbia, a free community after April 1862. By 1864 Democrats could raise few arguments to support a declining institution which was "melting away like a snowball in the sun."[100] Instead party members complained of federal interference with a local institution, insisted on state–or,

[99] J. C. G. Kennedy, *Preliminary Report on the Eighth Census, 1860* (Washington, D.C.: Government Printing Office, 1862), pp. 126–32. In 1810, Maryland had 111,502 slaves; in 1860, only 87,189. While slavery in Maryland was disappearing, the number of slaves in the United States was increasing at a rate of over 20 percent a decade.

[100] Frederick *Examiner*, April 2, 1862.

somewhat inconsistently, federal–compensation for "the taking of private property," and questioned the future status of freedmen in Maryland.[101] Such objections, aired in repetitious speeches of an hour's length, did not delay the vote on emancipation which, after only a week's debate, passed by a strict party vote.

Slavery could not simply go out, like a candle, in a border state where hatred of a large free Negro population still raged. Throughout the convention, Democrats raised the question of the future status of Maryland's Negroes, and some convention delegates opposed emancipation because the freeing of slaves would double the state's Negro population. When Isaac Jones asked, "What is to be done with all these 80,000 Negroes you are to set free?" no one answered the delegate from Somerset, although Democrats unsuccessfully offered resolutions preventing free Negroes or mulattoes from emigrating to Maryland. Fines collected from violators would be used to encourage the state's own black population to leave Maryland. Democrats also introduced proposals for the apprenticeship of minor freedmen to protect the "white laboring man from equality with the Negroes."[102]

Behind such proposals lay the specter of "amalgamation, equality and fraternity" with blacks.[103] Increasingly, the Maryland press exacerbated such fears by printing reports of racial mixing; as a result, some delegates, excited and titillated by racist fantasies, accepted a domino theory of race relations. As one southern Marylander explained: "On, on, you go step by step. You recklessly go from one thing to another. You first liberate them, then give them the civil rights of citizens, and then for intermarriage and commingling of the races." Such fears led some delegates to see the "ballot-box" as the only protection "for your altars, your firesides, and your homes."[104]

Reluctant to discuss the future of the Negro in Maryland, Unconditional Unionists denied any commitment to the rights of black men. Even the hyperbolic Henry Winter Davis insisted that no one in Maryland, except the Democrats, raised the issue of equality,[105] and certainly few Unionists could be accused of supporting such a struggle. Said one:

[101] *The Debates of the Constitutional Convention of the State of Maryland*, 3 vols. (Annapolis: Richard P. Bayley, 1864), 1:61, 248, 538–60, 713–46. Hereinafter cited as *Debates*.

[102] *Debates*, 2:947, 1:627–31.

[103] *Ibid.*, 1:276.

[104] *Ibid.*, 1:664, 681.

[105] Baltimore *American*, April 4, 1864.

> Free them; give them equal human rights, the rights of husband and wife and parent.... Bring him to the point where he will desire to take a part in the civil government of the land and let him know he can never do so.... When he has become sufficiently educated to desire a voice in government and finds that here he can never be received as the equal of the white man, it is then that he will seek for himself a new country.[106]

In most cases, Unionists who clearly preferred to focus on less sensitive issues replaced considerations of the free Negro with their version of a new Maryland—"a young giant on the race of glory and reknown," freed now from the "dead weight" of slavery.[107] According to Governor Bradford, "the war was a special providence of God to tear loose from us a black idol"; cleansed of slavery, Maryland now could enjoy progress, happiness, and advancement of material wealth.[108] The familiar and insulting comparison of stagnant Maryland with progressive Massachusetts—Democrats preferred to compare Maryland with less bountiful Vermont—rested on the presumption that slavery had abused the state and caused economic, moral, and political harm. Unionists who were eager to be rid of slavery asked:

> Where are the majority of your seminaries of learning? Where are your great charities and enterprises? Where are your mammoth mills and factories giving employment to thousands of artisans? Where do the great and startling developments of science and art have their origin ... in the free North.[109]

As evidence of their interest in progress, Unionists included a provision in the Constitution for a state public education system. For the first time, Maryland would have a system of education, organized by a state superintendent and financed by a state tax. It was, concluded one Unionist, the beginning of "great work."[110]

Such a commitment to the future necessarily involved changes in Maryland's economy. Yet Unionists could never agree on the specific revisions in the Constitution that might encourage the state's economic development. Some wanted to sell the state-owned stock in Maryland's internal improvements, others wished the state to divest itself of investments in railroads and canals, and a few Unionists wished to repeal the constitutional prohibition on interest rates over

[106] *Debates*, 1:111.

[107] *Debates*, 1:615.

[108] Fragments of a speech, 1864, Bradford Papers.

[109] *Debates*, 1:555.

[110] *Ibid.*, 2:1210.

6 percent. Such disagreements fractured the party's voting unity and gave way to unusual alliances, which defied any political or regional patterns. On some economic issues, Baltimore Unionists joined Democrats from southern Maryland, only to vote with Eastern Shore Unionists on the next roll call affecting economic policy.[111]

Divided on racial and economic issues, Unionists united in supporting reapportionment, a registry system, and oaths for potential voters. For years, those who opposed the Democracy had suffered from an antiquated apportionment system which, because it was based on total population, favored southern Maryland and the Eastern Shore, both areas of Democratic strength with high black populations. In 1858, and again in 1862, Know-Nothings and Unionists had fought for a Constitutional Convention to change such arrangements, and in the Constitution of 1864, Unionists succeeded in their partisan desire to achieve more favorable representation. According to the provisions of the new Constitution, delegates from Baltimore who had represented 21,000 white Marylanders under the Constitution of 1851 would now serve 9,711. Certainly this adjustment was an improvement, but Unionists still chafed under the continued power of rural counties like Charles where a delegate represented only 5,796 white Marylanders.[112] Unionists fell silent, however, when Democrats suggested that, after emancipation, representation rightfully should be based on total population. When one Democratic leader, Ezekiel Chambers, charged that emancipationists were great friends of the Negro "up to a certain point," Unionists explained that Negroes—"a proscribed class"—should not be represented by their enemies from southern Maryland and the Eastern Shore.[113]

[111]A roll-call analysis of fifteen economic issues including selling the state's interest in internal improvements, repealing the prohibition on interest rates over 6 percent, regulating corporations, and revising the Board of Public Works does not reveal any sectional or political patterns except in isolated instances. Such an instance did emerge in voting on the Chesapeake and Ohio Canal, when delegates from western Maryland voted as a bloc to support resolutions preventing the sale of the state's interest in the Chesapeake and Ohio Canal without the approval of the General Assembly. The average index of cohesion for Unionists on these economic roll calls was 31, for Democrats, 45; the index of party likeness, 62. The influence of such important corporations as the Baltimore and Ohio on the state's political life awaits further study, but certainly the behavior of the legislature and Convention along with corroborative evidence from the Baltimore and Ohio papers suggests that the railroad had supporters in both parties and that its influence transcended party lines. See William B. Catton, *John W. Garrett of the Baltimore and Ohio: A Study in Seaport and Railroad Competition, 1820-1874* (Ann Arbor, Mich.: University Microfilms, 1959), pp. 329-44, 389-407.

[112]*Debates*, 2:1037-53.

[113]*Ibid.*, 2:1052, 1067.

In addition, Unionists agreed on the need for both a registration system and test oaths for prospective voters. Partly an attempt to prevent Confederate soldiers from voting in Maryland and partly an effort to assure the future of Unionism, such regulations also represented growing concern over political fraud and violence, as Marylanders, like other Americans, gradually accepted the need to regulate elections. While some Democrats protested that swearing past loyalty to the Union might disfranchise many Marylanders in the future, there was little objection to the registration procedures outlined in the Constitution. The need for more polling places as the population increased and the failure to regulate district and ward meetings where candidates were nominated evidently concerned Marylanders of diverse political background.

By September, the Constitution was complete. Democrats immediately announced their intention to oppose ratification, complaining that the Constitution violated "cardinal" principles.[114] Yet most of these new constitutional directions were in fact familiar byways. Reflecting established traditions in state political history, the Constitution of 1864 instituted alterations which were not so much imposed by the war as by the accumulated need for change. The most noteworthy contribution—the emancipation of the slaves—destroyed an institution which even supporters agreed was dead. Election controls, challenged by Democrats as reflecting military interference, in fact represented long overdue attempts to regulate the state's elections. The creation of new positions, such as the Attorney General, merely reintroduced to Marylanders officials whom their ancestors had elected earlier in the century. Even the provision for a state superintendent of education had been the concern of legislatures since 1849.[115] Neither the revolutionary document promised by the Unionists nor the result of "the passions, the excitement, and all the angry feelings . . . incident to a state of civil war," as Democrats charged,[116] the Constitution of 1864 introduced changes to Maryland's law which were skin-deep, not organic.

Inevitably the campaign for ratification of the Constitution merged with that to elect Lincoln and the Unionist candidate for

[114] *Ibid.*, 3:1873.

[115] Testimony of Libertius Van Bokkelen, November 14, 1867, Maryland Investigation, Records of Congressional Investigating Committee, House, 40th Cong., 1st sess., 1867, Record Group 233, National Archives.

[116] *Debates*, 2:917.

governor, Thomas Swann.[117] This campaign played on expressive symbols long familiar to Marylanders—the importance of Union, the necessity of allegiance to the United States, and the need for a new Constitution. "Free Union, Free Constitution, and Free Labor," proclaimed the party's ballots.[118] Support of Unionism and the Constitution assured progress, for, as one candidate proclaimed, "new factories will spring into being, and your workshops will resound to the busy hum of well paid labor, and the productive power of your rich fields will be tasked to the utmost under improved culture."[119] Opposition to Unionism meant support for the slave oligarchy of the past—and the secessionists of the present.

Yet when the state voted in October, only the favorable soldiers' vote saved the Constitution. Traditional areas of Democratic support overwhelmingly rejected the new charter, and the failure of some Unionists to vote nearly defeated the Constitution. This referendum represented the second statewide campaign undertaken by the Democrats since the war had begun, and the results clearly indicated the continuing influence that party exerted on Maryland politics. Even friendly newspapers concluded that Unionism was in danger.[120]

Three weeks later, on a rainy day in November, the state voted again—this time for local officials, congressmen, governor, and President. The issues were those which Unionists had raised throughout the year: the Union must be preserved, and the country saved by war. "The path to peace," according to Thomas Swann, "lies across the battlefield."[121] Consistent with their traditional emphasis on national issues, Unionists paid little attention to local concerns, although Marylanders elected state and county officials in November. Instead, from Cumberland to Elkton and Salisbury to Port Tobacco, Unionists urged voters to sustain the government until the end of the rebellion. A vote for Lincoln's opponent, the Democrat General George B. McClellan, was a vote for "the politics of treason."

[117]One of the most partisan provisions of the Constitution, this section called for elections of new state officers in 1864 who would not take office until 1866. If the Constitution had been defeated, no state officials would have stood for election until 1865.

[118]"Ticket for the Constitutional Convention," Bradford Papers, Hall of Records.

[119]Baltimore *American*, September 22, 1864.

[120]Referenda on constitutions traditionally fail to bring out a high proportion of voters, as Marylanders learned again in 1968. In 1864, 27,541 Marylanders voted for the Constitution, and 29,536 against. The soldier vote of 2,633 for and 263 against saved the Constitution. Three weeks later, Maryland's Unionist vote in the presidential contest, omitting the soldier vote, jumped 10,000. Baltimore *Clipper*, October 31, 1864.

[121]Thomas Swann, Scrapbooks, "Address to Unionists," 1864, Swann Papers.

Despite such powerful appeals, Lincoln received only 54 percent of the state vote, and if the ballots of Union soldiers who voted in military camps are omitted, only a fraction over 51 percent of the home vote. Democratic support was greatest on the Eastern Shore, and in Baltimore, Harford, and Allegany counties, all areas of prewar party strength. While Lincoln did well in the rural, farming regions of other states "inhabited largely by native-born citizens, former Bell-Everett voters and the skilled urban workers and professional classes," in Maryland this was not the case.[122] On the Eastern Shore and in southern Maryland, both agricultural areas, the President received only 36 percent and 14 percent of the vote, respectively. The Unionist vote, like that of Know-Nothings, was higher in the towns and villages than in the surrounding countryside, and 83 percent of the Baltimoreans who voted supported Lincoln.[123]

Such divergences from the pattern of national politics revealed the state's loyalty to the past, for despite three years of war, Marylanders remained attached to ante-bellum institutions and political customs. Unionists like Reverdy Johnson and George Vickers who had taken temporary refuge in Unionism "as a patriotic association," now returned to the Democracy unable to vote against that organization in a national election.[124] Other Unionists, disturbed by anticipated racial problems, supported the political party which had neither associated itself with emancipation nor budged from its prewar positions on the status of free Negroes. Even the division within the Unionist party was a legacy of the prewar confusion among Know-Nothings, Constitutional Unionists, and Republicans. Such fervid loyalty to the politics of the past made it impossible for Henry Winter Davis and Montgomery Blair to reorganize the state's parties. If the attachment to the past continued to guide the present, Unionists had much to fear from the future and Maryland's Democratic party.

[122]Lincoln received 37,353 votes, McClellan 32,413; the soldier vote was Lincoln 2,800 and McClellan 321. Thus the soldier vote did not save the state for Lincoln, as has been suggested by Zornow, *Lincoln and the Party Divided*, pp. 204, 210, 214–15.

[123]Throughout the period 1858–70 there are few significant correlations between socioeconomic variables, such as number of manufacturing establishments, value of farm land, value of assessments, etc., and votes for political parties. The only consistent and significant correlation is the positive correlation between the Democratic vote and the number of blacks, on a county-by-county basis. In 1864 this coefficient of correlation is +.8326. It is therefore impossible to make any conclusion about the socioeconomic background of either the Lincoln or the McClellan voters. The coefficient of correlation of the American party vote for Comptroller in 1859 and the Unionist vote for Lincoln, on a county-by-county basis, is +.5863; between the Lincoln vote and Bradford vote in 1861, +7304.

[124]Baltimore *Sun*, September 21, October 8, 1864.

V. THE BONDS OF PARTY: DEMOCRATS DURING THE WAR YEARS

WHILE UNIONISTS CONTENDED with disruptive internal factions, Maryland's Democratic party, temporarily displaced by the States' Rights faction in 1861, struggled to maintain its organization during the war years. For the first time since the American Revolution, the legitimacy of the opposition party was suspect, and Democrats became victims of charges that theirs was a party of treason, disloyalty, and rebellion.[1] In the minds of some Marylanders, party conflict, long sanctioned by tradition and history, now threatened the Union. A plaintive Maryland Democrat poetically described his reaction to such treatment:

Our looks are call'd in question, and our words,
How innocent soever, are made crimes.
We shall not shortly dare to tell our dreams,
Or think, but t'will be treason.[2]

Similar problems afflicted Democrats throughout the North and West. A party split in two factions during the presidential election of 1860 found, a year later, that its most powerful and numerous wing had seceded with the South. There were 101 Democratic congressmen in the Thirty-sixth Congress; after the formation of the Confederacy less than fifty remained. The death of Stephen A. Douglas, the Illinois senator, and the departure of John C. Breckinridge for the Confederate army removed two of the party's national leaders. Without an effective congressional voice, national leadership, or the power that comes from control of patronage, many Democrats agreed with their national chairman, August Belmont, that this was "the most disastrous epoch in the annals of the Democratic party."[3]

For Maryland Democrats, the future seemed especially bleak. War forced many Marylanders to make their choice between North and South, and by the fall of 1861, at least one-half of the party's state central committee had chosen the Confederacy. Some Democrats

[1] Richard Hofstadter has detailed the gradual acceptance of the opposition party as a part of the political system. By the 1830s many Americans saw parties not as the iniquitous institutions that Washington and Jefferson described but rather as significant and beneficial organizations. Certainly Martin Van Buren and his friends in the New York Regency contributed to this change in attitude. Richard Hofstadter, *The Idea of a Party System* (Berkeley and Los Angeles: University of California Press, 1969); Michael Wallace, "Changing Concepts of Party in the United States: New York, 1815-1828," *American Historical Review* 74 (December 1968):453-91.

[2] *The Debates of the Constitutional Convention of the State of Maryland*, 3 vols. (Annapolis: Richard P. Bayley, 1864), 1:290.

[3] Irving Katz, *August Belmont: A Political Biography* (New York: Columbia University Press, 1968), p. 91.

joined the Maryland Line, recruited in Virginia during the summer of 1861; some, like former Governor Enoch Lowe, served the South as civilians. Unwilling or unable to take an oath of allegiance to the Union, others languished in northern prisons from Boston's Fort Warren to the forbidding Fort Monroe overlooking the Chesapeake Bay. A few party members, including Reverdy Johnson and Henry Goldsborough, gave temporary support to the Union party, while Francis Gallagher, an important figure in Baltimore city politics, immediately joined the Union army.

Such desertions—for whatever reason—left the party in the hands of older leaders who, scorning even the name Democratic, chose to rally support for a new organization—the States' Rights party. By August 1861, Democrats who had carried Maryland the preceding fall advised their constituents that "it is not expedient to recommend candidates for election. Let the people determine whether to send representatives to the meeting of the Legislature or leave the counties unrepresented." Affirming "love of country as well as obligation to aid the officers of the United States and support the Constitution," Democrats urged their followers to support States' Rights candidates—advice which some party members followed in the important 1861 elections.[4] Organized by elderly Democrats, the new party did best in areas of traditional Democratic strength, but its candidate for governor, Benjamin C. Howard, received only 33 percent of the total vote, as Unionists, led by Augustus Bradford, easily won control of the state.[5] Never certain of its position on the war, on the Confederacy, or even of its own name, the States' Rights party disappeared, hardly mourned, from Maryland politics after 1861.

For the next two years, the Democratic party survived in the form of county organizations.[6] Always the strongest link in the chain which made up the state organization, these local units became even

[4]*Cecil Democrat* (Elkton), August 17, 1861; M. Viers Bouic *et al.* to Nathaniel P. Banks, September 13, 1861, Banks Papers, Duke University Library, Durham, N.C.

[5]On a county-by-county basis, there are positive correlations between the percentage of States' Rights vote in 1861 and Democratic vote for Comptroller in 1859 of +.7830 and between the Breckinridge vote in 1860 and the States' Rights vote of +.9151.

[6]Despite the importance of county government throughout the nineteenth century, there are few adequate studies of local government. Fortunately there are some exceptions—notably Ralph Wooster, *The People in Power: Courthouse and Statehouse in the Lower South, 1850-1860* (Knoxville: University of Tennessee Press, 1969); Seymour Connor, "The Evolution of County Government in the Republic of Texas," *Southwestern Historical Quarterly* 55 (October 1951): 163-200; and Charles Sydnor, *The Development of Southern Sectionalism, 1819-1848, A History of the South*, vol. 5 (Baton Rouge: Louisiana State University Press, 1948), pp. 33-53.

more important after the abrupt disappearance of the central committee. For years the Democrats had encouraged the development of county conventions that served three functions—the stimulation of interest in party affairs, the nomination of candidates for the county's numerous elective jobs, and the election of delegates to the party's state conventions. In these annual conventions, the power of county political units was manifested by the influence of delegates on the choice of the party's official governing body—the state central committee. Although officially chosen by the president of the convention, the choice of representatives to this committee was in fact dictated by county delegations. Each county and the city of Baltimore also had its own central committee chosen by the head of the county convention as well as an executive committee which ran economic affairs.

For 200 years Maryland counties had played a significant role in state history, and the organization of political parties naturally reflected this power. As late as 1850, delegates to the Constitutional Convention argued that counties were political individualities with sovereign powers.[7] Although all Marylanders were not willing to accept this extreme position, most recognized that their state had developed a system that made the county a vital part, not just a peripheral attachment, of the state government. By 1860 counties held impressive powers, recognized in law and practice. In each county, executives called commissioners—elected at large rather than by district—administered local affairs, decided on important patronage appointments ranging from tax collector to election judge, organized support for commercial projects such as the construction of bridges and the incorporation of coal companies, and generally ran the affairs of the county. The traditional reluctance of the legislature to articulate general—as distinguished from local—policy enabled county commissioners and delegates to formulate, as well as administer, laws intimately affecting the lives of their constituents. Tax assessments accurately reflected the relative power of state and county governments. Most Marylanders paid more than seven times the amount of county as state taxes, and paid these assessments on their property to collectors appointed by county commissioners.[8]

[7]*Debates and Proceedings of the Maryland Reform Convention to Revise the State Constitution*, 2 vols. (Annapolis: William McNeir, 1851), 1:235, 437-41. According to Walter W. Bowie of Prince Georges county, state senators, elected by each county, represented the "sovereignty of the state." *Ibid.*, 2:260.

[8]For an example of the power of county commissioners, see "Minutes of Meetings of Cecil County Commissioners," Cecil County Courthouse, Elkton, Maryland. See also *Debates of the Constitutional Convention, 1864*, 2:878-86. County commissioners had the right to

The war served to augment, not diminish, the power of the county. In 1862 and 1864 the state legislature empowered commissioners to pay premiums to Maryland soldiers. Lacking a statewide bounty system until 1864, Marylanders and their families turned to county government for the financial remuneration which encouraged volunteering. At the same time, war legislatures, in an effort to simplify proceedings and reduce the amount of time spent on special issues, restricted their own powers over a variety of concerns including school budgets, election boundaries, and name changes. In the 1864 Constitution such limitations on state powers greatly increased the authority of county commissioners, for it was into these officials' province that control over such elemental matters as tax assessments, divorces, and election arrangements fell. During the convention when Henry Stockbridge, a Baltimore Unionist, complained of the evils of local legislation and county power, Oliver Miller of southern Maryland took the more popular position that "the most important propositions are such as affect the counties locally and the laws in relation to powers and duties of our county commissioners." By the end of the war, such additional duties kept the commissioners in longer session than had been the case in the 1850s.[9]

For some Marylanders the most important function of county commissioners was to prevent slaves from joining the Union army. Fearing both a Negro "stampede" as well as the disappearance of the state's laborers, Marylanders continually complained of the removal of slaves—a removal which most whites believed was the work of army recruiters rather than a movement toward freedom by individual slaves. As Governor Bradford angrily noted in an 1862 letter to Lincoln:

> A steamer in the government employ provided with a recruiting officer and armed guard [is] sent down the many rivers which our state abounds in and guards immediately make known their presence and find means of communicating with slaves at night. Slaves under cover of night quit their owners' homes and repair on board the boat.[10]

---

set tax rates in their counties and hence these rates varied in time and place, but were always more than those of the state. In 1860 Cecil countians paid 10 cents per $100 of assessed property to their state, 70 cents to their county. *Cecil Democrat* (Elkton), September 14, 1861.

[9] "Minutes of the Meetings of County Commissioners," Cecil, Howard, Frederick, and Anne Arundel counties, 1859–68. See also *St. Mary's Beacon* (Leonardtown), February 17, 1862 and *Debates of the Constitutional Convention*, 1:65; 2:878.

[10] Bradford to Lincoln, September 28, 1862, Lincoln Papers, Library of Congress.

Despite the assertions of Union officers that Negroes could not be restrained from coming into camps, Marylanders generally agreed with Baltimore Congressman Henry May that "the contented slaves of our people [are] happy until corrupted in their humble cabin homes . . . by officers of rank seeking promotion."[11] Planters, torn between their need for black labor and their hatred of free black men, complained of the war-induced agitation among the local black population and sought redress from local officials. Walter W. Bowie, a prominent planter from Prince Georges, urged the governor to call out a posse to prevent the escape of his slaves. Bradford refused to take any action, except to complain of the army's role in slave removals and to warn Montgomery Blair that such practices would lead to "Democratic rule."[12] Dissatisfied with these results, Bowie turned instead to sympathetic county commissioners, who responded by doubling the number of constables. When even this strengthened police force proved ineffective, the commissioners arrested local slaves. For two years, twenty slaves—who had never been charged, much less convicted of any offense—languished in the Prince Georges county jail at Upper Marlboro. Only the interference of a horrified Union lieutenant freed these captives—an action which resulted in bitter complaints from the county commissioners about unnecessary military intervention in local affairs.[13]

The existence of such powerful and self-sufficient county governments, complete with their own patronage, taxing authority, and even newspapers, enabled Democrats to retain their organization throughout the lean years of the war, although in some elections Democratic candidates bore no party label. A disgruntled Unionist complained that "the real and ulterior purpose of the selection of local candidates is to maintain the organization of the Democratic party."[14] Demo-

[11]*Congressional Globe*, 38th Cong., 3rd sess., 1863, 33, pt. 2:1071. For comments on the "flocking" of slaves toward camps, see the *Cecil Democrat* (Elkton), January 23, 1864. For evidence of concern over free Negroes, see the Baltimore *American*, October 6, 1862; Bradford to Blair, September 19, 1863, Bradford Papers, MHS; Civil War Diary of Samuel Harrison, September 25, 1863, Harrison Papers, MHS; George Vickers to Bradford, September 19, 1863, Bradford Executive Papers, Hall of Records, Annapolis, Md.; R. Bayne to Lincoln, March 17, 1862, Bayne Papers, MHS.

[12]Bowie to Bradford, May 12, 1862; Bradford to Bowie, May 19, 1862, Bradford Executive Papers; Bradford to Blair, September 11, 1863, Bradford Papers.

[13]Lieutenant D. B. Holmes to Colonel S. M. Bowman, April 5, 1864, Adjutant General Papers, Hall of Records, Annapolis, Md.; Lieutenant Colonel Joseph Perkins to Colonel S. M. Bowman, March 28, 1864, Bradford Executive Papers.

[14]Civil War Diary of Samuel Harrison, September 29, 1863, Harrison Papers.

crats frequently traded their support to Unionist candidates for state and national office in return for that party's votes at the local level. Complaining that their opponents were "always running to back doors for coalitions," perceptive Unionists correctly assessed this Democratic strategy as an attempt to confine party organization "to counties to prevent the flame from entirely dying out."[15] By 1864, Democrats controlled the Maryland Senate, where representation was by county, and by 1865 the commissioners of many Eastern Shore and southern Maryland counties were Democrats.

The success of the Democratic county organizations led some Unionists to attack the power of the county and to seek a new political structure. To this end, Henry Stockbridge and Alexander Stirling, Unionist delegates from Baltimore, urged the Constitutional Convention to divide counties into independent townships whose powers would dilute those of the county. Hugh Bond, the Unionist judge from Baltimore and close ally of Henry Winter Davis, agreed and urged the governor to support a plan to augment the power of municipalities and townships.[16] Such proposals were offensive to Marylanders long accustomed to the traditional power of their county governments. Furious Democrats complained that any diminution of county powers was "a complete revolution," "an entire change," and "a Northern Trick."[17] Although the final version of the Constitution of 1864 gave the General Assembly power to provide for township government, no townships were actually created or discussed before the Constitution of 1867 repealed this provision. The successful defense of the county system enabled the Democratic party, while politically invertebrate, to operate within the hostile climate of Unionism; by protecting and even extending the sources of its power, the party prevented any structural change in Maryland's government that would have undermined the power of counties.

☆ ☆ ☆

ENCOURAGED BY THEIR PARTY'S POWER of survival, Democrats made several attempts to gather support outside the state. U.S.

[15]Easton *Gazette*, September 26, 1863; *Cecil Whig* (Elkton), March 15, 1862; September 26, 1863.

[16]Bond to Bradford, November 23, 1865, Bradford Executive Papers; *Debates of the Constitutional Convention, 1864*, 3:1694.

[17]*Debates of the Constitutional Convention, 1864*, 2:1192; 3:1694–95.

Senator Reverdy Johnson, who had long been convinced of the importance of sympathetic newspapers in political campaigns, noted the importance of controlling the failing *National Intelligencer* and encouraged Samuel J. Tilden, a powerful figure in the New York Democracy, "to make arrangements and arrest its downfall."[18] Two influential Baltimore Democrats, William Kimmel and William Glenn, traveled to New York to seek financial aid for the party. It was a logical place to turn, for Marylanders enjoyed close financial as well as familial relationships with the New York Democracy, and the needs of the Maryland party were obvious.[19] The party could no longer collect funds from state or national officeholders; only county officials remained to pay assessments on their meager salaries. Yet neither Glenn nor Kimmel was successful in gaining such support. Returning instead with anti-Lincoln pamphlets, Glenn noted a New York politician's wry comment that "New York could not make common cause with Maryland because New York had as much as it could do to take care of itself."[20]

In May 1863, still without outside help, Maryland Democrats held a meeting at Barnum's Hotel in Baltimore.[21] State leaders invited Conservative Unionists of the Blair faction to these discussions, and although the meetings were closed to reporters, party-watchers speculated that negotiations would end in a coalition between Conservative Unionists and the Democrats. Yet no call to convention or appointment of a central committee issued from Barnum's. Apparently rejecting any joint action between the two groups, Democrats returned instead to their county conventions to contest local elections. In the Eastern Shore and northwest counties, Democratic conventions nominated partial tickets, while the southern Maryland counties of the

[18]Johnson to Tilden, September 1, 1863; Hiram Ketchum to Tilden, September 9, 1863, Tilden Papers, New York Public Library.

[19]Civil War Diary of William Glenn, November 28, 1862; August 5, 1863, Glenn Papers, MHS; Daniel Vorhees to Horatio Seymour, January 28, 1863, Tilden Papers; Peter Hagner to Alexander Hagner, January 29, 1863, Hagner Papers, Southern Historical Collection, University of North Carolina. In the period before the Civil War, a number of Baltimoreans had moved to New York, including Democrats like Elisha Riggs and James Brown. Many Baltimore merchants had New York branches or correspondents—that is, companies that maintained special relationships with each other. The most prominent were Alexander Brown Brothers, managed in New York by James Brown; the Wyman family correspondent, A. C. Tiffany; and the B. & O.'s correspondent, William O. Hoge.

[20]Civil War Diary of William Glenn, November 28, 1862, Glenn Papers.

[21]For descriptions of this meeting, see the New York *Tribune*, May 22, 1863; *Cecil Whig* (Elkton), May 27, 1863.

sixth congressional district nominated and subsequently elected Democrats—from county commissioners to Congressman Benjamin Gwinn Harris, a rich planter from St. Mary's.[22]

Lacking a central committee, Democrats turned to their legislative delegation in Annapolis for party leadership. Strength in many election districts enabled Democrats to continue sending delegates to the war legislatures. In fact, one of every three delegates during the war years was a Democrat from the Eastern Shore or southern Maryland. Strengthened by the correspondence of regional and party interest, these legislators were a highly disciplined and persistent force in state politics. Although only a few Unionists survived the high turnover of delegates in the legislature, approximately one-third of the Democratic delegates in the 1862 legislature returned to the 1864 and 1865 sessions.[23] Certainly the voting behavior of this coterie reflected the discipline of the delegates. On 144 roll calls during the war that were studied, Democrats voted as a party 85 percent of the time, compared with the Unionist record on the same roll calls of 69 percent.[24] Evidently, the pressure of minority group status within the legislature unified, rather than fragmented, the party.

As in past legislatures, Democrats still voted together more often as members of a party than as representatives of their region.[25] Democrats achieved their greatest unity when they voted for political issues such as the organization of the legislature, patronage appointments, the disposition of contested elections, and the calling of a Constitutional Convention, although roll calls on issues involving the state's free blacks also revealed considerable unity among Democrats. In 1864 and 1865 only a rare Democrat disagreed with his party on Negro apprenticeship and changes in the state's Black Code. Thus, in

[22]The wealthy Harris, scion of an old Maryland family, owned 1,600 acres, 45 slaves, and $130,000 in real and personal property. He proved no boon to the national party, as even fellow Democrats like Samuel S. Cox of Ohio opposed his hot-headed outbursts in Congress. Cox to Manton Marble, April 11, 1864, Marble Papers, Library of Congress; Manuscript Census Returns, Maryland, Eighth Census, 1860, National Archives.

[23]The turnover of legislators is a characteristic of the Maryland system throughout the period. In most cases, legislators did not disappear from politics, but instead ran for the state senate or local offices. Ralph Wooster has described the same attrition in other ante-bellum southern legislatures. See Wooster, *People in Power*, p. 42.

[24]These roll calls involve issues of general, rather than local or special, interest, and I have defined a party vote as a roll call in which the index of cohesion is 80 or above.

[25]Southern Maryland consistently displayed more regional cohesion than did the Eastern Shore, and in 1865, the index of cohesion among members of this region—85—approached that of the Democratic party—86. See Appendix Table D-14 for a cluster bloc analysis revealing agreement scores among Unionists and Democrats.

keeping with party rhetoric outside the legislature, the status of black men—along with partisan disagreements—unified Democrats.

Democrats failed, however, to agree on two important types of issues—those involving economics and war. Traditionally, economic measures had never divided Democrats from Know-Nothings. In the 1850s platforms rarely mentioned either state or national fiscal matters, and legislative caucuses seldom took positions on such issues. Instead, delegates voted as individuals or as sponsors of a particular regional or corporate interest, and this pattern continued in the 1860s.[26] Democrats also disagreed on a number of war-related issues. For example, bills on the organization of the state bounty system split the party. To demur was not, however, to challenge the war. As one party leader explained:

> We love our country and recognize our obligation to support the Constitution and laws of the United States and to aid the officers of the United States in the constitutional and legal discharge of their office. We recognize our obligation to support the constitution and laws of this state. . . . We are opposed to the Republican party and to its principles controling [*sic*] the administration of the Federal government.[27]

Distinguishing between the government, which they supported, and the administration, which they did not, Democrats were a loyal, if disagreeable, opposition.

In 1864, Democratic legislators, aided by strong county machines, reestablished the state party. The calling of the Constitutional Convention provided the impulse for such a reorganization. Defeated in the legislature on the vote for convening such a convention, Democratic legislators traveled throughout the state organizing local meetings with a zeal which accounts for the high absentee rate in the closing days of the 1864 session. Democratic gatherings soon gave party members the opportunity to attack the convention movement as illegal, unnecessary, and expensive; to air objections to Lincoln and his handling of the war; and to play on Maryland's fear of free Negroes.

[26]That the influence of corporations like the B. & O. transcended partisan lines is apparent in several letters in the massive collection of Baltimore and Ohio Papers at the Maryland Historical Society. The key issue for the railroad during the war years was to end state control exerted by state-appointed directors, and in an attempt to achieve the termination of what the railroad called "political influence," the B. & O. turned to partisans of both parties. See J. E. Smith to John Garrett, July 12, 1860; Barzillac Marriott to John Garrett, April 29, 1861, Garrett Papers, MHS; and William B. Catton, *John W. Garrett of the Baltimore and Ohio: A Study in Seaport and Railroad Competition, 1820–1874* (Ann Arbor, Mich.: University Microfilms, 1959), pp. 329–44, 389–407.

[27]M. Viers Bouic *et al.* to Nathaniel Banks, September 13, 1861, Banks Papers.

Although Democrats lost the April referendum on the Constitutional Convention, the party gained some satisfaction from its first statewide election since 1861.[28] One of every three delegates who traveled to Annapolis in late April 1864 was a Democrat, and all but three of this thirty-five-man delegation represented either southern Maryland or the Eastern Shore. While this minority was unable to fashion a constitution to its liking—and voted against the final version—the Democratic delegates again acted as a disciplined and effective voting bloc within the convention.

Despite the hopes of many Marylanders, the process of Constitution-making was as partisan an affair as the legislative sessions. When the convention dragged on through the summer and fall, it became a platform from which Democrats attacked their opposition. For example, when Unionists adjourned the proceedings to attend the Union National Convention that nominated Lincoln in Baltimore, Democrats complained of absenteeism and joked that Lincoln had been nominated by an assemblage of "office-holders, relatives, contractors and niggers."[29] When Unionists attempted to change the state's constitution, Democrats were quick to argue "for old things, old laws, old customs, old habits—anything that time has tried and proved good."[30] Not content to air such opposition within the convention halls at Annapolis, Democrats published their speeches in pamphlets that circulated throughout the state.

One such pamphlet printed the objections of a southern Marylander to a proposed new article in the Bill of Rights: "The Constitution of the United States and the laws made in pursuance thereof being the supreme law of the land, every citizen of this state owes paramount allegiance to the Constitution and Government of the United States." Using familiar arguments, Daniel Clarke, son-in-law of a former Democratic governor, Philip F. Thomas, and a leading politician in Prince Georges county, denied the power of the United States to command such sovereign allegiance and insisted that the federal government trampled on the rights of Marylanders. After a lengthy

[28]In April, 31,593 Marylanders voted in favor of calling a convention, 19,524 against. This vote is 73 percent of that cast for President seven months later, a remarkable turnout when compared with other referenda on constitutional calls. Usually such votes averaged 60-65 percent of the turnout for state and national elections held in the same year.

[29]*Maryland Union* (Frederick), June 16, 1864. Quoting an article from the New York *World*, the *Maryland Union* found "no Unionists in the Republican nominating convention opposed to arbitrary arrests, or in favor of liberty of the press, but 65 for the Negro and 10 for buncombe."

[30]*Debates of the Constitutional Convention, 1864*, 1:42.

historical exposition of the power of the states and the baneful effects of "consolidation," Clarke concluded his address with a partisan appeal to Democrats: "Where is this silent mighty throng of voters, 40,000 strong? They will speak some day through the ballot box. Take courage then, fellow Democrats. . . ."[31]

Such pamphlets—along with the coming national elections and the referendum on the Constitution—encouraged the party to organize a state convention. The faithful network of Democratic newspapers from the *Cecil Democrat* to Frederick's *Maryland Union* printed calls to elect delegates to a state convention. In June 1864, party members met in Baltimore, and although several northern counties did not send delegates, Oden Bowie, chairman-elect of the state central committee, immediately began the task of preparing for elections. Bowie used all the traditional forms of party machinery—the state central committee, the executive committee, the hierarchy of local conventions, and the ward and election district Democratic clubs. Only once, when he appointed the state's presidential electors, who hitherto had been nominated by special conventions, did Bowie stray from the party's familiar procedures. For the moment, Democrats adopted no platform. With the staggering tolls of Grant's Virginia campaign still unknown and with rumors of an impending Confederate invasion menacing the state, military events might help to determine the party's appeals.

The "new" Democratic leadership of 1864 was a carbon copy of that of 1860. Of fifty-two members of the central committee, forty-five had been associated with the party in 1860. None of the central committee whose allegiances are known had supported the Know-Nothings, Bell, or Lincoln, although a number had been Whigs in the 1840s. Unionists justly complained that Democrats were "old copperheads, old officeholders—on the list the former collector of that city, the postmaster, and a hatch of small fry, most of them well-remembered hunkers of the most undoubted stamp."[32] Certainly Oden Bowie, the party's replacement for Bradley Johnson, held impeccable Democratic credentials. The son of a Democrat and a member of one of Prince Georges's most powerful families, Bowie had fought in the Mexican-American war. While his sons, brothers, and nephews served in the Confederate army, the rotund Bowie ran the family's extensive

[31] *Speech of the Hon. Daniel Clarke to the Constitutional Convention* (Baltimore: Sherwood Co., 1864); *Debates of the Constitutional Convention, 1864*, 1:292. See also Article 5, Declaration of Rights, Constitution of 1864.

[32] Baltimore *Clipper*, June 17, 1864. "Hunker" was a pejorative term originally used to describe Democrats in New York in the 1840s.

estates, developed a stable of thoroughbreds, and planned for the Democracy's return to power.[33]

With high hopes, Bowie and thirteen other Democrats of long standing traveled to Chicago to nominate a candidate for President. Many Marylanders hoped their party would run a peace candidate on a platform of ending the war, but isolation from the national organization caused them to underestimate the growing popularity of General George B. McClellan. During the year, prominent northern and western Democrats had convinced each other that "Little Mac," former commander of the Army of the Potomac and veteran of the Peninsular and Antietam campaigns, could attract the support of both war Democrats at home and Union soldiers in the field. By August, McClellan had the backing of three important party leaders–August Belmont, national party chairman, Manton Marble, editor of the New York *World*, and Samuel L. M. Barlow, a prominent New York political leader.[34] But for Maryland Democrats, the nomination of a Union general associated with the coercion of civilians would be a catastrophe. Shocked at the popularity of the General within the convention, delegates made clear their objections. In a scene reminiscent of angry diatribes during the 1860 Democratic conventions, Benjamin G. Harris, the hot-tempered congressman from southern Maryland, complained

> that McClellan was a tyrant. He it was who first initiated the policy by which our rights and liberties were stricken down–Maryland which has suffered so much at the hands of that man will not submit to his nomination in silence. All the charges that can be brought against Lincoln and Butler, he could substantiate against McClellan.[35]

Despite such passionate objections, Democrats nominated McClellan on the first ballot, with the Maryland delegation unanimously supporting Horatio Seymour of New York. The subsequent passage of a resolution referring to the war as four years of failure and demanding the

[33]A few of Bowie's personal papers are in the Hall of Records, but evidently the bulk of his correspondence has been lost, discarded, or destroyed. A. Leo Knott, one of the party's leaders, has written a highly partisan account of the revival of the Democracy and the role Bowie played in reestablishing the party. See A. Leo Knott, *A Biographical Sketch with a Relation of Some Political Transactions in Maryland, 1861–1867* (Baltimore: S. B. Nelson, 1898). One of Bowie's nephews who fought for the Confederacy was killed in a raid on Rockville just before the Convention met. *Cecil Democrat* (Elkton), October 15, 1864.

[34]S. S. Cox to Manton Marble, August 7, 1864; S. L. M. Barlow to Marble, August 21, 1864, Marble Papers.

[35]Baltimore *American*, September 1, 1864.

cessation of hostilities provided little consolation for angry Democrats insulted by the nomination of a man who, while military commander of the Army of the Potomac in 1861, had ordered the arrest of Democratic members of the legislature.

Hurriedly, leaders tried to absolve their candidate of charges that he had trampled Maryland's ballot. Both Barlow and Marble sought to prove that McClellan had not been responsible for the orders to arrest the Democratic legislators, and a hopeful Reverdy Johnson urged McClellan to refute the charges that he was as culpable as Lincoln "in the suppression of Maryland liberties."[36]

Such efforts failed to convince some influential Democrats. When McClellan modified the peace plank by stressing the importance of Union as well as his military record, some Maryland Democrats urged the convening of a new convention. T. H. Buckler, who had voted "Democratic all my life from President down to ward managers," complained to Glenn that "since the performance of the so-called Democratic convention at Chicago the word is odious and it is necessary now to establish a new party. Call it the peace convention." Glenn agreed that "Democratic leaders of influence here who favor peace will withhold their support for McClellan."[37] Daniel Clarke, a delegate to the Constitutional Convention, announced publicly that he would not vote for McClellan, and some Democrats printed election ballots with the name of the vice-presidential candidate, George Pendleton, who had long been associated with opposition to Lincoln's war measures, in larger type than that of McClellan.[38] Opposition papers noted with delight the disagreement among the Maryland Democracy. "Every point they would use against Lincoln—the draft, arbitrary arrests—they have virtually thrown away by the nomination of General McClellan," concluded the Baltimore *Clipper.*[39]

Certainly McClellan's nomination effectively neutralized the issue of the trampled ballot in Maryland, although occasionally Democrats sought to show their candidate as a more sincere advocate of Constitution and Union than Lincoln. In one widely circulated pamphlet, the

[36]Johnson to McClellan, September 16, 1864, McClellan Papers, Library of Congress; Barlow to Manton Marble, August 26, 1864, Marble Papers.

[37]Buckler to Glenn, September 14, 1864; Civil War Diary of William Glenn, September 1864, Glenn Papers.

[38]Stinnecke Scrapbook, Peabody Library, Baltimore, Md.; *Debates of the Constitutional Convention, 1864*, 1:292.

[39]Baltimore *Clipper*, September 1, 1864.

President was tried and found guilty of war crimes by the great statesmen of the Republic—Washington, Jackson, Clay, and Douglas.[40] On the other hand, McClellan was "for Union in its integrity, for the Union under the Constitution, for the Union at all hazards."[41] McClellan's own statements fitted neatly into these same themes: "I assert my fidelity to the Union under the Constitution. Every true patriot desires above all things, restoration of Union, Constitution, ancient harmony and fraternity of states as they existed in the days of Washington, Jefferson, Madison and Monroe."[42] Yet at the same time that national leaders found the Republican violation of constitutional liberties a more effective campaign issue than the Democratic search for peace, Marylanders had concluded that McClellan could never lead what the Ohio Democrat Clement L. Vallandigham called the "grand army of constitutional liberty."[43]

During the ensuing campaign, the confusion over McClellan's nomination led most Maryland Democrats to resort to vague appeals similar to those of 1860. Unable to agree on the proper approach to ending the war and unwilling to accept McClellan as a candidate, they talked instead of "Union as it was and Constitution as it is."

> If you are opposed to the old Union [urged a Frederick editor], join the abolitionist party, for you will then be among its enemies. If you are in favor of it as it was formed and upheld by Washington, Jefferson, Madison and Monroe, join the Democratic party.[44]

Such paeans to Constitution and Union enabled Maryland Democrats, while saying little of the future, to invoke party heroes and issues of the past. Neglecting state concerns entirely, stump speakers concentrated instead on invocations to Washington, Jefferson, and Clay and incantations to the Republic, Constitution, and Union.

Certainly these protean concepts of Constitution and Union meant different things to different Democrats. Indeed such vague symbols afforded the only opportunity for those who disagreed on the purpose of the war and the future of the Union to share a political

[40] *The Trial of Abraham Lincoln by Great Statesmen of the Past, A Council of the Past on the Tyranny of the Present* (Baltimore: William Inness, 1864).

[41] William Schley, *Appeal to My Fellow Citizens of Maryland*, October 24, 1864, Tilden Papers.

[42] Fragment of a statement by McClellan during the campaign, 1864, McClellan Papers.

[43] Vallandigham to S. S. Cox, October 28, 1863, Marble Papers.

[44] *Maryland Union* (Frederick), June 2, 1864.

platform.[45] To Democrats like William Glenn, the term "Constitution" implied the protection of states' rights, the importance of individual liberties, and the need for a negotiated peace with the Confederacy. To Reverdy Johnson, the same term meant the continuation of war until the South surrendered. To both men the expressive symbolism of the past provided a convenient meeting ground.

On one issue, the status of free blacks, Democrats were quite specific. Rejecting any need for state protection or aid to freedmen, the party categorically denied Negro equality, insisted that theirs was a white man's party, and condemned Unionists for encouraging race-mixing. Often the only local matter amid a number of national concerns, Negrophobia had become a Democratic issue in the 1850s, and the war served only to sharpen the political impact of what Marylanders called "niggerism." In 1862, Senator Anthony Kennedy had noted the growing antipathy between "laboring white" and free blacks. Anticipating "deeds of violence" between the two races if Negroes were freed, Kennedy described to his Senate colleagues race riots in the 1850s between Baltimore's Negro and white caulkers. His congressional colleague, Henry May of Baltimore, was even more specific. Amused by theories of "sentimental gentlemen" who believed in "the perfectability of the negro," May elaborated on "the inert nature, slovenly habits, clumsiness, want of vigilance, and timidity" of Negroes.[46]

Influenced by such attitudes, local Democrats drew lurid pictures of race-mixing and miscegenation. In 1862, after the lynching of a Negro accused of the rape and murder of a white girl near Denton, an

[45]I devised an index of specificity to measure the frequency of specific programs enunciated by Democrats and Unionists in various campaign platforms. Any specific recommendation such as a resolution for a negotiated peace or a plea to support a specific candidate counts as a specific recommendation and is divided into the total number of such resolutions adopted. General statements of support for Constitution and Union, and references to the "brave Union soldiers" are not counted as specific references. In 1864, the index of specificity for Democrats was .20, meaning that of every 5 resolutions passed by county or state conventions, only one contained a specific reference. By comparison the index of specificity for Unionists in 1864 was .43, for Unionists in 1862, .35. In the 1840s and early 1850s, Democrats were far more specific than in the 1860s. A study of resolutions passed at Democratic conventions in 1844, 1848, and 1852 reveals an average index of specificity of .52. For other uses of such indexes, see Louis Galambos, "AFL's Concept of Big Business: A Quantitative Study of Attitudes toward the Large Corporation, 1894-1931," *Journal of American History* 7 (March 1971):852.

[46]*Congressional Globe*, 37th Cong., 2d sess., 1862, 32, pt. 2:1358; *ibid.*, 37th Cong., 3rd sess., 1863, 33, pt. 1:685.

enterprising reporter found the black community "influenced by national affairs, vaguely calculating to appropriate white women for the wives of black men."[47] The racist doggerel of "Major Jack Downing" found receptive audiences throughout the state:

White man, white man sure's yo's born,
The crows are going to take your corn,
They surround your fields on every tree,
And they blacken the sky as far
As we see,
Lubly Rose,
Sambo stay,
In the land of Dixie,
Far away.[48]

Gradually Democrats translated this pernicious racism into a useful political weapon. Presenting the Democracy as the party of white men, county conventions called for a "white man's party formed on the single issue of opposition to abolitionism. Too long already has the Negro been pushed forward and the white man thrust back."[49] Democrats frequently passed resolutions opposing Negro equality at the polling windows, in the jury box, and on the witness stand. The Constitution of 1864 became, in Democratic rhetoric, an attempt to have integrated schools, and the struggle of Negroes themselves to achieve freedom heightened such fears.[50] By opposing any change in the status of Negroes, Democrats made it appear that their Unionist opponents favored race-mixing. Such a conclusion was both unwarranted and chimerical, for hatred of blacks was a nonpartisan failing in Maryland, but the emancipation of the state's slaves by a Unionist convention just seven days before the presidential election of 1864, hardly abated racial fears cultivated by the Democratic party.

While the Negro issue greatly embarrassed Unionists, "the politics of loyalty" frequently discomfited Democrats during the campaign.

[47] *Cecil Democrat* (Elkton), November 8, 1862.

[48] *Ibid.*, May 24, 1862. The "Jack Downing" letters were written by the Maine satirist, Seba Smith.

[49] *Maryland Union* (Frederick), March 3, 1864.

[50] Baltimore *Daily Gazette*, August 3, 1864. In March 1864, Baltimore Negroes held what Philip Foner calls "the first meeting of Negroes ever held in the city of Baltimore or in the state of Maryland" to encourage the enrollment of Negroes in the Union army. See Philip Foner, "The First Negro Meeting in Maryland," *Maryland Historical Magazine* 66 (Spring 1971):60-67. It is questionable whether this is the "first" meeting of Negroes in Maryland, for free Negroes often met to discuss African colonization. See James M. Wright, *The Free Negro in Maryland, 1634-1860*, Columbia University Studies in History, Economics and Public Law, vol. 97 (New York: Columbia University Press, 1921), p. 289.

Throughout the war, but most frequently in 1864, Democrats were the party of "Dixie, Davis, and the devil."[51] Even the uncomplimentary epithet "copperhead," which attached itself to the party during the war, suggested a hatred that went beyond the bounds of normal partisan billingsgate. The gravamen of Unionist charges against the Democrats was quite simple: during the war there could be only two parties—the loyal and the disloyal—and as the Unionists had taken the loyal ground, Democrats were therefore traitors.[52] According to this argument, parties had caused the war, and now it was time for a patriotic association which transcended the petty issues of politics. A Unionist pamphlet entitled *No Party Now but All for Our Country* made the point profusely:

> Party has no meaning in far the greater number of the highest and common relations of human life. When we are ailing, we do not take money by party prescription. We do not build ships by party measurement. We do not enjoy the flowers of spring, nor do we harvest the grain by party line. . . . We do not, and we must not love and defend our country and our liberty, dear to us as part and portion of our very selves according to party rules. . . . We know no party in our present troubles.[53]

To offset such criticism, Maryland Democrats drew on a body of doctrine developed before the war that maintained parties were not the corrupt institutions so long vilified by Americans, but were instead a significant and beneficial part of the political process. In 1856, a Baltimore lawyer and Democrat, Philip Friese, had noted two important "uses" of party within a democracy: first, political organizations created and stimulated public opinion; and second, parties helped to organize and accomplish the election of persons motivated by certain principles to elective office. During the Civil War, Maryland Democrats used Friese's arguments to insist on the need for two parties "to strive for the mastery of the government."[54] Pressed to defend their very existence during the 1864 campaign, Democrats contended that every government must have an opposition, that parties were thus unavoidable in free countries, and that the existence of such a perverted

[51] Baltimore *American*, April 1, 1864.

[52] For examples of this reasoning see Civil War Diary of Samuel Harrison, January 14, September 28, 29, 1863, Harrison Papers; Baltimore *Clipper*, August 22, 1864; Governor Bradford, Notes for a speech in Harford County, September 1865, Bradford Papers; and "Immorality in Politics," *North American Review* 98 (January 1864):105–27.

[53] *No Party Now but All for Our Country* (New York: C. S. Wescott, 1863). A copy of this pamphlet is found in the Lincoln Papers, May 1863.

[54] Philip Friese, *An Essay on Party Showing Its Uses and Abuses and Its Natural Dissolution* (New York: Fowler and Welles, 1856), pp. 10–12.

organization as Unionism justified the continuance of the Democracy during the war. Using an argument developed by Democratic congressmen, Marylanders maintained that without parties the best government would degenerate into the worst of tyrannies. In the Democratic view, Unionism was a corrupt faction controlled by a clique of radical and selfish politicians.[55]

With politics at a white heat in 1864, only a few Marylanders had either the time or inclination to engage in philosophical considerations of the role of party within a democracy; most partisans were concerned with more mundane, but no less important, tasks of organization and campaigning. Democrats called for the formation of a "cabinet" of prominent national leaders as well as for the appointment of various campaign officials, a financial secretary to devise ways and means of raising money, a superintendent of the public press, a secretary of correspondence to keep in touch with state committees, and even a detective force, as the committee explained pointedly, "for obvious reasons."[56] Yet these national agents paid little attention to Maryland. Except for an occasional visit by Charles Mason, head of the executive committee, county machines remained isolated from the national party. Noting the apathy of some Democrats in the state, Mason described the "standing aloof of men of wealth" and "working men without much means. . . . A few thousand dollars would probably turn the scale in Maryland." John Bishop, a local leader, agreed. "A number of men speak favorable [*sic*] of your nomination for President," he wrote McClellan. "I think with a little money to treat around with Baltimore city and county are yours."[57]

Such estimates were too optimistic. McClellan failed to carry the state by 5,000 votes, although he received 48 percent of the total vote—nearly the same proportion of Maryland's popular vote that Breckinridge received in 1860. McClellan ran well in areas that had supported the Democratic party in the late 1850s, and his greatest strength was in rural areas. Even in the Unionist territory of northern and western Maryland, McClellan's vote was higher in rural districts than it was in the cities of Cumberland and Frederick, or even towns

[55] *Cecil Democrat* (Elkton), May 17, 1862; *National American* (Bel Air), July 31, 1864; *Baltimore County Advocate* (Towson), March 22, 1862; *Cecil Democrat* (Elkton), October 11, 1862, November 21, 1863.

[56] "Plan of the Democratic Campaign," October 1864, Executive Campaign Committee, Marble Papers.

[57] Charles Mason to Manton Marble, October 25, 1864; John Bishop to General McClellan, September 10, 1864, Marble Papers.

like Boonsboro and Ellicott City. Although urban and foreign-born voters in other states supported McClellan, he did poorly in those wards of Baltimore city with high proportions of German- and Irish-born. As in past elections, the Democratic vote was heaviest in areas where the black population was highest.[58] (Map 3 shows the geographic distribution of the Democratic vote.)

Democrats demonstrated remarkable discipline in their voting. While Thomas Swann, the Unionist gubernatorial candidate, ran some 1,000 votes ahead of Lincoln, Ezekiel Chambers, the Democratic candidate, received exactly the same number of votes as McClellan. Apparently those Democrats who did vote heeded the advice of their newspapers "to vote the whole ticket."

After the election, some Democrats charged that military interference had prevented their victory. Generally accepted by past and present writers on Maryland history, this charge omits any consideration of the closeness of the results, for McClellan lost by only 5,000 of nearly 70,000 votes cast. These returns belie the familiar image of federal troops under General Lew Wallace refusing to allow Democrats access to the polls.[59]

Actually, it was less the presence of the military than the necessity of taking an oath of past loyalty to the government that kept Democrats from the polls. The 1864 legislature required the prospective voter to swear that he had never expressed a desire for the triumph of the "rebels" or given aid to any Confederate. Such an oath was a difficult one in the border state of Maryland, where many

[58]William Frank Zornow, *Lincoln and the Party Divided* (Norman: University of Oklahoma Press, 1954), pp. 210–13. In the city's Second and Eighth wards, where over 35 percent of the population was foreign-born in 1850, the McClellan vote was under 20 percent. The coefficient of correlation on a county-by-county basis between the percentage of population that was black and the percentage of Democratic vote for President is +.8326. Throughout the period 1858–70, there are few significant correlations between socioeconomic variables, such as the number of manufacturing establishments, value of farm land, value of assessments, and votes for political parties. The only consistent and significant correlation is that between the percentage of Democratic vote and the percentage of population that was black. There are high correlations, again on a county-by-county basis, between the McClellan vote of 1864 and that for Democratic congressmen in 1859 (+.6367); that for Breckinridge and Douglas in 1860 (+.5658); and Howard in 1861 (+.7034).

[59]In 1864, the Maryland legislature set up machinery for its citizens to vote in army camps outside of the state. Only 3,121 of approximately 15,000 Union soldiers took advantage of this opportunity, although certainly some soldiers received convenient furloughs and returned home to vote. The voting procedures in the field, which permitted officers to collect ballots, probably intimidated some Democrats from voting. Josiah H. Benton, *Voting in the Field* (Boston, 1915). There is evidence that a few Maryland units, such as the Purnell Company, used viva-voce voting. See Joseph Cushing to Bradford, October 7, November 21, 1864, Bradford Executive Papers.

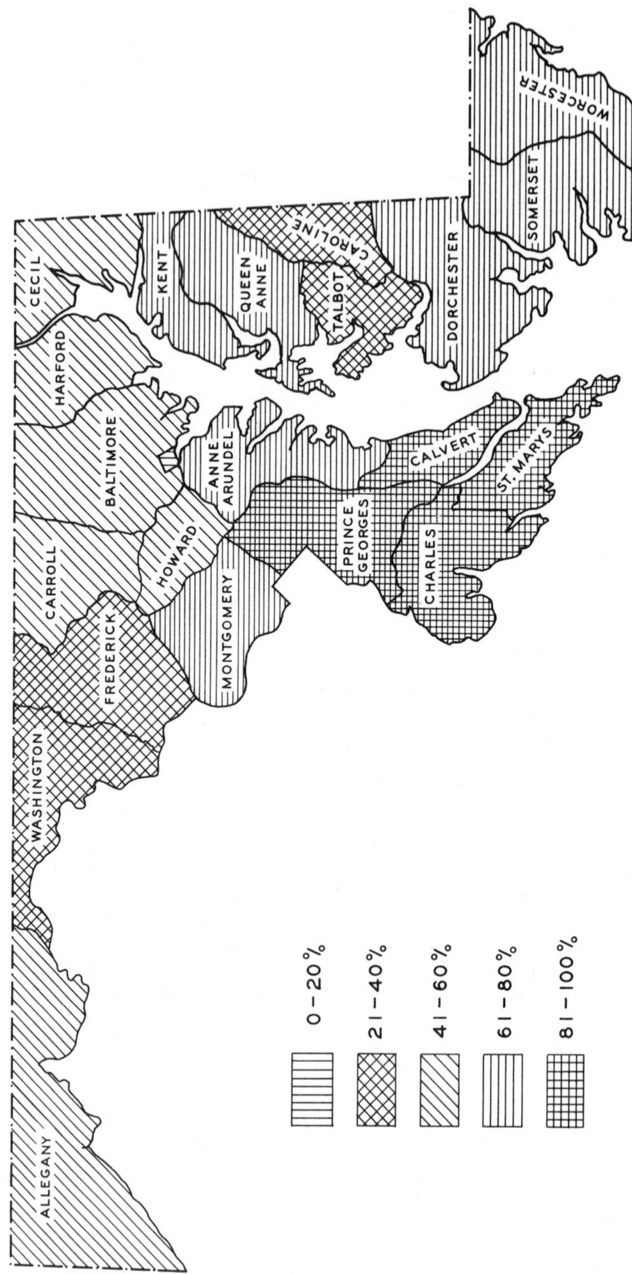

Map 3. *Geographic Distribution of the Democratic Vote for President in 1864*

families, including those of congressmen, delegates, and even the governor, had relatives who were fighting for the Confederacy. Some Democrats refused to vote for the sake of principle and argued that such provisions were bills of attainder. Others decided "to face the music and take Lincoln's oath," but in some areas of the state, particularly in districts where election judges were Democratic and less than zealous in its application, the oath was seldom used.[60]

Many Maryland Democrats did not vote for two other reasons: first, whether fighting in the Union or Confederate armies or in temporary exile, Democrats who were not physically in the state could not vote. Furthermore, state law which required residence for six months in a county before voting disfranchised many Baltimoreans who had moved to the country. In Baltimore, the community that had lost the most population during the war, the vote declined more than 35 percent from 1860. Yet in Somerset, the county that Democrats described as controlled by "blue-coated hirelings," voting was down only 9 percent.[61] The second reason for the decline in the Democratic vote lay with the refusal of some party members to vote either because they disliked taking an oath, or because confronted with the choice of an unacceptable nominee, McClellan, they preferred not to vote at all. Absence and confusion, not interference and coercion, prevented a Democratic victory.[62]

☆ ☆ ☆

BY THE FALL OF 1864, Democratic prospects had improved under the leadership of Oden Bowie. The party's organization was now

[60] Charles Lanman to McClellan, October 8, 1864, McClellan Papers; H. Valentine to Bradford, November 4, 1864; G. P. Leach to Bradford, November 9, 1864, Bradford Executive Papers.

[61] House of Delegates, *Documents of the State Legislature, 1865*, "Contested Election for Judge in Somerset County," Document V (Annapolis: Richard P. Bayley, 1865), p. 122.

[62] Recent research in political behavior has suggested that voters presented with conflicting ideas often resolve these cross-pressures by not voting at all. In 1864, the conflict between a vote for McClellan, considered by many a war candidate who had trampled Maryland's rights, and the desire for peace and the restoration of the state's constitutional liberties ended in some abstentions. "When people desire and shun a course of action in about equal degree, they often do not decide for or against it, but rather change the subject or avoid the matter altogether." According to Kurt Lewin's field theory, psychological cross-pressures often result in movement away from both forces—in this case, not voting. See Angus Campbell *et al.*, *The American Voter* (New York: John Wiley and Sons, 1960), pp 33–36, 80–88. The quotation is from Paul Lazarsfeld, Bernard Berelson, and Hazel Gaudet, *The People's Choice*, 3rd ed. (New York: Duell, Sloan, and Pearces, 1944), p. 62.

statewide, a central committee helped direct financial affairs, and Democratic candidates for state office had received 46 percent of the Maryland vote. The vibrant county machines, so long a factor in keeping the party alive, elected 26 Democrats out of 80 delegates to the 1865 legislature. Certainly appeals for "Constitution as it is, Union as it was and a white man's party" proved effective rallying cries—particularly when voiced by leaders long familiar to Maryland voters. With Grant poised in Northern Virginia and Sherman inching northward through the Confederacy, even the long war seemed near an end, and in political terms, the termination of the fighting meant the return of Democratic voters to the state and the assurance of that party's return to power.

Faced with the prospect of defeat, the Conservative wing of the Unionist party tried to incorporate Democrats into a new political alliance. In the early months of 1865, Conservative Unionists, eager to elect Montgomery Blair to Thomas Hicks's Senate seat, urged Democrats to join supporters of Constitution and Union.[63] The possibility of such an arrangement had long enlivened Maryland politics, and on many editorial pages the metaphor of a wedding or "nuptials" described the anticipated coalescence of Democrats and Conservative Unionists. As the *Kent News* noted, the two organizations could join on a platform "upholding the principles of Constitution, with the motto of Union under the Constitution and the protection of the rights of habeas corpus. . . ."[64] In 1865 the advantage of such a coalition was obvious to Democrats who lacked the necessary legislative votes to elect their own candidates or institute their own programs. As one Democratic delegate wrote Montgomery Blair, a candidate in 1865 for a Senate seat:

> It will afford me much pleasure to aid you. . . . You are conservative in your views and will much better represent the present feeling of Maryland than the more radical of the [unionist] party and again you belong to my county and have a greater personal interest in what honors she may obtain. From what I know of Democratic sentiment they would prefer you to anyone named.[65]

[63]In poor health for many years, Hicks had a leg amputated in 1864, and the former governor longed to retire from his Senate seat and accept the rich patronage plum of Collector of the Port of Baltimore. Before resigning, Hicks died in February 1865.

[64]Quoted in the Chestertown *Transcript*, January 18, 1865. For other reports of the possible merger, see the *Civilian and Telegraph* (Cumberland), March 17, 31, 1864; Baltimore *American*, March 2, 1864.

[65]Benjamin Fawcett to Montgomery Blair, January 25, 1865, Blair Papers, Library of Congress.

Despite Blair's appearance in Annapolis, fusionists could not deliver the Democratic vote. On two important roll calls involving procedures for the senatorial election, Democrats either did not vote or they cast ballots against the Blair position.[66] Eventually the legislature elected the Unconditional Unionist and protégé of Henry Winter Davis, John Creswell. Evidently the strong bonds of party prevented Democrats from voting for a Unionist, no matter how similar their positions. Later a Democratic newspaper explained that Blair had been a part of the Lincoln administration and therefore deserved the "opprobrium" of Democrats.[67]

The same failure of fusion was apparent in the 1865 legislature. Democrats continued to display their unity, despite the temptation to join a sympathetic faction of the Unionist party. With only one defection, Democrats voted against the Thirteenth Amendment, which prohibited slavery. The party also voted as a bloc against Conservative efforts to rewrite the state's militia law and against a Conservative-supported bill to change the state's apprenticeship laws. While Democrats gave little support to the Conservative wing of the Unionist party, that faction occasionally voted against their party and with the Democrats.[68]

The Radical wing of the Unionist party favored a very different strategy to prevent the Democrats from returning to power. Late in the session, Unconditionals, without the votes of some sixteen Conservatives, adopted a much-needed registry law. For years, reformers of both parties had urged some form of voter registration to prevent fraudulent election practices. In the past, losers had frequently complained that the lack of any enrollment system permitted unnaturalized citizens and boys under twenty-one to vote, and in some cases, enthusiastic partisans to vote more than once. Indeed that nefarious local custom, "cooping"—a political version of the shanghai—grew quite naturally from this lack of control over voters. To prevent such fraud, the Constitution of 1864 provided for the enrollment of qualified voters in poll books, and in 1865 the legislature implemented this provision by setting up procedures for registration. The final Registry

[66]According to Maryland law, one of the state's U.S. senators had to come from the Eastern Shore. In 1865 an attempt was made to repeal this law, with Blair's supporters urging repeal, because their candidate lived in the western shore county of Montgomery. On the procedural votes to change this anachronistic provision, Democrats voted no.

[67]Baltimore *Daily Gazette*, October 26, 1865.

[68]The index of party likeness was 45 during the session; the Democratic index of cohesion was 86, that of the Unionists, 68.

Bill, which Democrats unanimously opposed, empowered the governor to appoint three registrars in each district and ward who would in turn register all prospective voters on one page, all qualified voters on another.

The political advantages of such a system were immediately obvious to Marylanders, since the "iron-clad" oath of past allegiance now became a qualification for registration.[69] In the hands of unsympathetic Unionist registrars, appointed by a Unionist governor, such machinery could effectively disfranchise many Democrats. While Unionists defended the measure as a safeguard to the purity of the ballot box, Democrats saw the registry law as the work of "political cliques straining every nerve to perpetuate their powers. They declare in effect that none should register who do not think as they do."[70]

In retaliation, Democrats organized local meetings to protest the registry law; neither the freeing of the slaves, nor the convening of a Constitutional Convention, nor even the institution of a draft had merited such political reaction. In 1865, a year without statewide elections, returning soldiers relearned their politics while complaining of the new law. At one such meeting, a Democratic speaker inveighed against the registry system and noted that "with the passage of this disappears all hope for a restoration of the state to her ancient status."[71] Gradually Democrats connected the iniquitous registry law with attempts by Unionists "to force their doctrines of negro equality upon the country."[72] A symbol of the "politics of the trampled ballot," the Democratic fight against the registration law came to include all that party's vigorous disagreements with its opponents.

☆ ☆ ☆

EARLY IN THE WAR, a faithful Democrat had suggested "that the Democratic party neither dies nor changes, being a party of principle,

[69] According to Section 4 of Article 1 of the Constitution of 1864, "no person who has at any time been in armed hostility to the United States or the lawful authorities thereof, or who has been in any manner in the service of the so-called Confederate States of America and no person who has voluntarily left this state and gone within the military lines of the so-called Confederate States of America or armies with the purpose of adhering to said States or armies and no person who has given any aid, comfort, countenance, or support to those engaged in armed hostility" could vote. It was, of course, this latter provision of "aiding, comforting, countenancing or supporting the Confederacy" by sending money or goods or letters, or wishing for a Confederate victory that infuriated many Marylanders.

[70] *Maryland Journal* (Towson), August 5, 1865.

[71] *St. Mary's Beacon* (Leonardtown), March 13, 1865.

[72] Bel Air *Aegis and Intelligencer*, August 4, 1865.

it is indestructible, full of vitality and durable as the everlasting hills."[73] The war clearly revealed both the vigor and durability of the Maryland Democracy, despite the removal of its leaders, the organization of the States' Rights party, and the attraction of Unionism. In the view of loyal Democrat William Preston, "[it is] better to be a tortoise in a shell than a crippled lion baited by the blood wounds of faction."[74]

While Democrats in other states have been variously interpreted as precursors to the Grange Movement of the 1870s, disloyal adjuncts to the Confederacy opposed to the war, and western sectionalists fighting Wall Street, Maryland's Democratic organization represented an attempt to hew to old values, traditions, and loyalties during a period of great turmoil and change.[75] In the words of one Democrat, the party meant to "preserve the time-honored principles of the past."[76] Built on nostalgic appeals long familiar to Marylanders, cries of "Constitution as it is, Union as it was, and Negroes where they were,"[77] won support in areas of traditional Democratic strength. Never disloyal to the Union as their opponents charged, Democrats in Maryland played down the peace issue, preferring instead, at least until the nomination of McClellan, to emphasize the "politics of the trampled ballot." By 1865 only a registration law, the vagaries of national politics after the death of Lincoln, and Blair's persistent dreams for a new Conservative party stood between Democrats and control of the state. The military metaphor of party stalwarts reflected Democratic optimism: "Not a man must leave the ranks now. Not only must the veterans remain where they gallantly met the enemy . . . but new soldiers of Union and Constitution must be marshaled into line."[78]

[73] *Southern Aegis* (Bel Air), October 9, 1863.

[74] William Preston to Ida Preston, April 22, 1863, Preston Papers, MHS.

[75] For various interpretations of so-called "copperheadism" during the war, see Richard Curry, "The Union As It Was: A Critique of Recent Interpretations of the Copperheads," *Civil War History* 13 (March 1967):25-39; Frank Klement, *Copperheads in the Mid-West* (Chicago: University of Chicago Press, 1960); Wood Gray, *The Hidden Civil War: The Story of the Copperheads* (New York: Viking Press, 1942); Frank Klement, "Midwestern Copperheadism and the Genesis of the Granger Movement," *Mississippi Valley Historical Review* 39 (June 1952):29-44; and Ronald Formisano and William Shade, "The Concept of Agrarian Radicalism," *Mid-America* 52 (January 1970):4-30.

[76] Clarke, *Speech to the Constitutional Convention, 1864*, p. 21.

[77] Eugene Roseboom, "Southern Ohio and the Union in 1863," *Mississippi Valley Historical Review* 39 (June 1952):42.

[78] Chestertown *Transcript*, December 22, 1864.

VI. THE FAILURE OF FUSION: MARYLAND PARTIES DURING RECONSTRUCTION, 1865-1866

ON JUNE 6, 1865, a procession of Union soldiers paraded through the streets of Baltimore. These veterans of the Maryland Line, among them survivors of military engagements from Antietam to Monocacy Junction, marched through the city to the new public park at Druid Hill. Here an impressive ceremony marked both the conclusion of the war and the end of a period of mourning for the assassinated Lincoln. Soldiers stacked their arms and then received the thanks of the community "for brave and glorious deeds." Since Lincoln's successor, Andrew Johnson, had declined an invitation to speak,[1] Baltimoreans listened instead to the bombastic oratory of Governor Bradford, who welcomed "the long loitering dove back with the olive branch of peace in her beak." Bradford greeted the veterans with fulsome praise:

> If in their return to civil duties they are as true to themselves as they have been to [their country], they will by the same application of their industry, energy, and talents add to the vast productiveness and resources of the land and pay off the debt, while the politician and the visionary are yet discussing the best means of entering upon the task.[2]

In the following months Bradford traveled throughout the state to welcome returning soldiers. His themes were always the same: praise of the veterans, hope for the future, and condemnation of the politicians who had started the war. Like other Marylanders, Bradford viewed the conflict as a "challenge to the American Republic, sent by the Almighty to tear away from us a black idol." Reflecting his party's distaste for politics, the governor saw the schemes and ambitions of corrupt politicians as the cause of the war. In his closing remarks he welcomed the veterans to "the prosperous tide on which everybody now admits old Maryland is at last fairly launched."[3]

Yet the return of Maryland's soldiers to civilian life was not the easy process Bradford envisioned. Clashes between Confederate and Union veterans often ended in violence. Some communities attempted to bar citizens who had served the Confederacy, while others made Yankee soldiers the victims of "social isolation."[4] Many veterans returned to farms untended since the emancipation of slaves in November 1864 and the subsequent departure of many freedmen to Baltimore. Indeed, neighbors of the once wealthy Tilghman family in

[1] Mayor John Chapman to Johnson, June 1865, Johnson Papers, Library of Congress.

[2] Baltimore *American*, June 7, 1865.

[3] "Notes on Speeches," 1865, Bradford Papers, MHS.

[4] *Civilian and Telegraph* (Cumberland), May 4, 1865; Civil War Diary of Samuel Harrison, May 9, 22, 1865, Harrison Papers, MHS.

Talbot county found the young ladies of the family milking the cows while old Colonel Tench Tilghman held an umbrella over their heads. Angry white farmers complained that so many Negroes had left the region that the cultivated acreage in southern Maryland was halved. Declining land prices, a burgeoning population in Baltimore, and decreased farm production belied Governor Bradford's optimism.[5]

The early years of Reconstruction were further complicated by the deterioration of relations between the races. In the summer of 1866, whites in Anne Arundel county invaded a black religious meeting and assaulted Methodist worshipers.[6] Intrepid Negroes who tried to institute an educational system found their efforts impeded by the state government which callously refused to use taxes collected from Negroes for black schools and by the hostile actions of white Marylanders who burned Negro schools and harassed Negro teachers. The treatment of a black teacher in Havre de Grace, who was assaulted and beaten by a white gang, was not unusual, nor was the disposition of the case unique, when a local jury refused to award damages.[7]

In their struggle to maintain control over the freedmen, many Maryland whites tried to return blacks to virtual slavery by means of an anachronistic apprenticeship system. Hurrying to Orphans Court, farmers and planters, manufacturers and merchants applied for apprenticeship contracts until by 1867 more than 3,000 black minors had been bound over to their former masters.[8] Negro parents pro-

[5]Civil War Diary of Samuel Harrison, November 9, 13, December 13, 25, 1864, Harrison Papers; Lieutenant S. N. Clark to Colonel John Eaton, August 21, 1865, Bradford Executive Papers, Hall of Records, Annapolis, Md.; John Gibbon to Benjamin Henry Latrobe, September 7, 1865, Gibbon Papers, MHS. For a narrative account of Maryland during the early years of Reconstruction, see Charles Wagandt's chapter, "Redemption or Reaction?—Maryland in the Post Civil War Years," in *Radicalism, Racism and Party Realignment: The Border States during Reconstruction*, ed. Richard O. Curry (Baltimore: Johns Hopkins Press, 1969), pp. 146-87.

[6]A neglected incident in Maryland history, this attack in Anne Arundel county was an unprovoked assault by a band of whites who attacked a religious meeting of Negroes and later plundered the camp grounds. Some Maryland papers minimized the incident and described the stones hurled by attacking whites as "water-melons." See the Baltimore *American*, September 1, 1866; Baltimore *Daily Gazette*, September 3, 1866; and testimony of William Downs, January 29, 1867, Maryland Investigation, Record Group 233, Records of the Congressional Investigating Committee, House, 40th Cong., 1st sess., National Archives.

[7]Testimony of John A. Hopper, November 14, 1867, Maryland Investigation, Records of the Congressional Investigating Committee. According to Maryland law, Negroes could not testify in any matter concerning a white. For the reaction of veterans to their treatment see "Petition of Colored Veterans to Andrew Johnson," March 17, 1866, Johnson Papers.

[8]Baltimore *Sun*, March 17, 1866; October 17, 1867. See the Civil War Diary of Samuel Harrison, November 1, 2, 1864, Harrison Papers, for evidence that children were bound to former masters.

tested this vestigial form of slavery, but the practice continued, despite passage of the Civil Rights Act in 1866, despite the opposition of Hugh Bond, a Baltimore judge who issued writs of habeas corpus to free apprentices, and despite the surveillance of the Freedmen's Bureau which investigated literally hundreds of Negro complaints.[9] Adult Negroes had reason to fear for their own freedom; two months after the Civil Rights Act passed over President Andrew Johnson's veto, five black Marylanders convicted of petty larceny became the first victims of a peonage system when they were sold by the courts to local farmers for periods ranging from six to eighteen months.[10]

To deal with these problems of Reconstruction, Marylanders turned to the governor they had elected in November 1864–Thomas Swann. Born in Virginia, Swann was that rarity in Maryland politics–a transplanted Virginian.[11] A descendant of the powerful Byrd family, he was born, and had lived, in Virginia until the 1830s. Despite a parental request that he stay in Washington where his father was a District Attorney, or near Morven Park, the family estate in northern Virginia, Swann moved to Baltimore, "to stand," as he remarked to his friend Salmon Chase, "on my own resources."[12] By the 1840s these resources were considerable, as Swann became first a lobbyist and then an investor in Maryland and Virginia railroads. His marriage to Elizabeth Gilmor Sherlock, a member of Maryland's respected Gilmor family, increased his wealth and social prominence. Soon his business success was equally legendary, and in 1848, he became president of the Baltimore and Ohio Railroad. Thereafter one of Mary-

[9]The Civil Rights Act of 1866 guaranteed persons of every race and color the right "to sue, give evidence, inherit, hold, and convey property." Negroes were also entitled "to full and equal benefit of all laws and proceedings for the security of person and property, as is enjoyed by white citizens." For evidence of the complaints of Negroes, see Charlotte Brown to the Freedmen's Bureau, July 2, 1866; E. M. Gregory to General Oliver O. Howard, October 13, 1866; William J. Anderson to the Freedmen's Bureau, July 9, 1868; Jeremiah Dorsey to the Freedmen's Bureau, August 3, 1868; William H. Gale to the Freedmen's Bureau, February 23, 1867; all in Letters Received, Record Group 105, Records of the Bureau of Refugees, Freedmen and Abandoned Lands, National Archives.

[10]George Helmick to the Freedmen's Bureau, December 1, 1866, *ibid.*; Baltimore *American*, June 27, 1866; William Van der Lip to Swann, July 21, October 12, 1866, Swann Executive Papers, Hall of Records, Annapolis, Md.

[11]One of the more fascinating figures in Maryland politics, Swann still lacks a biographer, partly because his papers are privately owned. The following biographical sketch is based on Nancy Miller, "Thomas Swann–Political Acrobat" (master's thesis, Virginia Polytechnic Institute, 1969); the Swann Executive Papers in the Hall of Records; Swann's private papers owned by Mrs. Page S. Gillet, Glyndon, Maryland; and a number of Swann letters in the Salmon P. Chase Papers in the Historical Society of Pennsylvania, Philadelphia, Pa.

[12]Swann to Chase, November 13, 1830, Chase Papers.

land's wealthiest men, Swann's income from local investments and Baltimore real estate was $43,848 in 1857, a figure which excluded his salary as mayor, his returns from the estate in Virginia, and his dividends from Baltimore and Ohio stock. In the years before the Civil War, the Swann mansion on the corner of Charles and Franklin, the present site of the Enoch Pratt Library, was a popular meeting place for Maryland socialites, some of whom joined the Swanns at the family's estate in Newport during Baltimore's long hot summers.

Gradually Swann's tremendous energy and ambition led him into politics. A Whig, then a Know-Nothing, the handsome, sideburned entrepreneur invested in the Baltimore *American* in the early 1850s.[13] By the end of the decade Swann had joined the American Protestant Association, an organization dedicated to excluding Roman Catholics from public office.[14] Such zealous nativism combined with Swann's executive talents led to his nomination as the Know-Nothing mayoral candidate. Elected in 1857, Swann was responsible for many improvements in the city's administration during his four-year term. "He was," admitted Hugh Bond, "the best mayor Baltimore ever had. She is indebted to him for most of her public works and improvements."[15] In the 1860s Swann made the switch to the Union party with no difficulty, and after a bitter struggle with Henry Winter Davis for a congressional nomination in 1863, he became the head of the Union central committee in 1864. His reward was that party's gubernatorial nomination, and although he spent the campaign summer at Saratoga and Newport, he ran 1,000 votes ahead of Abraham Lincoln in November.

Under the provisions of the Constitution of 1864, Swann did not take office until Bradford's term ended in December 1865. In his inaugural address the following month, Swann made little mention of his state's racial and social conflicts, except to praise emancipation and at the same time to warn that any insistence on equality would lead to "irrepressible conflict" between the two races. Instead he focused on the financial plight caused by the Civil War. To help pay off the war-imposed state debt the governor recommended the sale of various securities as well as a policy of financial retrenchment. Swann also touched briefly on the proper use of the resources of the Chesa-

[13] Charles C. Fulton to Swann, May 6, 1853, Swann Papers.

[14] *Booklet of the Constitution, By Laws, Rules, and Regulations of Baltimore, Lodge No. 1, American Protestant Association* (Philadelphia: J. Craig, 1856). Swann was initiated on April 27, 1857, and his nomination for the mayoralty came four months later.

[15] Bond to Salmon Chase, August 18, 1863, Chase Papers. For dissenting testimony on Swann's effectiveness as mayor, see the Baltimore *Daily Gazette*, January 20, 1866.

peake Bay, his support of the registry law, and the need for revision in property assessments.

Yet such state concerns were of secondary importance; the longest section of Swann's speech dealt with national policy. Taking sides in the important postwar controversy on the proper relation of former Confederate states to the Union, the governor made clear his contempt for Congressional Republicans who, by repudiating the idea of an "unbroken union," wished to reduce the South to "the condition of dependent territories." For Swann, the future of the South must be determined by the "Anglo-Saxon race." While some states with few Negroes might be indifferent to black suffrage, the southern and border states could not. The governor closed his lengthy address with an analysis of the Monroe Doctrine and placed his state on record as approving any plans to remove the French from Mexico.[16]

While Swann made no explicit reference to politics, his inaugural marked the opening of a new attack on the Maryland party system. In the months following the death of Lincoln and the end of the war, both parties were challenged by a new conservative organization. This proposed coalition of war Democrats and Conservative Unionists—united as much by hostility to the state's registry law, Negro suffrage, and the much despised Congressional Radicals as by devotion to Andrew Johnson, Constitution, and Union—sought to destroy the state's allegiance to its prewar parties. For a time the survival of both the Democrats and the Unionists seemed doubtful.

The principal engineer of this new party movement was Montgomery Blair, the state's perennial political manager and senatorial candidate. During the war Blair had tried unsuccessfully to restructure Maryland's parties. Now he was to try again. His contacts with the state's Democrats, his extensive network of post-office employees, and his friendship with Governor Swann gave him the leverage to attempt such a reorganization. After the assassination of Lincoln, Blair moved to cement his relationship with the new President. In fact, Blair was already well known to Johnson; it was to the Blair family estate in Silver Spring that Johnson had retreated after his unfortunate speech on his inauguration day in 1864.[17] The presence of Blair when John-

[16]"Message of Governor Swann to the General Assembly of Maryland," Swann Executive Papers.

[17]Although not a heavy drinker, Johnson had taken some liquor on inauguration day to calm his nerves. Either an abnormal sensitivity to alcohol or weakness from a typhoid attack resulted in a drunken speech which enemies never forgot nor friends forgave. See William E. Smith, *The Francis Preston Blair Family in Politics*, 2 vols. (New York: Macmillan Co., 1933), 2:328.

son took the presidential oath, only thirteen months later, indicated the close relationship between the two men.

By the summer of 1865 Blair was widely acclaimed as Johnson's closest adviser. Charles Sumner, the Massachusetts senator, complained that "the ascendancy is with the Blairs,"[18] while Democrats and Unionists proved the point by deluging Blair with requests for presidential appointments. "I am getting a little afraid of overdoing the business of advising the President," Blair confessed to his frequent correspondent, Samuel L. M. Barlow. "I have flooded him with letters from my correspondents till I am pretty sure he knows my views and those of my Democratic and Republican friends."[19]

As Blair struggled to reorganize America's postwar politics, he was playing for higher stakes than the realignment of Maryland's party system. Basing his tactics on a plan long entertained by his family, whose political activism and partisan energies had survived the war, Blair hoped to organize a new national coalition of southern moderates, border state Democrats and Unionists, and conservative Northern Republicans under the leadership of the former Democrat, President Andrew Johnson.[20] Such a national organization, as Blair himself recognized, must rest on the control of state political organizations, and it was to these local parties, particularly in his home state of Maryland, that Blair turned in 1865.

As was his practice, Blair made effective use of the patronage. Maryland officeholders, suffering the habitual fears attending a presidential change, naturally turned to Blair for protection, and many federal employees, gratefully acknowledging Blair's aid, pledged support to the former postmaster. There was, however, a great deal of confusion over the federal patronage in the state, as warring factions within the Union party tried to control such appointments.[21] Partic-

[18] *Ibid.*, p. 329.

[19] Blair to Barlow, August 15, 1865, Barlow Papers, Huntington Library, San Marino, Calif. For letters from Marylanders to Blair relating to the patronage, see Oliver L. Jenkins to Blair, May 13, 1865; Thomas Pratt to Blair, December 5, 1865, Blair Papers, Library of Congress; and William H. Purnell to Blair, May 27, 1865, Blair-Lee Papers, Princeton University Library.

[20] For an intricate study of this conservative movement, see Lawanda and John H. Cox, *Politics, Principle and Prejudice, 1865–1866; Dilemma of Reconstruction America* (New York: Free Press of Glencoe, 1963).

[21] Johnson's use of the patronage has been criticized by some historians and defended by others. Despite the counsels of Blair, the President never effectively employed the Maryland appointments—at least not as a tool in the formation of a new party. Johnson irritated many by his indecisiveness. In 1866 when the struggle to create a new party was most intense, Johnson's use of the patronage was sporadic and inconsistent. See Edwin Webster to Colonel____[?], June 9, 1865; H. H. Neilson to Johnson, October 3, 1866; William E. Cole to

ularly intense were the struggles for the key jobs in the Custom House and Post Office, and although early rumors of the Johnson appointments included several of Henry Winter Davis's political lieutenants, Davis, in an angry letter to his protégé Senator John Creswell, described Blair "as conspiring with the rebels to defeat you and the whole Union party." By July, factions within the Unionist party were so clearly defined that one Marylander associated with the Davis-Creswell faction inquired if it would be disloyal for him to apply for a position under a Blair man.[22] Only Davis's death six months later ended the long feud between Davis and Blair for control of Maryland's patronage.

Yet even before Davis's death, Blair's hand was apparent in many of these appointments. Edwin H. Webster, the corpulent Bel Air congressman, Union colonel, and a long-time Blair associate, received the important Custom House post. Johnson also appointed Washington Bonifant, another Blair lieutenant, as Maryland's Provost Marshal. For a man who held no official position within either the state or national administrations, Blair had remarkable influence on the Maryland appointments.[23]

With patronage providing one lever for an assault on Maryland's party system, Blair used the unpopular registry law, which required prospective voters to register and take an oath of past loyalty, as a wedge to detach Democrats from their party. Small turnouts in the local elections of 1865 convinced Democrats that three-quarters of Maryland's voters were disfranchised. While this figure was inflated, the state's registration law was certainly among the most restrictive in the nation. It was far more stringent, for example, than registration procedures used in the southern states during military Reconstruction.[24] For Democrats, the most galling aspect of the law was the power of registrars appointed by a Unionist governor to disqualify voters. Occasionally a refusal to register was based on nothing more than the prospective voter's prewar allegiance to the Democratic party. In one election district in Anne Arundel county, 302 citizens

---

Johnson, September 17, 1866; and Blair to Johnson, August 9, 1866, Johnson Papers, Library of Congress.

[22]Davis to Creswell, April 1865, Cecil County Historical Society, Elkton, Maryland; John Russum to Creswell, July 31, 1865, Creswell Papers, Library of Congress.

[23]"A Friend of the Party" to Creswell, July 27, 1865, Creswell Papers.

[24]In most Confederate states, only civil officers of the Confederacy or those who had sworn to uphold the Constitution and who later joined the Confederacy were barred from voting. Elizabeth S. Nathans, *Losing the Peace: Georgia Republicans and Reconstruction* (Baton Rouge: Louisiana State University Press, 1968), p. 33.

attempted to register and 90 qualified. Yet only 79 prospective voters failed for cause—that is, a legitimate reason such as membership in the Confederate army or failure to take the oath; the other 133 were given no reason for their disqualification, and the assumption was made that they were not registered because of their allegiance to the Democratic party.[25]

Blair became the leader of the impassioned attempt to modify this proscriptive law. At first he simply helped angry Democrats gain access to President Johnson. One such group presented a memorandum to Johnson describing both the iniquitous registration laws and the consequent disfranchisement in Maryland. The President's ambivalent reaction disappointed these Democrats; according to William Glenn, the President "smiled and talked of his early commitment to Democratic principles but said nothing about attacking the registration law."[26] By 1866, the year the "new party" was founded, Blair became the acknowledged head of the Anti-Registry movement. To a group of Democrats meeting to protest the law, Blair joined a vituperative attack on registration with a denunciation of the Union party and its pro-Negro policies.

Later, Blair traveled to Annapolis with an anti-registration petition measuring 800 feet and signed by 11,000 Baltimoreans. In a speech before the legislature he combined exhortations to Democrats "to bring the country together" with complaints about Unionists who proscribed whites "by putting up" blacks. Furious Unionists, who had written the law just a year before as protection from the state's Democrats, saw in his strategy an attempt to destroy their party. One Baltimore legislator complained that Blair's visit was "a piece of unparalleled presumption and unwarranted interference."[27]

[25]House of Delegates, *Documents of the State Legislature, 1866*, "Testimony in the Contested Election Cases before the Delegates of Maryland," Document D (Annapolis: Richard P. Bayley, 1865), pp. 11–27. Such partisan use of registration was a two-way street. In some areas Democrats who controlled the machinery barred Unionists from voting. For an example of such practices, see Shelby Clark to Swann, July 28, 1866, Swann Executive Papers. Also John Crisfield to Augustus Bradford, November 16, 1865, Bradford Executive Papers, and testimony of Thomas S. Hodson, Maryland Investigation, Records of the Congressional Investigating Committee.

[26]A. Leo Knott, *A Biographical Sketch with a Relation of Some Political Transactions in Maryland, 1861–1867* (Baltimore: S. B. Nelson, 1898), p. 49; Diary of William Glenn, February 7, 1866, Glenn Papers, MHS.

[27]*Journal of the Proceedings of the House of Delegates, 1866* (Annapolis: Haverstick & Longneckers, 1866), p. 194. For Blair's speech and a description of the anti-registry petitions, see the Baltimore *Sun*, February 3, 1866, and Montgomery Blair, *Proscription in Maryland: Speeches of the Hon. Montgomery Blair to the Convention and to the Legislature of Maryland, 1866* (Washington, D.C.: Joseph L. Pearson, 1868), p. 7.

Following Blair's arguments, complaints that the registry law disfranchised whites gradually broadened into the charge that the framers of the statute intended Negro suffrage. There was, in fact, no logical connection. The state constitution specifically required voters to be white males over twenty-one, and the most radical of registrars could not have made voters of Maryland's blacks. Before 1867, only one Maryland politician, Henry Winter Davis, publicly urged Negro suffrage, and he delivered his muted appeal in a speech delivered far from the state. Yet even Davis had reservations about allowing Negroes the ballot, and his support of black suffrage emanated as much from political expediency and the need to enfranchise a new constituency loyal to the Unionist party as from ideological conviction and the importance of protecting black men's rights. Negroes were, in Davis's view, an "integral part" of the southern states, and their support for the government was necessary to offset the votes of southern whites. In a letter to Edward McPherson, the clerk of the House of Representatives, Davis declared that he was not "an enthusiast for Negro suffrage. It is not a question of abstract right, but of political dynamics."[28]

Because Republicans in other states were gradually moving toward the support of Negro suffrage, Blair used this issue to unify Maryland Democrats, who had long feared Negro equality, and Conservative Unionists, who were out of step with their own national party's stand on issues relating to the freedmen. Even before the end of the war Blair had outlined his strategy in a series of letters to his Democratic friend, Barlow:

> . . . it is necessary to get rid of slavery to demonstrate that the North is not fighting for Negro equality . . . to get rid of the slavery question in order that we may get at the Negro question which lies behind it. If we can dispose of the slave question we shall have the miscegenators in a party to themselves and can beat them easily but while they can cover themselves behind the slave question they will. . . .[29]

[28]Davis to McPherson, May 27, 1865, McPherson Papers, Library of Congress. The lines quoted were crossed out, but are still clearly legible. In July 1865, Davis addressed a meeting in Chicago where he supported the principle of universal suffrage. In May 1865, Davis had written a letter to James Scovel of St. Louis in which he accepted the principle of Negro voting. This letter was printed after Davis's death in several papers. Baltimore *American*, March 19, 1866.

[29]Blair to Barlow, May 11, 1864, Barlow Papers. In his letters to Barlow, Blair frequently referred to Negro suffrage and equality as a wedge to divide the Radicals. See Blair to Barlow, January 12, 21, and November 18, 1865, Barlow Papers. For an examination of Blair's influence in New York politics, see Lawanda and John H. Cox, *Politics, Principle and Prejudice*.

After the war Blair moved to implement this strategy by branding Unionists the champions of black suffrage. In an 1866 speech in Baltimore, he insisted:

> The great desire of the radicals is to keep possession of power until they can introduce the black element by which to override the whites in the South, and keep control of the country. . . . Our Governor [Swann] is striving to fasten upon Maryland the proscription of white men inaugurated here by Henry Winter Davis in order to introduce black suffrage. Negro suffrage is the absorbing political question of the future.[30]

The charge that the Maryland Unionist party planned to enfranchise the state's 180,000 blacks led to vociferous Unionist denials. One county convention assured voters that "we are not in favor of extending the elective franchise to any class of persons now excluded from the same by the Constitution of Maryland and the registry law." The Unionist state convention of 1866 agreed that Negro suffrage was not an issue, but was rather "a great bugaboo raised by the enemies of the Union party for the purpose of dividing and distracting it." Before the November elections in 1866, Marylanders reached complete unanimity on the issue of Negro suffrage. Even candidates for sheriff who usually managed their campaigns without taking positions on any issue other than personal competency and party loyalty found it necessary to announce their repugnance to black voting. Nowhere in the state could a candidate, faction, or convention be found publicly supporting universal suffrage.[31]

Gradually the discussion of Negro suffrage degenerated into race-baiting. Again Blair played a part. In an April 1866 speech, he announced that Congress was using "the African race" to control the government. "The hired beagle of the Civil Rights Bill will hunt the white man down at his home or drive him from it."[32] The editors of the Frederick *Republican Citizen* were even less restrained:

> Rampant fanatical abolitionism gloated with its success, drunk with blood-raving and with its insane heresies is pressing furiously onward to its legitimate consequence—the goal of full social equality for the Negro with all the degrading horrors of amalgamation. Be not deceived: our very firesides are threatened and unless men act and act with vigor, even race itself as well as home will be prostituted to the orgies of this great Moloch of America.[33]

[30] Baltimore *Sun*, January 25, 1866.

[31] Baltimore *Sun*, August 16, 1866; *Mountain Valley Register* (Middletown), June 15, 1866; Baltimore *American*, June 5, 1866; J. M. Wheeler to John Ridgley, n.d., Swann Executive Papers, Hall of Records.

[32] Baltimore *Daily Gazette*, April 16, 1866.

[33] Frederick *Republican Citizen*, June 22, 1866.

With similar animus but more brevity, Democratic and Conservative Unionist transparencies—the political placards of the nineteenth century—carried slogans such as "This Is a White Man's Government," "No Negro Equality," and "No White Niggers Here."[34]

Struggles in Congress during the winter of 1865-66 only reinforced Blair's contention that Republicans and Unionists intended racial equality. When Andrew Johnson vetoed the Freedmen's Bureau Bill in February 1866, most white Marylanders supported his position. Many viewed the measure as unconstitutional as well as unnecessary.[35] Members of the Blair coalition added a new racial twist to these objections; the bill favored blacks at the expense of whites. Blair's allies organized meetings throughout the state to announce their objection to the bill and their support of Johnson. John Frazier, Speaker of the House of Delegates, found a receptive audience in Baltimore for such appeals:

> When they talk to me of the Freedmen's Bureau, . . . when they talk about taking care and providing for the defenseless negro, if they would say one or two words about the white—the orphans and the soldiers who fought the battles of his country [great applause], if they would attempt to make some provisions for the education of the orphan children of those gallant soldiers [renewed applause], if they would attempt to find homes and provide lands for the crippled soldiers who fought their battles [general applause], then my fellow citizens we might believe in their sincerity. But I stand here tonight to make a short appeal for the poor white man. What has the white man gained by the war? [Cries of Nothing] What has the negro gained by the war? [cries of Everything].[36]

Unionists who supported the Freedmen's Bureau or Civil Rights Bills were called extremists and "nigger lovers." As the break between Johnson and the Congressional Republicans widened amid a welter of presidential vetoes and congressional recriminations, Blair continually stressed the allegiance of Maryland Unionists to "the wily politicians who know no interest but their own" and the consequent need for a new party based on Jacksonian principles of Conservatism and Unionism.[37]

[34]Baltimore *American*, June 22, September 28, 1866.

[35]*Der Deutsche Correspondent* (Baltimore), April 13, 1866. A number of Marylanders complimented Johnson on the veto. T. F. Bowie to Johnson, March 2, 1866; B. F. Benson to Johnson, February 28, 1866, Johnson Papers. One enthusiastic Marylander sent the President a traditional Maryland gift of three pairs of redhead ducks to express his appreciation of the veto. E. T. Sweeting to Johnson, February 24, 1866, Johnson Papers.

[36]Baltimore *American*, February 27, 1866.

[37]Baltimore *Sun*, January 25, 1866.

Blair's plans for such a new party led him to condemn national leaders who would not accept his strategy for a Conservative party dominated by former Democrats. In letters to Samuel Barlow in December 1865, the former Postmaster outlined a plan to reform parties on "the platform from which we will see an overwhelming triumph next fall";[38] now as the opportunity for such a reorganization presented itself, Blair found Republicans like his ancient enemy William H. Seward committed to a Conservative party dominated by former Whigs. To President Johnson, Blair complained that Seward was trying to keep the "so-called Union party together," and such a stance would prevent "the restoration of the Union and might even involve us in another civil war." Appealing to President Johnson's self-interest, Blair later wrote: "It is . . . indispensable to your success and to the preservation of the government that the so-called Union party be broken up. Your policy . . . your actions, your personal success are therefore directly antagonistic to the policy of Mr. Seward."[39]

Blair's "conservative offensive"[40] would, of course, isolate extremists, whether southern revolutionaries or northern fanatics, and the successful formation of a National Union organization would make it extremely difficult for any opposition party to survive. Indeed an alliance of Democrats and Conservatives would dominate the political future and would create a one-party system for decades. Such a return to an era without party conflict had long appealed to Maryland's Know-Nothing, Constitutional Unionist, and Unionist leaders, who had never agreed on the benefits of a two-party system and who thus found pleas "to come out of old parties" familiar and alluring slogans.

Occasionally, however, the intricacies of Blair's national maneuvers were overlooked by his followers in Maryland, who simply focused on racial matters. Despite the differences in their positions on the rights of freedmen, Southerners, and Confederate states, Secretary of War Edwin M. Stanton, Senators Charles Sumner of Massachusetts and Benjamin F. Wade of Ohio, and Pennsylvania's Representative Thaddeus Stevens were all guilty, according to Blair's Maryland supporters, of elevating the Negro above the white man. "No one," an-

[38]Blair to Barlow, December 9, 1865, Barlow Papers. For letters outlining the Blair strategy and Blair's efforts to gain Democratic support for Johnson, see Blair to Barlow, January 21, February 9, April 7, 18, June 14, 1865, Barlow Papers.

[39]Blair to Johnson, April 11, 1866, Johnson Papers; Blair to Johnson, April 9, 1866 [copy], Blair Papers.

[40]Lawanda and John H. Cox, *Politics, Principle and Prejudice*, p. 31.

nounced a Blair Unionist in Baltimore county, "who reads the debate and proceedings in Congress can doubt that the real object of that party is to establish universal Negro suffrage. It is folly to say that this question is not at issue in this state. This is a great national party; their measures are intended to embrace the whole country. . . ."[41]

Certainly the preoccupation of Maryland's Conservative Unionists with national concerns led to the neglect of important state issues. There was, for example, considerable disagreement on whether to accept Negro testimony in Maryland's courts; yet little partisan comment ensued on this issue. Blair and his colleagues never discussed this point, although they continually expressed their repugnance to Negro suffrage, the Freedmen's Bureau, and the Civil Rights Bill. On those issues where virtual unanimity existed, discussion was extensive, passionate, and redundant; on local concerns where disagreement existed between parties, such debate was muted, infrequent, and unobtrusive.

As Swann's inaugural suggested, the Blair party planned to introduce another unifying issue into Maryland politics—foreign policy. Shortly after Lincoln's death, Blair bitterly denounced Secretary of State Seward's failure to oust the French from Mexico. In a speech in Hagerstown on July 12, 1865, Blair defended the Monroe Doctrine as the inviolable foundation of American foreign policy. As he explained to Barlow in a letter written two days after the speech, the Monroe Doctrine was "a good issue to start to right the old Democracy." Privately, Blair also encouraged an invasion of Mexico for two reasons: first, to rid the Hemisphere of the French; second, "to secure pacification among ourselves." Black soldiers would carry out this venture, and after the collapse of Maximilian's regime, these same Negroes, joined by their families, would settle in Mexico, thus relieving "the pressure on the Southern people."[42]

As a result of Blair's policy, even the Maryland legislature became entangled in foreign affairs. A series of resolutions complimenting Secretary of State Seward's "firmness and judgment without compromise to the national honor"[43] were tabled when some delegates refused to commend one of Blair's enemies. Throughout the state, Conservatives who took their cues from Blair found the Monroe Doctrine a convenient point of agreement between Democrats and themselves in the campaign of 1866.

[41]Baltimore *Sun*, June 2, 1866.

[42]Blair to Barlow, July 16, 1865, Barlow Papers.

[43]*Proceedings of the House of Delegates, 1866*, p. 407.

This focus on illusory national, and even international, issues was nothing new in the state's history. In 1860 public discussion had focused on the threat of abolitionism; yet neither the abolitionists of 1860 nor the supporters of black suffrage in 1866 ever numbered a handful. As the Baltimore *American* pointed out, "Men who favor Negro suffrage hold exactly the same relation to the Union party that old abolitionists did to Republicans."[44] In both cases, however, discussion centered on these issues, in part because the cultivation of racial prejudice served as political capital in a border state with a significant black population. Before and after the war the attempt to remake the state's political parties into a new conservative coalition dictated the use of issues which had not arisen locally. Political agreement on such concerns as Negro suffrage and foreign policy served as a possible bridge which both Unionists and Democrats could travel on their way to a new Conservative coalition. By constantly reiterating a position with which all voters agreed, Blair hoped to detach Marylanders from their old party habits.

Blair's new party movement demanded more than unifying issues. Holding no public office after the fall of 1864, the former postmaster required the active support of Maryland's elected officials. The most important, of course, was Governor Thomas Swann. Swann's friendship with Blair was of long duration; during the war both had been important members of the Union party. As head of the Union state central committee Swann had frequently adopted positions encouraged by Blair. By 1865, Henry Winter Davis, wary of attempts to ostracize radicals from the party, had assigned Swann to the Blair "wing" of the party.[45]

Swann's election to the governorship made him a crucial figure in Blair's plans, for he now controlled the important patronage appointments so necessary for the formation of a party. The correct use of such powers would go far toward the creation of a new political coalition. Furthermore, in the spring of 1866 Swann would appoint officials to register Maryland's qualified voters. If Swann chose "liberal" registrars—men who would moderate the harsh provisions of the 1865 Registry Act—Democrats could expect to contest the 1866 state elections. If Swann continued in office the Bradford registrars, the Unionist party would retain its hegemony.

[44] Baltimore *American*, June 5, 1866. Another newspaper could find only ten native Marylanders in favor of Negro suffrage. *Maryland Journal* (Towson), May 19, 1866.

[45] Blair to Swann, October 17, 1863, Swann Papers; James W. Clayton to John Creswell, October 7, 1864, Creswell Papers; Davis to Creswell, April 1865, Cecil County Historical Society.

By May 10, 1866, Swann had made his choice. In a letter to a Union party committee, he denounced the Unconditional Unionists and supported Andrew Johnson. A few weeks later Swann announced that he would appoint "liberal" registrars, and his appointment books reveal a change in policy as Democrats and Conservatives replaced the Bradford registrars, some of whom Swann and his secretary now classified as "radical."[46] Not long after Swann's appointments, Maryland newspapers complained that the governor had made a deal with the Democrats: the price for liberal registrars was Democratic support for Swann as senator.[47]

Swann's arrangement with the Maryland Democracy reflected his lack of commitment to the Conservative party. By acting with the Democrats, Swann not only refused to serve Blair's plans for a new coalition, but he also rejected the possibility of a Unionist party strengthened by black voters or one dominated, as Seward urged, by former Whigs. Having made his choice, the pragmatic and ambitious Swann paid far more attention to Democrats than to Blair's Conservatives. For example, the patronage recommendations of two Democratic leaders, William Maulsby and Oden Bowie, were often approved, while the pleas for favors to his own party went unheeded.[48] Clearly, Swann, one of the few "party acrobats" in Maryland politics,[49] recognized the strength of the state's Democratic party, and accordingly saw that his own future rested with the old Democracy, and not Blair's new Conservative-Democratic coalition.

Grateful Democrats who had earlier condemned the governor now congratulated him. One wrote that "the Governor supports the national and liberal policy of the President. . . . sensible and patriotic voters of the state will be with Governor Swann."[50] By the summer of

[46]Baltimore *Sun*, May 14, 1866; Annapolis *Gazette*, May 17, 31, 1866; Swann Appointment Books, Hall of Records, Annapolis, Md.; J. H. Franklin to George Gale, July 7, 1866, Gale Papers, MHS.

[47]Swann vigorously denied the charge and accused the Unionists of raising a false issue. He announced his "cooperation with only Conservative men," not Democrats. Baltimore *American*, May 26, September 25, 1866. Ferdinand Latrobe, Swann's son-in-law, apparently owned letters between Swann and election judges which described the arrangement whereby Swann would appoint sympathetic registrars in return for support of the governor as a senatorial candidate. William S. Myers, *The Self-Reconstruction of Maryland*, Johns Hopkins University Studies in Historical and Political Science, ser. 27 (Baltimore: Johns Hopkins Press, 1909), p. 56.

[48]Maulsby to Swann, September 17, 1866; Bowie to Swann, June 26, 1866; G. B. Westcott *et al.*, to Swann, January 9, 1866, Swann Executive Papers. See also the Swann Appointment Books, 1866.

[49]The phrase is from Miller, "Thomas Swann."

[50]*Harford Union* (Bel Air), May 17, 1866.

1866 Swann had achieved the honored status among Democrats that Andrew Johnson had attained. "We endorse Governor Swann for the patriotic stand he has taken for Constitution and Union," exulted one Democrat.[51] While Radical Unionists observed that Blair had forced Swann into the Democratic party and Conservative Unionists refused to admit his defection, Thomas Swann, an adept politician, had hedged his bets.

☆ ☆ ☆

IN THE SPRING OF 1866, at Blair's urging, a call for a national convention was issued from Washington. The purpose of the convention was to organize a new political party.[52] Editorials in Maryland heralded "the coming of a grand conservative national army."[53] Throughout the state, district and primary meetings responded by nominating delegates to a national convention to be held in Philadelphia in August.

Though welcomed by many Marylanders, the call for the Philadelphia Convention did not produce the political fusion that Blair desired. While the Democratic state central committee enthusiastically supported the idea of a Conservative movement, the party maintained its autonomy by refusing to meet with Blair's Conservatives in joint conventions. Eventually, Democrats elected their own delegates—all prominent party members of the past—to participate in the Philadelphia meetings, and disappointed Conservatives chose a separate delegation.

Despite such local failure, Blair had reason to be optimistic about the national progress of the new coalition. In August, delegates from thirty states crowded into Philadelphia. Even the inconveniences of a leaky convention hall did not dampen this exuberant reunion of southern and northern conservatives. While the band played "Rally 'Round the Flag" and "Dixie," a symbolic reunification occurred: the tiny General Darius Couch of Massachusetts walked down the aisle arm-in-arm with the physically more prepossessing Governor James Orr of South Carolina. Later the convention approved a series of

[51] W. W. Cunningham to Swann, June 8, 1866, Swann Executive Papers.

[52] Certainly Blair was the moving spirit behind this attempt to form a new political party, although the first invitation to join a National Union convention came from Senator James R. Doolittle of Wisconsin. Doolittle to Gideon Welles, July 10, 1866, Welles Papers, Library of Congress; Smith, *Blair Family*, 2:362.

[53] Annapolis *Gazette*, March 1, 1866.

resolutions supporting Andrew Johnson, the return of the southern states to Congress, the constitutional right of each state to determine its voting qualifications, the inviolability of the federal debt, the invalidity of rebel debts, and federal aid for soldiers and their families.[54]

Marylanders played a prominent part in these convention proceedings. Blair helped to write the resolutions and organize convention committees, while Reverdy Johnson, the state's senior senator, demanded better treatment for the South. It was the same Senator Johnson with his appropriate surname who received the honor of presenting the resolutions to the President in a White House ceremony. The appointment of ex-Governor Thomas Pratt and Governor Thomas Swann to a national committee demonstrated the desire of convention leaders to form a permanent organization.

Yet the party had little impact on Maryland politics. Despite public support from important Maryland leaders and despite favorable newspaper coverage, the new coalition floundered on an insurmountable obstacle—the firm attachment most Marylanders felt for their prewar parties. The powerful Democratic party had no reason to abandon its organization to support such a feeble new movement, although in 1866 it was willing to test conservative waters at the National Union Convention. Furthermore, Democrats simply could not join a former opponent, Montgomery Blair; party loyalties prevented such a liaison. Eventually, as a Unionist leader noted, "the old Democratic leaven was superior to the new element of conservatism."[55]

Certainly Maryland's political system with its powerful and established county organizations diminished the chances for a new party. In their haste, Blair and the leaders of the National Union party neglected the lowest, but most important, denominator of state politics—the ward and district meetings, county conventions, and county executive committees. In Carroll county, for instance, leaders of the "new party" waited for direction from Blair and Swann. Pleas for aid went unanswered, and eventually the Democratic county machine swallowed the fledgling National Union organization.[56]

[54]Baltimore *Daily Gazette*, August 13-18, 1866; *Proceedings of the National Union Convention Held at Philadelphia*, August 1866, Pamphlet Collection, MHS.

[55]Baltimore *American*, September 19, 1866. A variety of explanations have been given for this failure of the Conservative party. William Smith cites the lack of newspaper support and the President's failure to exploit economic grievances as well as his Fenian policy. Eric McKitrick stresses the ambiguity of the party's platforms and the American political tradition of a two-party system. See Smith, *Blair Family in Politics*, 2:370-71; and McKitrick, *Andrew Johnson and Reconstruction* (Chicago: University of Chicago Press, 1960), pp. 364-420.

[56]C. W. Renaters [?] to H. McCauley, July 2, 1866, Vertical File, MHS.

Occasionally, Democrats and Conservatives did unite in an uneasy alliance. The *St. Mary's Gazette*, voice of the Democratic party in southern Maryland, asked "who shall carry the political flag" and answered:

> The Democratic party could merge into the Johnson (conservative) party or the Johnson party could take service with the Democratic party. If both these were objectionable, let the two parties come to an understanding by caucus or convention or elsewhere. In localities where Democrats have an undisputed or clearly ascertained majority, the Johnson men shall support the Democratic ticket and in communities where Johnson men are relatively stronger than Democrats, Democrats shall support the Johnson ticket.

Later the paper came to feel that the Democrats were stronger, and hence Conservatives should give up their own organization to join the established party.[57] In most cases, it was indeed "the Johnson party" which took service with the Democrat organization. In only a few election districts did Conservatives run with Democratic support. Leaders in Allegany county, for example, presented a ticket for state and local offices, but Democrats vigorously complained that in fact the nominees were all Unionists. In Baltimore, the reverse was true, and Unionists resented "the bad faith of the Democrats" who, despite agreements to split the nominations, had in fact chosen an entire slate of their own party members.[58]

In southern Maryland and the Eastern Shore there was very little fusion of Democrats and Unionists. Democratic conventions, although they welcomed voting support, had almost nothing to do with Conservatives. Summer talk of a new party disappeared in the fall when Democrats began the serious job of organizing a political campaign. Benjamin G. Harris, the Democratic congressman from St. Mary's county, wrote his friends to arrange their own convention: "I will presume there will be no motives operating on the minds of its members other than those which will promote Democratic [interests] and [there must be] no sacrifice made of Democratic men because of their determined adherence to these principles. Such conduct would be fatal to any party organization."[59] Local leaders agreed and insisted

[57] *St. Mary's Gazette* (Leonardtown), May 3, 10, 24, 1866; Baltimore *American*, May 26, 1866.

[58] Baltimore *Daily Gazette*, September 25, 1866; Chestertown *Transcript*, June 9, 1866; Baltimore *American*, September 25, 1866. For a description of similar friction between Unionists and Democrats in Baltimore county, see the *Maryland Journal* (Towson), September 1, 1866.

[59] Harris to William Billingslea, quoted in Baltimore *Daily Gazette*, September 15, 1866; *St. Mary's Gazette* (Leonardtown), August 23, 1866.

that Democrats, not Conservatives, make the nominations. Disgruntled Conservatives complained that the nominations were a "grab game" on the part of the Democracy, but most Democrats agreed with the *St. Mary's Gazette* that the party "with an historic name, thoroughly drilled and already in the field should carry the flag."[60]

Blair soon learned the strength of party bonds when the Democrats of the Fifth District refused to nominate him for Congress and chose instead a lifetime member of their party. During the convention the Democrats made their position perfectly clear. "Blair can't command the votes of Prince Georges, Charles, St. Mary's, and Calvert," insisted one delegate.[61] Piqued, Blair's friends met to nominate him as a Conservative, but as the former postmaster general explained in a letter to his wife: "I have declined the nomination to Congress. The Democrats nominated another man and that rendered the election doubtful."[62]

This failure to nominate the national leader of the National Union party symbolized the difficulties of partisan mixtures in Maryland. The new coalition required the allegiance of Democrats and Conservative Unionists to achieve a realignment; local leaders who refused to nominate candidates from another party effectively scotched any hopes for fusion. Blair's plan thus failed because it would have required Democrats to give up their own organization to share offices with Unionists whom they had been fighting for years, and to shuck off the pro-southern element of the party in return for a doubtful increment of strength from Conservative Unionists. Such conditions were unacceptable to Marylanders who ridiculed the idea that

> a handful of officeholders who have abandoned principle merely to retain or to obtain places of profit should be allowed to swallow up the great National Democratic party. . . . The children of a Protestant or Roman Catholic usually attach themselves to the churches of their parents and think all other denominations on the road to perdition. So it is with the Democrats. They live and die in the faith of their fathers and are not easily drawn off to any new organization.[63]

Disgusted, Blair soon recognized his failure. Forgetting Maryland, he campaigned extensively in Pennsylvania for Conservative candidates.

[60] *St. Mary's Gazette* (Leonardtown), May 3, 1866; Baltimore *American*, October 25, 1866.

[61] Baltimore *American*, September 27, 1866.

[62] Montgomery Blair to Mary Elizabeth Blair, October 9, 1866, Blair Papers.

[63] Baltimore *American*, October 15, 1866.

Gradually the plan for a new party deteriorated in Maryland, as organizations of the past—Unionist and Democrat—dominated the election. In Baltimore, where the Democrats organized mass meetings, a Unionist newspaper noted "the whale (Democratic) has swallowed Jonah (Blair)."[64] In other areas of the country, National Union candidates also failed to win election to Congress, and Republicans continued to control the new House elected in 1866.

☆ ☆ ☆

THE STRONG DEMOCRATIC ORGANIZATION which successfully resisted the blandishments of Blair and his party did not disagree with the principles of the Conservative Unionists. Recognizing this ideological similarity, a Democratic newspaper in southern Maryland compared the relationship between Democrats and Conservative Unionists to that of "the allies in their late war against Austria. We are all anti-radical, but we still maintain our distinctive faith and we hold our primary allegiance to be due to the Democratic party alone."[65] Both organizations opposed Negro suffrage, the registry law, and congressional Reconstruction. Both supported Governor Swann, President Johnson, and the immediate restoration of the South "to the councils of the Union." While the sympathy of Maryland Democrats with the South was obvious, the party took care not to make its support too generous. Hence, Confederate heroes played little part in Maryland's Reconstruction politics. When Governor Swann appointed former Confederates officers in the Maryland militia, a number of newspapers promptly and vociferously complained.[66]

Democrats easily matched the undercurrent of racism apparent in Conservative appeals. One Democratic parade included a transparency emblazoned with the words: "We are in favor of Negro suffrage as they suffered in New Orleans."[67] Before the war, Democrats had culti-

[64]Baltimore *American*, October 4, 1866. Earlier the New York *World* had used the same phrase to describe the relationship between Democrats and Conservatives. "The Democratic party will not merge its existence in the proposed new organization. It is beyond the realm of possibility that Jonah should swallow the whale." New York *World*, June 27, 1866. The relationship between the two organizations seems to encourage metaphors. According to McKitrick, "The Democratic tail was getting bigger and fatter than the Unionist dog." McKitrick, *Andrew Johnson*, p. 407.

[65]*St. Mary's Gazette* (Leonardtown), August 23, 1866.

[66]Baltimore *American*, July 11, 13, 1867; Civil War Diary of William Glenn, May 20, 1866, Glenn Papers.

[67]The reference was to the attack in New Orleans by whites on a procession of Negroes who supported Negro suffrage. Thirty-seven blacks and three whites were killed. Baltimore *American*, September 28, 1866.

vated the racial prejudice of Marylanders who feared the Negro as a free man; now after the war, the party unofficially encouraged the formation of white men's clubs. Philip C. Friese, an influential Baltimore Democrat, wrote President Johnson condemning "attempts to enforce the forbidden union of white and dark skinned races in our midst" and lamenting "treason to the [white] race."[68]

Such appeals were similar in tone and substance to those of earlier Democratic propaganda. In the 1850s, Democrats had accused the Republicans of threatening the Union with their "extremist" positions against slavery; during the war, Democrats had condemned Republican violations of the Constitution and Union; now after the war, Democratic demonology found its villain in the Republican refusal to seat southern congressional delegations. In an appeal to Baltimore's ethnic vote, Democrats compared the Republican treatment of the South to English oppression of the Irish.[69]

Even in a year when Marylanders did not elect national officials, state issues were neglected in the 1866 campaign. The Democrats had a great deal to say about the iniquity of the registration law, but they remained mute on other local problems. Such questions as the state's relationship to its corporations, the improvement of Baltimore's harbor, and even the perennial question of oystering were seldom discussed during the campaign.

If the Democrats sounded the same as they had in the past, they also looked much the same. Of 106 postwar party leaders, 67 had served the Democrats in the 1850s. The Baltimore *American*, a stanchly Unionist paper, identified the postwar party as "the resurrection of the dead . . . a number of old political hunkers who used to flourish under the dynasties of former years. . . . as well as a number of Buchanan office-holders, who are trying to rally the scattered forces of that rebellious phalanx."[70] Among these "resurrected Democrats" were the leaders of Maryland's prewar Democracy: ex-Governor Philip F. Thomas, a Buchanan cabinet officer; John T. Mason, Buchanan's Collector of the Port; Oden Bowie, head of the state central committee and a former Buchanan appointee; William T. Hamilton, a former state committeeman and future U.S. senator; and Patrick Hamill, an

[68] Friese to Johnson, August 7, 1865, Johnson Papers. For evidence of "white men's clubs," see G. L. Knorr *et al.*, to Swann, May 1, 1866; William Lowdermilk to Swann, April 14, 1866, Swann Executive Papers, and *Civilian and Telegraph* (Cumberland), April 12, 1866.

[69] Baltimore *Daily Gazette*, March 1, 1866; Baltimore *Daily Commercial*, July 25, 1866.

[70] Baltimore *American*, January 25, 1866. See Appendix Tables D-15, D-16, and D-17 for a profile of these Democrats.

influential delegate from western Maryland. Only three Know-Nothings and Constitutional Unionist leaders emerged as Democratic leaders after the war, although some Unionists whose prewar allegiance is unknown did become Democrats. As in the 1850s, many Democratic leaders were well-off farmers, and important landed families such as the Bowies, Thomases, Blackistones, and Hamiltons continued to provide sons for the Democratic hierarchy.

It was hardly surprising that Democratic party managers organized their party in much the same way as they had before the war. The identical pattern of ward and local meetings culminated in nominating conventions; the weak central committee chosen by the head of the party's state convention still served as a link between county organizations. Positions on the county executive committees where important party decisions were made continued to carry as much power as those on the state committee.

☆ ☆ ☆

OF ALL MARYLAND'S PARTIES, the Unionists were most changed by the political currents of Reconstruction. Yet even this party, despite the defection of some of its leaders and constituency, displayed remarkable continuity. Certainly the factions within Unionism were not entirely the result of differences over the immediate issues of Reconstruction or Blair's attempt to create a new party. Rather, these divisions reflected the past weakness and instability of the Know-Nothing organization of the 1850s.

In the summer of 1866 both wings of the Union party organized the usual hierarchy of local meetings and county conventions. One faction led by Blair, Swann, and William H. Purnell, the former Postmaster of Baltimore, supported the Philadelphia Convention, Andrew Johnson, and repeal of the registration law. The other led by Senator Creswell and two congressmen, John L. Thomas of Baltimore and Francis Thomas of Allegany,[71] defended congressional Reconstruction and the registry law. The so-called Conservative Unionists soon dropped their second name and became known in Maryland politics as

[71]The surname Thomas complicates the story of Maryland's Reconstruction politics. Francis Thomas, the ex-governor from western Maryland, was no relation to John L. Thomas, elected in 1865 to fill the congressional seat vacated by Edwin Webster. A third Thomas, Philip Francis, a former Democratic governor and friend of President James Buchanan from Talbot county, was elected to the Senate by the Maryland legislature in 1867, but the Senate refused to seat him.

Conservatives, while the other wing of the party was designated Unconditional Unionists. Opponents often used more expressive epithets; thus Conservatives became rebels, Blairites, traitors, and Copperheads, while Unconditionals were denounced as extremists, fanatics, and Radicals.

By the summer of 1866 the Unconditional Unionists held a precarious position in state politics. Blair's strategy of cooperation with former Democrats offended many Unionists whose politics had been defined by antagonism to the Democrats. Without the protection of Unionist registrars, the return of Maryland's Democrats would inevitably lead to defeat in 1866. The bleak political future would then include, according to one pessimist, a repeal of the registration law and even a rewriting of the state's two-year-old Constitution. "With a Democratic Governor, a Democratic legislature and patronage of the general government in the hands of Democratic politicians," predicted the Baltimore *American*, "ex-slave owners will carry almost any measure they choose to demand."[72]

To prevent such a catastrophe, Unconditional Unionists appealed to Maryland voters to support the registry law and allow only loyal men in the government of Maryland. Waving "the bloody shirt" of war remembrances, Unionists insisted that their Democratic opponents still wore the yellow coat of treason. A Baltimore leader questioned why "the party should throw away victory. Men who with Gilmor and Johnson sought to raze our city now want power back."[73] As the campaign progressed, appeals to wartime loyalties became more explicit: "Do your armless sleeves and limping steps excite no sympathy?" The military metaphors popular after the war led to assertions that "every ballot is a dead shot. Let every shot that is fired into the ballot-box . . . prove a death wound to the disorganizers."[74] Unionists emphasized their point by nominating members who had been maimed in the war, and many of the party's candidates for Baltimore's local offices had lost an arm or leg while serving in the Union army.[75]

Unionists also protested that the issue of Negro suffrage was "a delusion and an attempt by Democrats and silly Unionists afflicted

[72]Baltimore *American*, August 6, 1866.

[73]The reference is to two prominent Maryland Confederates, the dashing cavalryman Colonel Harry Gilmor and the Confederate General Bradley T. Johnson. Baltimore *American*, May 9, 1866.

[74]*Ibid.*, August 10, 1866; *National American* (Bel Air), November 3, 1866.

[75]Baltimore *American*, October 5, 8, 19, 1866.

with Negrophobia to deceive Union men. They run around with their miserable cry nigger, nigger."[76] Consistently denying its support of Negro suffrage, the party nonetheless found the Fourteenth Amendment a political embarrassment. Passed by Congress in June 1866, this amendment, among other provisions, made Negroes citizens, thereby eliminating the three-fifths ratio for slaves as a basis for representation, and provided for reduction of representation if a state denied suffrage to any of its citizens. Democrats, sensing a ripe issue, charged that such requirements would force Maryland to enfranchise her Negroes or lose a congressman. Tepidly Unionists defended the amendment. According to Congressman John Thomas, the section on suffrage neither enfranchised Negroes nor diminished the state's representation in Congress; rather the Fourteenth Amendment, now that Negroes counted as "political persons," prevented rebels "from voting the Negroes." In congressional debate, Thomas denied that support of the amendment meant support of Negro suffrage which he opposed "at this time, in any manner, and any and everywhere."[77] Following Thomas's logic, most Maryland Unionists plaintively objected that without the Fourteenth Amendment, southern Maryland and the Eastern Shore, prewar Democratic strongholds with many Negroes, would increase their political power.

Confronted with the return of white Democratic Southerners to the polls, Republicans in other states sought the enfranchisement of Negroes, as often for reasons of political expediency as belief in black equality.[78] Certainly Maryland leaders were aware of the possible political benefits of enfranchising Negroes, who made up over 20 percent of the Maryland population and whose concentration in certain counties assured control of these communities. Despite encourage-

[76] *Ibid.*, May 15, 1866.

[77] *Ibid.*, June 15, 1866. *Congressional Globe*, 39th Cong., 1st sess., 1866, 36, pt. 5, Appendix, p. 60.

[78] Republican reasons for support of black suffrage have been interpreted quite differently. William Gillette concludes that the primary object of the Fifteenth Amendment, passed in 1870, was "first to enfranchise the Northern Negro, and second to protect the Southern Negro against disfranchisement," while the Coxes insist that race prejudice was so strong that Republican leaders could have acted only from ideological motives. See William Gillette, *The Right to Vote: Politics and the Passage of the Fifteenth Amendment* (Baltimore: Johns Hopkins Press, 1965), p. 77, and Lawanda and John H. Cox, "Negro Suffrage and Republican Politics: The Problem of Motivation in Reconstruction Historiography," *Journal of Southern History* 33 (August 1967):303-30. For support of Gillette's position, see Felice Bonadio, *North of Reconstruction: Ohio Politics, 1865-1870* (New York: New York University Press, 1970).

ment from out-of-state Republicans to support Negro suffrage and thereby offset the votes of returning Democrats, Unionists hesitated.[79] Many party members apparently believed that there were not enough Negroes to make such a strategy worthwhile, while others, long-time victims of border-state Negrophobia, saw black voting as a weapon to destroy the Unionist allegiance of many whites who detested any step toward Negro equality. By 1866, few had committed themselves to follow what Henry Winter Davis had earlier called "the strength of niggerdom." "So be on the right side," encouraged Davis, "and go with its sturdy friends."[80] Yet the official party did not heed Davis's advice in 1866; instead it rejected any form of Negro voting. In September, at the meeting of the Southern Loyalist Convention, the "radical" counterpart of the National Union Convention, Marylanders walked out of the convention when Southerners introduced a resolution in favor of Negro suffrage.

To demonstrate their orthodoxy, Unionists accused the Democrats in the South as well as in the border states of attempts "to perpetuate and strengthen their dynasty by means of Negro votes."[81] Clearly the proportion of Negroes in the state as well as Maryland's intense Negrophobia made the political effectiveness of black suffrage questionable in the uncertain days of 1866.

Nor did Maryland Unionists use economic issues with the vigor of party members in other states. While talk of economic progress and a new era was constantly on Unionist lips, this rhetoric never gave way to specifics. In other states Unionist Republicans fought for railroad charters, encouraged the retirement of Greenbacks, and argued for tariff increases, but in Maryland, platforms remained curiously bereft of such issues and politicians remarkably uninterested in financial concerns.[82] Such behavior was reflected in the 1866 legislature, where economic issues continued to produce substantial agreement between Democrats and Unionists.[83]

[79] James Whitall to Hugh Bond, November 1866, Bond-McCulloch Papers, MHS.

[80] Davis to Creswell, October 1865, Creswell Papers.

[81] Cumberland *Union*, July 21, 1866.

[82] Curry, *Radicalism, Racism and Party Realignment.* See also Nathans, *Losing the Peace.* For a different position, see Howard K. Beale, "The Tariff and Reconstruction," *American Historical Review* 35 (January 1930):276-94. Beale argues that Republicans in the midwest realized that economic issues would divide their party, and hence leaders avoided taking positions on the tariff and currency.

[83] An analysis of fifteen economic issues, which includes ten votes on incorporations, three votes on issues involved in changing the state's code on corporations, and two votes on

While there were important disagreements between the postwar parties, particularly on the registry law and on Andrew Johnson's Reconstruction policies, Unionists spent most of their time attacking not Democrats but defectors from Unionism. Blair and Swann were continually criticized as political manipulators who had joined the "rebels." A Baltimore county meeting condemned both of them as "changing politicians, professional office-seekers ready to yield principles and conditions to the highest bidder and betray the people's trust."[84] In a state which revered political faithfulness, party inconstancy—not ideological disloyalty—represented the greatest sin, and Unionist heretics—not Democratic disbelievers—received the greatest opprobrium.

☆ ☆ ☆

THE NOVEMBER ELECTIONS in 1866 clearly revealed the durability of Maryland's parties, as Democrats gained control of the legislature. Their ranks replenished by returning soldiers, new voters, and former Unionists, Democrats won 61 percent of the state vote for comptroller as well as sixty seats in the eighty-man Assembly. The sectional character of Maryland politics kept Democrats from a clean sweep, as Unionists won only in the northern and western counties of the state. The same regional coalition of southern Maryland, the Eastern Shore, and Baltimore which had given Democrats control of the legislature in 1860 gave heavy support to the party again in 1866.[85]

Democrats did not achieve their victory without a struggle over Baltimore. In a political sequence remarkably similar to the confrontation between Governor T. Watkins Ligon and Mayor Swann in 1857, Governor Swann ousted two of the city's Unionist police commis-

state fiscal policies indicates the considerable agreement between the two parties in the 1866 legislature. The index of party likeness on these roll calls was 85, the index of party cohesion correspondingly low, 22.

[84]Baltimore *American*, August 23, 1866.

[85]There are significant positive correlations on a county-by-county basis between the Democratic vote for comptroller in 1866 and the Democratic vote for the legislature in 1859 (+.6034), the Democratic vote for governor in 1861 (+.5621), the Democratic congressional vote in 1863 (+.6209), the Democratic vote for President in 1864 (+.7219). The Unionist vote of 1866 also reveals positive correlations with the Know-Nothing vote of 1859 (+.4105), the Unionist vote in 1863 for Congress (+.7218), the Lincoln vote in 1864 (+.8343), the Unionist vote for governor in 1864 (+.8342). The only other significant positive correlation is that between the Democratic vote in 1866 (and, of course, other elections) and the number of blacks, +.6738.

sioners and appointed Democrats.[86] Not to be outdone, the Unionist Judge Hugh Bond arrested Swann's new commissioners. At issue was the power of police commissioners sympathetic to the Unionists to appoint election judges who might prevent Democrats from voting. Because of fears that election day might end in violence, Swann persuaded President Johnson to alert federal troops, and, on Johnson's direction, General Ulysses S. Grant dispatched a regiment to convenient posts near Baltimore.[87]

Yet the election was calm and orderly, as 68,000 registered voters cast ballots. With its voting population diminished by registration procedures, Marylanders saw the Unionist party lose heavily in Baltimore. Even the old trick of coloring election tickets so that only those with correct ballots were allowed to the voting windows failed to prevent a Democratic majority. Disappointed, the Baltimore *American* announced the thorough rout of the Union party as well as the end of the Conservatives: "With the deposit of the last ballot yesterday the mock name of conservatives ceased to exist. . . . We are henceforth Democrats and Republicans."[88]

Now Maryland's political future belonged to the Democracy, as that party completed its control over state politics—a process that had begun just before the war. An institution of remarkable durability and consistency, the Democratic organization managed to survive both the war and the postwar threat of a new party. Such a triumph had been achieved because of dedicated leaders, local control of political machinery, the neglect of divisive grass-roots issues, the constant reiteration of Negrophobia, and a loyal—and conservative—constituency. Even the attempts by the "stormy petrel of Maryland politics,"[89]

[86]In 1857, election irregularities attributed to Know-Nothings encouraged Democratic Governor Ligon to call up troops to prevent unfair elections in Baltimore. The American party mayor resisted the encroachment on the city's prerogatives. It was this same Know-Nothing mayor—Thomas Swann—who was governor in 1866. Lawrence F. Schmeckebier, *History of the Know Nothing Party in Maryland*, Johns Hopkins University Studies in Historical and Political Science, ser. 17 (Baltimore: Johns Hopkins Press, 1899), pp. 72-73. See Ligon to Swann, October 3, 1857, Swann Papers, and Bradley T. Johnson, "Memo on Governor Ligon's Proclamation," 1857, Bradley T. Johnson Papers, Duke University Library, Durham, N.C.

[87]General Edward Canby to Grant, October 23, 1866; Grant to Johnson, October 23, 1866; Johnson to Swann, November 2, 1866, Johnson Papers.

[88]Baltimore *American*, November 7, 1866.

[89]Reinhard Luthin, "A Discordant Chapter in Lincoln's Administration: The Davis-Blair Controversy," *Maryland Historical Magazine* 39 (March 1944), p. 47.

Montgomery Blair, to jettison the Union party and include Democrats in a new coalition had failed to splinter the party. Unionists, on the other hand, held much the same position in Maryland as they had in 1860; divided, distracted, and disorganized, the party had only a precarious future in Maryland.

VII. POLITICS OF THE PAST: THE TRIUMPH OF THE MARYLAND DEMOCRACY, 1867-1868

IN EARLY JANUARY 1867, during one of the state's most severe winters, Maryland legislators traveled to Annapolis for the biennial session of the legislature. The sleepy capital city had changed little during the war, but triumphant Democrats, celebrating their return to power, hardly noticed the inadequate accommodations.[1] Delegates still represented the same privileged social and economic status as before the war. A majority were lawyers or farmers, traditional occupations for Maryland politicians, and, as in previous legislatures, a smattering of business and professional men completed the delegation.[2] Democratic newspapers noted with favor the political experience of the delegates, and though the Speaker of the House modestly admitted his own lack of parliamentary training, he and thirty fellow delegates had served in previous legislatures or Constitutional Conventions. Gradually the continuity of Maryland politics had produced a more experienced legislative membership than that which represented the state before the war.

Scarcely had legislators unpacked, when Governor Swann in his address to the delegates referred to a number of state problems which merited attention. In Swann's view, Maryland should sell its assets in several corporations, the militia law should be revised, and improvements should be made in the Baltimore harbor and Maryland penitentiary. Yet the Governor's recommendations on state policy carried little weight with legislators. Swann accepted his lack of influence with equanimity, for like his predecessors in Annapolis, he regarded himself as an executive and not a legislative leader. "It is not my province," he announced, "it is not my appropriate duty to interfere with legislation engaging the attention of the two houses of the General Assembly. I am the executive officer of this state. I am here to see that the laws are faithfully executed."[3]

As in the past, much of the governor's message dealt with national problems such as the relations between Congress and President, Negro suffrage, and the Fourteenth Amendment. Oliver Miller, the legislature's choice for Speaker of the House, seconded Swann's concerns. In his address Miller said nothing of state problems; instead he

[1] Diary of Richard H. Townsend, 1867, Enoch Pratt Library.

[2] Of eighty delegates, there were thirty-three lawyers, thirty-two farmers, eight merchants, one accountant, one editor, one miller, one president of a canal, and three manufacturers. There were sixty Democrats and twenty Unionists in the 1867 House of Delegates; in the Senate there were nine Unionists and fifteen Democrats.

[3] Baltimore *Sun*, February 27, 1867. For Swann's address, see "Proceedings of the Governor, 1867," Swann Executive Papers, Hall of Records, Annapolis, Md.

devoted his entire speech to an indictment of Congress and the Fourteenth Amendment. Reflecting the interest of their governor and Speaker, delegates themselves did not hesitate to take positions on such issues. Resolutions placed the 1867 legislature on record as supporting Andrew Johnson's policies, while at the same time condemning congressional Reconstruction. Notwithstanding the press of other business, members spent two days of a sixty-day session discussing Reconstruction in Louisiana.[4]

Despite such interest in national affairs, the 1867 legislature, like its predecessors, spent a disproportionate amount of time on the local matters which had so engaged the attention of previous legislators. Seventy-three percent of all roll calls, nearly the same proportion as before and during the war, involved the perennial problems of special incorporations, hogs running at large, and county whiskey, school, and voting regulations.[5] The Baltimore *Daily Gazette*, forgetting that such concerns had always dominated the legislature's attention, complained that "a considerable number of delegates are thinking more about petty matters of local or personal interest than of those reforms which are so eminently necessary for public security and welfare."[6] More understanding of such behavior, the Baltimore *Sun* explained that "the pressure for legislation affecting private interests is always so much greater than that which relates to the public, the latter is liable to be neglected or postponed to a late period of the session. There are 1,000 nameless bills relating to private and local affairs which ought to be left until last."[7] Apparently neither the provisions of the 1864 Constitution which supposedly limited such legislation nor the exhortation of political leaders to pass general legislation altered the lawmakers' concentration on county and district issues.

This continuing neglect of general issues helped to perpetuate Maryland's manifold voluntary associations. Ad hoc committees and semi-permanent organizations, long a part of state tradition, served to enlist opinion and seek solutions for problems that political parties

[4] *Journal of the Proceeedings of the House of Delegates, 1867* (Annapolis: Henry A. Lucas, 1867), pp. 5-9, 28, 29, 431.

[5] In 1858, for example, 70 percent of the roll calls involved special and local legislation that did not affect the state as a whole. In 1860, the figure was 74 percent; in 1864, 68 percent; in 1865, 74 percent; and in 1866, 76 percent. This emphasis on local and special legislation has been a consistent pattern in Maryland. In 1902, 45 percent of all bills passed by the Maryland legislature were local; 35 percent, special; and 20 percent, general. Paul Reinsch, *American Legislatures and Legislative Methods* (New York: Century Co., 1907), p. 302.

[6] Baltimore *Daily Gazette*, February 20, 1867.

[7] Baltimore *Sun*, February 6, 1867.

sometimes avoided. From sorghum growers who wanted better transportation facilities to railroad managers who wished to reduce the number of state-appointed directors in their companies and Sunday school teachers who wanted more effective "Blue Laws," Marylanders met in conventions. Many of these organizations had existed before the war; some like the Maryland Convention of Colored Men were postwar creations. Their importance in 1867 reflected, in part, the legislature's continuing focus on local problems.[8]

Some Marylanders were aware of this failing of their government. Well after the end of the session, the influential Baltimore *Sun* complained that Maryland suffered from "a want of uniformity of public law," and "the loose customs of passing local law." If, argued the *Sun*, the legislature treated the counties as separate sovereignties, then inhabitants were not Marylanders, but were citizens of a particular county. The system of legislating for counties accounted for the fact that there were two volumes of Maryland statutes, and the one containing local laws was 250 pages longer than that containing general laws. There was not a lawyer in the state, concluded the *Sun*, "who pretends to know anything about any county save that where he practices."[9]

Despite Unionist threats that the Republican Congress might intervene and "territorialize" the state, Democrats passed three general laws toward the end of the 1867 session, which cemented their political control over Maryland. A bill calling for a referendum on the convening of a new Constitutional Convention, a bill to enfranchise citizens who could not vote under the restrictions of the present registry law, and a bill changing the oath necessary for registration—all passed by strict party votes before adjournment in March. A leading Unionist sadly noted that "the legislature has tied us hand and foot."[10]

The most spectacular display of political disagreement between the two parties involved the election of a U.S. senator to replace John Creswell, whose radical proclivities made his reelection unlikely. Promised Democratic support in return for the appointment of sympathetic registrars in 1866, Swann now claimed his share of the bargain, but to elect the Baltimorean Swann in place of Creswell necessitated the

[8] For examples of such conventions, see the Baltimore *Sun*, March 5, April 1, 3, 1867; January 8, 1868; *Civilian and Telegraph* (Cumberland), January 17, 1868; Baltimore *Daily Gazette*, February 14, 1867.

[9] Baltimore *Sun*, June 25, 1867.

[10] Hugh Bond to William Kelley, quoted in the Baltimore *Sun*, March 28, 1867.

repeal of an eighteenth-century statute which required that one of Maryland's senators be a resident of the Eastern Shore. Representatives from the Tidewater counties complained that the law was their last vestige of power, for the Constitution of 1864 had ended the rotation of the governorship among Maryland's regions. A future U.S. senator from Kent county, George Vickers, insisted that the protection of the region's interest was "above party."[11] Yet in a series of roll calls, disciplined Democratic Eastern Shore delegates voted with their party to rescind the law for a year.

A joint session of the legislature then elected Swann to the Senate, but he postponed his resignation from the governorship after receiving a warning from the ever-watchful Montgomery Blair. In a letter marked "confidential," Blair apprised the governor of the "Radical conspiracy" to reject him in the Senate. Playing to Swann's ambitions and ego, Blair compared the governor to John Wilkes, the English reformer refused a seat in Parliament in the 1760s:

> If you now resign in the face of these dangers to the rights of our people and abandon them to Cox [the Lieutenant Governor], it may affect your popularity and prevent that accord among the people in sustaining you against the Senatorial proscriptions contemplated and thus defeat us in the contest. The only sure way to put down the conspiracy against the state and against you personally in my opinion is for you to hold on to the gubernatorial chair.[12]

As Lieutenant Governor Christopher Cox's family prepared to move into the Executive Mansion—and on the very day designated for the Cox inauguration—Swann announced his decision to continue as governor. As he explained " . . . I have been visited by such appeals from the representative men of the state, urged with an earnestness and unanimity which could hardly be mistaken, asking my continuance in the Gubernatorial chair, that I did not feel at liberty to

[11] Baltimore *Sun*, January 25, 1867.

[12] A copy of this letter is in the Blair Papers, Library of Congress. See Blair to Swann, February 22, 1867. Blair said nothing of his own desire to become a Maryland senator, but this old ambition was clearly expressed in letters between J. F. Lee and Blair during February and March 1867. Frank Kent, in his delightful but frequently inaccurate account of Maryland politics, has suggested that the first word of the "Radical plot" to refuse Swann came when Creswell's wife told a Democrat that Congress would never accept Swann. Frank Kent, *The Story of Maryland Politics*, rev. ed. (Hatboro, Pa.: Tradition Press, 1967), p. 11. The accession of Cox to the governorship frightened Democrats because while Swann had made clear his opposition to Republicanism and his desire to join the Democratic party, Cox, a well-known physician, had not. Indeed, the indecisive Cox had hoped for a diplomatic mission, and Swann and others gladly recommended his appointment, perhaps to get rid of him. Thomas Swann to Andrew Johnson, August 30, 1865. Letters of Application and Recommendation, Microfilm 650, Department of Treasury Records, National Archives.

consult my own preferences."[13] Swann said nothing of his fears that Congress, because of an oath of allegiance he supposedly made to the Confederacy, would reject him. His slight to Cox who pledged he would never speak to Swann again ended the friendship between the two men and increased discord within the Union party.[14]

Charitably the Baltimore *Sun* called Swann's decision a reversal of the trend of resigning state jobs to join the federal government.[15] For weary legislators Swann's retention of the governorship meant the election of another senator. Again party lines held fast, but now, freed of their bargain with the former Know-Nothing Swann, Democrats quickly elected ex-Governor Philip Thomas, a Democrat of long standing whose brief tenure as Secretary of the Treasury in 1860 along with a loan to his Confederate son made him an insulting choice to Republicans. When Congress refused to seat Thomas, the Democratic legislature elected George Vickers, who hastened to Washington in 1868 to vote against the presidential impeachment proceedings.[16]

While partisan issues clearly separated the voting records of the two parties in the 1867 legislature, there was also substantial party disagreement on legislation affecting the state's black population. Of twelve roll calls involving Negroes, eight were party votes. In some instances, such as votes on apprenticeship, miscegenation, and the admissability in state courts of Negro testimony, only a handful of Unionists voted against the Democrats, the rest preferring to abstain. Yet when Democrats urged passage of a bill to take a slave census, Unionists voted overwhelmingly against this supposed first step toward state compensation of slave-owners. Generally Democrats, as before the war, were united on all issues relating to freedmen.[17]

Although Unionists and Democrats disagreed on political and racial questions, there was substantial concurrence on other state problems which cut across party lines. Few roll calls on economic,

[13]*Proceedings of the House of Delegates*, 1867, p. 650.

[14]There is some evidence that in order to collect interest on his extensive holdings of Virginia bonds, Swann empowered his brother-in-law, who lived in Virginia, to take an oath of allegiance to the Confederacy in his name. See *St. Mary's Gazette* (Leonardtown), March 7, 1867, and a clipping in the Swann Papers from the Boston *Journal*, July 13, 1883. For evidence on Cox's reaction, see the Baltimore *Daily Gazette*, February 27, 1867 and the Civil War Diary of William Glenn, February 26, 1867.

[15]Baltimore *Sun*, February 27, 1867.

[16]Baltimore *American*, January 7, 1868; Baltimore *Sun*, March 7-9, 1868; *Congressional Globe*, 40th Cong., 2d sess., 1868, 39, pt. 1:321, 656-62; pt. 2:1271.

[17]On votes to change part of the state's judicial and apprenticeship codes, only four Unionists out of twenty voted. The index of cohesion among Democrats on twelve roll calls involving Maryland's black population was 86.

judicial, and sumptuary issues were party votes.[18] For example, an important bill prohibiting children under eighteen from working more than ten hours a day split both parties. Even the battle between two railroad companies—the Baltimore and Ohio and the Baltimore and Potomac—over trunk lines to Washington found the leader of the Maryland Democracy and president of the Baltimore and Potomac, Oden Bowie, opposed to important Democratic interests in Baltimore. Unionists voted on both sides of this and other railroad issues. Such intra-party feuding made it possible for the Baltimore and Ohio to deny, quite correctly, any role in Maryland politics and to continue its nonpartisan efforts to reduce the number of state-appointed directors.[19] Legislation affecting another Maryland corporation, the ailing Chesapeake and Ohio canal, also split the parties.[20]

Press reports to the contrary, there were no significant or consistent voting blocs within either the Unionist or Democratic parties. The Conservatives, although frequently mentioned by newspapers, simply did not exist as an organized faction in Annapolis, a fact noted by a perceptive Baltimore Unionist, Archibald Stirling. According to Stirling, the Conservatives "were played out and were now under the name Democrat."[21] A special election in Baltimore illustrated Stir-

[18]I studied thirty such bills. The average index of cohesion was 40; the index of party likeness, 73.

[19]House of Delegates, *Documents of the State Legislature, 1867*, "Memorial from the Directors of the Baltimore & Ohio Railroad," Document G; "Communication from the President of the Baltimore & Potomac Railroad," Document Q; and "Counter Memorial of the President of the Baltimore & Potomac Railroad," Document T (Annapolis: Henry A. Lucas, 1867). For the company's attitude on the Maryland legislature, see John King to John W. Garrett, July 12, 18, 20, 1867, Garrett Papers, MHS. In Maryland, the great issue for the Baltimore and Ohio involved the company's attempt to decrease the number of state and Baltimore city directors on the railroad's board. In 1864 the state appointed ten directors, Baltimore eight, and private sources twelve. Thomas Swann's desire to sell state-owned stocks emanated, in part, from his desire as a former B. & O. president to end state control of the railroad. Baltimore *American*, March 28, 1867; William B. Catton, *John W. Garrett of the Baltimore and Ohio: A Study in Seaport and Railroad Competition, 1820–1874* (Ann Arbor, Mich.: University Microfilms, 1959), pp. 407–85. Apparently the railroad followed a different strategy in Virginia, where conflict over routes led the Baltimore and Ohio to play an important role in state politics. See Nelson M. Blake, *William Mahone of Virginia, Soldier and Political Insurgent* (Richmond: Garrett and Massie, 1935).

[20]There is evidence that economic factions such as the coal interest determined legislative policy toward the Chesapeake and Ohio Canal. Alfred Spates to Neilson Poe, November 15, 1869; Thomas McKaig *et al.*, to the Honorable Board of Public Works, n.d., Alfred Spates Papers, University of Virginia Library, Charlottesville, Va.; Proceedings of the President and Board of Directors, Record Group 79, Records of the Chesapeake and Ohio Canal, National Archives.

[21]Baltimore *American*, March 28, 1867.

ling's point. When Reverdy Johnson's son ran as a Conservative against a Unionist and a Democrat for a Baltimore judgeship, he received only 6 percent of the total vote.[22] Such a showing, along with the failure of so-called "Conservative" legislators to vote together, proved, according to one reporter, that the Maryland Conservatives had suffered the same fate as the "goat in the fable [who] aided the fox in escaping from the well by the use of his horns and remained at the bottom himself."[23]

☆ ☆ ☆

AMONG THE MOST IMPORTANT political measures passed by the 1867 legislature was a bill calling for a referendum on convening a new Constitutional Convention. According to Democratic litany, the re-writing of the 1864 Constitution was essential if the state was to be "regenerated and redeemed," for Maryland's present Constitution had been imposed by federal bayonets.[24] Urging their followers to vote in favor of a new Constitutional Convention, Democrats promised to expunge proscriptive oaths. To the state's 14,000 ex-slaveholders, party leaders held out a faint hope that they would receive compensation for their property. On other constitutional issues, Democrats gave vague assurance of a return to the ideals of the Constitution of 1851 and other "ancient landmarks."[25]

Shortly after the adjournment of the legislature in March 1867, Marylanders again found themselves engaged in the strenuous political activity so characteristic of this period in state history. Delegates from the legislature joined county executive committees in organizing the April referendum. Ward and district meetings started the familiar procedure designed to produce candidates for the Constitutional Convention. Such frenetic activities served to revive and stimulate the Democratic organization—again at the expense of Conservatives, for even Montgomery Blair failed to be nominated as a delegate from Montgomery county. Instead, as opposition papers noted, the convention was composed of old Democratic secession sympathizers, and "the same old steeds were in the valley of democracy jaded, worn, and fit

[22] Baltimore *Sun*, April 29, 1867.

[23] New York *Times*, August 20, 1867. If there had been a bloc within the Democratic party, it would have had some effect on that party's index of cohesion which was 85 for the 1867 session. For a cluster-bloc analysis, see Appendix Table D-18.

[24] Baltimore *Daily Gazette*, February 16, 1867.

[25] Baltimore *Sun*, April 3, 1867.

only for the paddock."[26] Other Unionists complained of "the resurrected ghosts of former Democrats on the street corners, in the groggeries chattering, hobnobbing and convincing unterrified idlers that their day has come again."[27]

Bold in their criticism of the Democrats, dispirited Unionists were less effective in organizing their opposition to a new convention. Even after the state central committee had described the call to convention as illegal, extravagant, unneeded, and a sop to former slaveholders, local Unionist organizations did not nominate any delegates to run against Democrats. In western Maryland, the heart of Unionist strength, the party did not contest the referendum, and throughout the state, Unionists paid no heed to Senator Creswell's exhortation "to organization and effort and assertion of principles."[28] Increasingly, Unionist political strategy came from a few leaders who had little interest in stimulating the party's decaying local organization.

Instead Unionists turned to Washington for help. In March 1867—the month in which Congress passed the first of a series of military Reconstruction Acts affecting southern states—Maryland Unionists sent a petition to Congress urging that body to guarantee republican government and to protect the people "from any revolution in their form of government."[29] In the view of many party members, what Congress could do for the South, Congress should do for Maryland. Captivated by hopes that black suffrage might increase their weakened electoral strength and convinced by Democratic victories that otherwise their party faced extinction, many Maryland Unionists concluded that only congressional intervention could support their declining fortunes. Determined to implement this strategy, Congressman Francis Thomas of western Maryland spent most of his legislative efforts encouraging the House of Representatives to investigate Maryland.[30]

[26]New York *Times*, August 20, 1867.

[27]Baltimore *American*, April 5, 1867.

[28]*Ibid.*, March 22, 1867; Cumberland *Alleganian*, April 13, 1867.

[29]"Resolutions of Both Branches of the City Council of Baltimore," 1867, Creswell Papers, Library of Congress. See also Francis Thomas to Creswell, February 22, 1867, Creswell Papers; and Charles O. Lerche, "Congressional Interpretations of the Guarantee of a Republican Form of Government during Reconstruction," *Journal of Southern History* 15 (May 1949):192–211.

[30]*Congressional Globe*, 39th Cong., 2d sess., 1867, 37, pt. 2:889; pt. 3:1790; 39, pt. 1:230; 40th Cong., 1st sess., 1867, 38, pt. 2:656, 657. Thomas also wrote Marylanders asking for the names of those who would testify concerning "the bargain of Swann to secure his election." Thomas to Creswell, February 22, 1867, Creswell Papers.

In the spring of 1867, Thomas was successful, and the investigation of Maryland began, as Unionists trooped to Washington to testify that their state was in the hands of "disloyal politicians." Most witnesses insisted that state officials, from registrars to judges, were traitors who did not believe in "coercion of the South."[31] Others found the 1867 legislature guilty on two counts—the disloyalty and corruption of its Democratic members. According to the testimony of David Pinckney West, a clerk in the city collector's office, a lien had been placed on his salary in order to raise money for political purposes. Such monies were then used to buy the votes of Democratic state senators.[32] Appealing to other congressional concerns, Libertus van Bokkelen, the respected state commissioner of education, testified that Maryland's school fund was unfairly distributed because "the black man's property" in the form of taxes was used for the education of white children.[33] Yet only van Bokkelen and John Hopper of Harford county contended that the violation of Negro rights justified congressional interference in Maryland; most Unionists instead argued that it was Democratic corruption and "rebellious spirit" that merited national attention.

Certainly the growing dependence of Unionists on Congressional Republicans required that these Maryland leaders fall in line with the national Republican party and its platforms. In April, the Maryland Unionist organization, so long resistant to association with a party still despised as "abolitionist" by many Marylanders, changed its name to the Republican Union party and by May, the party officially supported universal manhood suffrage, a tidy euphemism for black voting. In Maryland's first integrated state political convention both black and white Republicans called on Congress "to carry out the principles of the Declaration of Independence and abolish all legal distinctions on account of color and give the suffrage to the colored classes of this and all other states."[34] Implicit in the convention's resolution was the threat that unless Negroes could vote, Maryland would not have a republican form of government, and Congress then had both reason

[31] Testimony of John Hopper and Curtis Davis, Maryland Investigation, Record Group 233, Records of the Congressional Investigating Committee, House, 40th Cong., 1st sess., 1867, National Archives.

[32] "Report of Committee of the Senate into Corrupt Practices to Influence Legislation at the Last Session of the General Assembly," *ibid.*

[33] Testimony of Libertus van Bokkelen, *ibid.*

[34] *Civilian and Telegraph* (Cumberland), April 4, 1867; Baltimore *American*, April 6, May 15, 1867.

and right to intervene in the state. Such logic led Baltimore Republicans to threaten that if Democrats persisted in their plans for a Constitutional Convention there would be two conventions—one composed of delegates elected by universal suffrage.[35]

This policy reversal by a party which had opposed Negro voting less than six months before suggested that political expediency dictated the change—a change described by political satirist Petroleum Nasby as " 'straordinary changes in politix—some so very sudden that the movement perdoost conjestion uv the conshence."[36] Men who in 1866 consistently rejected the possibility of black voting now, in the face of political oblivion, embraced it. Unionists who in 1866 walked out of the Southern Loyalist Convention at the mention of Negro voting now declared their support for this principle. Certainly some Unionists like Hugh Bond, who had avoided discussion of slavery before the war, were influenced by considerations other than political expediency. As Bond explained:

> There cannot be one slave without being two. There must be a man who is tied and the man who he is tied to and when you were emancipated, I, too in common with the white people of the state, was emancipated. . . . The movement in your behalf has been largely political. When we have added to the power of our political truth the energy of religious fervor, our triumph is secure.[37]

Yet most advocates of Negro suffrage were less concerned with the justice of Negro voting than Hugh Bond. Some, like the leaders of the Union League, resolved in favor of black voting so that the entire Union Republican vote "may be polled against the disloyal vote lately enfranchised in direct violation of the Constitution and laws of the state."[38] Democrats who likened Unionists to "political acrobats after votes" complained with outrage that "when [Republicans] discover they can't carry states without the franchise of colored men, they become specially anxious that colored men should be voters. Now they would use [the Negro] if they could simply for party purposes, making him a mere chattel in their political market."[39]

Such logic was not lost on Maryland's Negroes who recognized the political motives behind sudden Unionist support for their en-

[35] Baltimore *American*, March 28, May 15, 1867.

[36] *Ibid.*, April 11, 1867; David R. Locke, *The Struggles of Petroleum Nasby* (Boston: Lee and Shepherd, 1888), p. 408.

[37] Baltimore *American*, July 1, 1867.

[38] Baltimore *Sun*, July 10, 1867.

[39] *Ibid.*, May 14, 1867; Baltimore *Daily Gazette*, August 3, 1867.

franchisement. William Sanders, a Negro delegate to the Republican Unionist convention, explained the role Negroes might play in Maryland politics:

> There is no need of advising the colored men of the state why and how they should vote. I desire to impress upon the people of the State . . . that we are true to the men that have given us the privileges we now enjoy. You desire to preserve the state of Maryland from its present oligarchy. The colored men will sustain you at the ballot-box, accordingly that continued aid that you depend on will be on hand. I pledge you the entire vote of the 30,000 black men of the State of Maryland.

At the same convention, Alfred Handy, a Negro tailor from Baltimore, outlined a political *quid pro quo*:

> We demand of the Radical Republican Union Party that when they shall have gotten into power that they will stand by their colored brethren—that they will not forget the assistance we tendered them in their hour of greatest need. We need when we get the right to vote some other things. . . .[40]

☆ ☆ ☆

IMPEDED BY NEITHER BLACK VOTING nor congressional interference, Democrats easily won the April referendum. By May the Constitutional Convention, composed entirely of Democrats, convened in Annapolis and by October, Marylanders had a new Constitution, which, though often amended, still serves the state today.

In rewriting the Constitution without the interference of any Unionist-Republican delegates, Democrats did little to change the state's organic law, for the Constitution of 1867 accepted far more than it changed. Most Unionist innovations of 1864 continued unchallenged, unrevised, and largely untouched. Registration procedures, restrictions on the assembly's power to pass local legislation, and even the prohibition on compensation to ex-slave-owners remained. Unionist newspapers wondered why Democrats kept so closely to the 1864 document. According to Archibald Stirling, there was nothing new in the Constitution "except new offices," and an unhappy delegate wrote Montgomery Blair that the convention was "much gabble about nothing."[41]

[40] Baltimore *American*, May 15, 1867.

[41] *Ibid.*, September 12, 1867; J. F. Lee to Montgomery Blair, June 12, 1867, Blair Papers.

The final document omitted the phrase that all men were created free and equal, and in a slap at fervent Unionist and nativist clergy, it forbade ministers from holding state offices. On the other hand, the Constitution gave Negroes the right to testify in court. With the example of deteriorating congressional-presidential relations before them, delegates provided a veto for the governor which could be overridden by three-fifths—of fifty-one votes—of the General Assembly. Yet since the Constitution required the votes of a majority—or forty-four votes—of the legislature to pass a bill, such a structural revision was not a notable change.[42] Delegates also abolished the lieutenant-governorship introduced in the 1864 Constitution.

Most of the Constitutional changes instituted in 1867 were political in nature. The final document omitted the despised iron-clad oaths as qualifications for office-holding and provided a new court system of eight judicial districts which made it easier for Democrats to elect judges of their own persuasion. The political motives of the Constitution were clearly manifest in provisions calling for reelection of all state officials in November. Consistent with their partisan purposes, Democrats increased the size of the Eastern Shore and southern Maryland delegations, and even created a new Eastern Shore county—Wicomico.[43]

With little but political changes to show for their effort, Democrats successfully used the Constitutional Convention for the purpose it was designed—a partisan forum. A policy of financial retrenchment forestalled the printing of Convention proceedings; hence newspapers published—and commented upon—the debates. In many instances such discussions, in an all-Democratic assemblage, degenerated into attacks on the Republicans. Such was the case during debate on allowing Negro testimony in state courts, when a delegate attacked "the Yankee Congress."[44] The summer visit to the convention of President

[42]According to one Baltimore delegate, who argued for the veto, "a fanatical Congress passed law after law and the vetoes of President Johnson were interposed." Baltimore *Sun*, June 5, 1867.

[43]According to the Baltimore *American*, "the southern counties of the Western Shore and the southern counties of the Eastern Shore having altogether at the last census a white population of only 130,331 will have in the Legislature under the proposed new Constitution, thirty-four delegates and fifteen Senators, whilst the rest of the state including Baltimore city and all the most wealthy and populous counties with 385,700 white inhabitants will have but 52 Delegates and ten Senators. Thus one-third of the State will have a majority of five in the Senate and nearly two-fifths of the Lower House." Baltimore *American*, August 27, 1867. In the 1864 Constitution, representation was based on white population; in 1867 it was based on total population, a change which favored the Democrats.

[44]Baltimore *Sun*, July 24, 1867.

Johnson, who lauded "the preservation of principles and the importance of Constitution," further highlighted the partisan nature of the meetings in Annapolis.[45]

Certainly the political energy generated by the Constitutional Convention helped Democrats to prepare for the election of a governor and new legislature in the fall. While Republican Unionists remained inert—their faithful press trumpeting the need for Negro voting even though their followers grimaced at what the New York *Times* called "the negro suffrage medicine"[46]—Democrats held mass meetings urging ratification of the new Constitution in October. Campaigning which had begun in the spring and summer continued into the fall. Party members met often in state conventions, and again the powerful county and district organizations, many run by the same professional politicians as before the war, revealed the remarkable durability of the party. "I saw many," a Democratic leader told his southern Maryland audiences, "who rallied around the Democratic banner as far back as 1840."[47]

The themes of the 1867 election campaign were those of the past. Reviving ancient cries of abolitionism, Democrats accused Republicans of radicalism, extremism, and race-mixing. The forbidding specter of the free Negro—"a savage, a laggard, and a vagabond" according to one convention delegate—led Democrats to insist that any attempts at equality would create a race, like the Indians, "arrayed in public hostility against white men."[48] Party leaders often exaggerated racial friction to buttress their opposition to the Fourteenth Amendment, the Freedmen's Bureau, and black suffrage. In the hands of such propagandists, racial troubles in Queen Anne's county, for example, became the equivalent of a black insurrection which justified the formation of white men's clubs. Decorating their placards with anti-Negro sentiments, Democrats made it clear that their party was dedicated to "a white man's government for the benefit of white men."[49]

Party appeals to the ancient symbols of Constitution and Union continued to fit neatly into the Democratic campaign strategy. The

[45]Baltimore *American*, July 1, 1867.

[46]New York *Times*, August 20, 1867.

[47]*St. Mary's Beacon* (Leonardtown), September 5, 1867. See also Baltimore *Daily Gazette*, July 25, 1867, and "List of Elected Officials of Maryland," MHS.

[48]Baltimore *American*, July 24, August 7, 1867; see also *St. Mary's Beacon* (Leonardtown), August 8, 1867.

[49]Baltimore *Sun*, June 24, 1867; William Lowdermilk to Swann, April 14, 1867, Swann Executive Papers.

refusal of Republicans to admit southern states into Congress and the gathering storm over Presidential impeachment were clear examples of "the politics of the trampled ballot." Charged one Democrat: "They have abolished the Union, the Constitution, trial by jury and the courts."[50] Other campaigners were less specific—"I stand upon the platform of maintenance of the Constitution. I stand by the Constitution and Union of the fathers of the country,"[51] announced Governor Thomas Swann. Focusing on national rather than state affairs, Democrats printed Reverdy Johnson's complex arguments on constitutional violations while local concerns went unmentioned.[52]

With some justification, opponents charged that Democrats lacked any progressive ideas. "Like the crawfish, they would rather go backwards than forwards," concluded the Baltimore *American*.[53] In fact, the party preferred to go sideways, repeating, often in almost the same words, its prewar appeals. When Democrats complained of New England textbooks and called for a Chinese wall across the Mason-Dixon line,[54] they parroted Maryland's fears of abolitionists during the 1850s. When Democrats announced their determination to restore the spirit of Andrew Jackson, they invoked nostalgic memories of a quieter, and presumably happier, time.

Led by Oden Bowie, great-grandson of a former Maryland governor, Democratic candidates were familiar faces to voters. Only a few Conservatives or Unionists were included on Democratic tickets, as length of service to the party became, in some instances, a criterion for nomination. In many Eastern Shore and southern Maryland counties, every candidate for office had served the party either before or during the war.[55] While the state patronage rested securely in the hands of old professionals like John Thompson Mason, Baltimore's Collector of the Port in 1859, the favors of Andrew Johnson went to Maryland's Democrats.[56]

[50]*St. Mary's Beacon* (Leonardtown), August 8, 1867.

[51]"Fragment of a Speech," Swann Papers, owned by Mrs. Page S. Gillet, Glyndon, Md.

[52]Baltimore *Daily Gazette*, October 29, 1867. See Reverdy Johnson, *The Dangerous Condition* (Baltimore: Baltimore Sun Book and Job Printing, 1867).

[53]Baltimore *American*, April 5, 1867.

[54]*Ibid.*, February 20, 1867; Baltimore *Daily Gazette*, March 11, 1867.

[55]Baltimore *Sun*, September 7, October 17, 1867; "List of Elected Officials in Maryland," MHS.

[56]Thomas Ligon to J. Thompson Mason, April 11, 1867, Aldine Papers, MHS. See also Applications for Office, Maryland, 1866-1867, Johnson Papers; U.S. Department of Interior, *Register of Offices and Agents, 1868* (Washington, D.C.: Government Printing Office, 1869).

Hugh Bond, the Unionist-Republican candidate for governor, provided little competition for the strong Democratic machine. The son and brother of Methodist ministers, the grandson of an old and respected Baltimore family, whose members had long served in local politics, Bond had attended New York University before his law training in Baltimore. In 1861 Governor Hicks appointed him to the Baltimore bench to replace the inebriate Henry Stump. No early abolitionist, Bond only gradually accepted the principle of Negro equality, but once accepted, the principle became a crusade. As his friend James Partridge affectionately explained:

> Bond is like the Athenians . . . always after some new thing. . . . he went nearly crazy with 'photography.' He bought a camera and used to practice on the chimney tops in the neighborhood until he nearly drove Mrs. Bond out of the house. . . . After this he nearly lost his mind living in the green air. . . . Then he took up with prayer meetings and then with revival and sailors mutual societies. . . . next he got hold of politics and the judgeship.[57]

By 1865, Bond had also "got hold of" the Negro, and serving as a dedicated missionary to the freedman, the Judge compared himself to an "Ishmaelite." "Equip me for the war and teach my hands to fight."[58]

In the fight for governor, Bond viewed himself as a reformer, not a politician, and therefore he campaigned mostly among the state's nonvoting Negro population. After the passage of the 1864 Constitution, Bond had realized the role he might play in state politics: "The men that made and carried [the new Constitution] have met the fate of all reformers. Like the advance in a charge, they all are killed while their less promising followers rush into the works, which the valors of the dead has [*sic*] rendered it less dangerous to do."[59] With the image of such sacrifice before him, Bond, accompanied by a retinue of Freedmen's Bureau officials, criss-crossed the state urging Negroes to work and educate themselves. To the freedmen who made up most of his audience, he emphatically urged the virtues of hard work, perseverance, education, and chastity. "I don't think you have learned to work to advantage during the period of your slavery. Will you learn how to labor? You can not lay down on the shovel and hoe and subsist upon the mere empty title of freedom. . . . Eschew intoxicating drinks,

[57]"J. R. P." [James R. Partridge] to Henry Winter Davis, March 21, 1865, Bond-McCulloch Papers, MHS.

[58]Hugh Bond to Kate Bond, March 1, 1866, *ibid.*

[59]*Ibid.*, n.d.

avoid thieving, get homes for yourselves."[60] Gradually the campaign, despite continuing complaints of some Unionists "that the Bond party is too severely radical," became a humanitarian effort to aid Negroes, rather than a political contest designed to elect a governor.[61]

Some members of the Republican-Unionists, unsure of black suffrage or its efficacy as a campaign issue, focused instead on familiar appeals to vote against the traditional enemy—the Democracy. According to one such Republican, Negro suffrage was not the issue, nor was Negro equality. Rather the issue was the "rebelized" and disloyal Democratic party which "had no principles and did not dare to put out any platform."[62] Some Republicans violated the traditional reluctance to discuss divisive local issues and accused the Democrats of opposing education.[63] Others, with perhaps a touch of jealousy, charged the Democrats with instituting "one party rule—a worse system of bondage than Negro slavery in its domination over thoughts, opinions, and actions of members."[64]

Although such anti-party spirit always came easiest to those in the minority, in Maryland, Republicans were repeating the reservations about political organizations long entertained by both Know-Nothings and Unionists. Parties, according to most Republicans, were unnecessary, corrupt, and guided by office-seeking politicians. In the words of the Baltimore *American*:

> Political parties in this country are to a large extent managed by a set of artful and unscrupulous men who are governed by no sound moral principles. Good men don't attend primary meetings and never interest themselves in the selection of candidates, and fail to vote. They denounce the corruption and that is all.[65]

Lieutenant Governor Cox's harsh comparison of parties to "old and effete carcasses which reeking with decay of the years offend the very nostriles [*sic*] of the nation"[66] was both picturesque and typical.

[60] *St. Mary's Beacon* (Leonardtown), September 5, 1867. For other examples of Bond's campaign speeches, see the Baltimore *American*, July 1, 30, September 5, October 22, November 2, 1867.

[61] A. Wallace to Bond, April 25, 1866, Bond-McCulloch Papers.

[62] Baltimore *American*, November 2, 1867.

[63] The Democratic convention had placed the responsibility for Maryland's public school system in the hands of the next legislature. According to Republicans, this constitutional provision was a move to strike down public education in the state.

[64] *Cecil Whig* (Elkton), September 3, 1867.

[65] Baltimore *American*, February 18, 1868.

[66] Baltimore *Sun*, February 13, 1867.

Neither the minority status of their party in Maryland nor the condition of political analysis in the United States gave the Republicans any reason to agree with the Democratic position that parties were "an admitted necessity and an actual outgrowth of free institutions."[67]

In an effort to reform political parties, Republicans encouraged the best men to go into politics, or at least to participate in local meetings. A few Marylanders attacked the convention system, where nominations were too easily controlled, it was thought, by corrupt "wirepullers." Some Republicans approved the suggestions of a Philadelphia Union League that parties give up the convention system and allow constituents the right to make nominations at primary meetings. Only then could the "sober, industrious, self-respecting [be expected] to leave their shops, their country homes, their factories and periodically repair to party headquarters, redolent of noisome odors, and reeking with ribaldry. . . ."[68] Echoing the complaints of prewar nativists, such criticism of parties continued in Maryland, until at the urging of Republicans and reformers, the state adopted its first primary law in 1886.[69]

In contrast with their Democratic opponents, many Republican-Unionist candidates in 1867 and 1868 were young and unfamiliar to the Maryland voters.[70] In some cases the mirage of expected congressional intervention provided an impelling reason for such inexperienced candidates to neglect both organization and campaigning. One Republican leader urged the Baltimore Congressman John Thomas "to use your influence with our friends in Congress to save us from the merciless hands of these rebels."[71] The influential Baltimore *American* seconded such appeals: "It would seem that in this hour, when we are weak and powerless, when of ourselves we can do nothing, but wait

[67] Baltimore *Sun*, April 15, 1867. There were few interpretations of American political parties available in the nineteenth century. Three such analyses—Charles Wright's *Our Political Practice* (Boston: A. Mudge, 1865), Simeon Nash's *Morality and the State* (Columbus: Follette, Foster & Co., 1859), and Martin Van Buren's *Inquiry into the Origin and Cause of Political Parties in the United States* (New York: Hurd and Houghton, 1867)—had little to say about political organizations. Nash and Wright found parties unnecessary and corrupt appendages to the democratic system, and while Van Buren's analysis extends into the 1850s, his interest in political parties diminishes after the Federalist period.

[68] Union League, *Essay on Political Organization* (Philadelphia: Collins, 1865), p. 4.

[69] James Crooks, *Politics and Progress: The Rise of Urban Progressivism in Baltimore, 1895 to 1911* (Baton Rouge: Louisiana State University Press, 1968), pp. 72-75.

[70] See Appendix Tables D-19, D-20, and D-21 for a comparison of Democratic and Republican leaders.

[71] J. M. Humphreys to John L. Thomas, January 11, 1867, Thomas Papers, MHS.

until the strong arm of the general government comes to our assistance, we might be united, presenting a solid front to our opponents. . . ."[72] Few Republicans heeded Bond's admonitory mixed metaphors: "If the Republican party, while the waters are troubled, waits beside the pond for Congress to push it in, it will have the palsy forever. It must put its own shoulder to the wheel and do its best before it has the right to call on the national Hercules for aid."[73]

In form, the Republicans retained the structure of their prewar political organization. Local meetings chose delegates to a plethora of nominating conventions. Gradually, however, the party's district and ward organizations had atrophied from faction and disuse, and by 1867 the state central committee controlled the party, occasionally making nominations without benefit of a delegate convention. In some cases conventions were open to all Republicans, rather than elected delegates. The Baltimore *American* sadly noted the "Republican apathy" and attributed Democratic success "to the activity and perseverance of its members."[74]

With so many Republican weaknesses and Democratic strengths, only the size of the Democratic victory in 1867 surprised Marylanders. As cannons boomed from Federal Hill, Baltimoreans learned the Democrats had elected Oden Bowie with 75 percent of the vote as well as an entirely Democratic legislature.[75] While the party's strength was statewide, the traditional Democratic strongholds rolled up the highest majorities. Even the local governments in northern and western Maryland fell into the hands of the party, as a happy Democrat noted: "The Rads are dead."[76] Only the refusal of a number of Marylanders to vote—some 70 percent of the registered voters cast ballots—gave Republicans any hope for the future. This failure to vote was greatest in the old nativist and Unionist election districts where some Marylanders, faithful to their traditional hostility toward Democrats, refused to support Bowie or Bond.

☆ ☆ ☆

[72]Baltimore *American*, April 27, 1868.

[73]*Ibid.*, September 28, 1867.

[74]*Ibid.*, October 1, 1867.

[75]Correlations again reveal the consistency of Maryland politics. There are significant positive correlations between the Democratic vote of 1867 for governor, on a county-by-county basis, and the Democratic vote for the legislature in 1866 (+.7169), the Democratic vote for President in 1864 (+.6595), and the Democratic vote for President in 1860 (+.5291).

[76]Jonathan Norris to Harry Norris, November 8, 1867, Norris Papers, MHS.

THE PRESIDENTIAL YEAR OF 1868 deepened the fissure within the Republican organization. As in 1863, the split involved both disagreement over policy and a leadership struggle. Republicans disagreed on the extent of Negro participation in primary meetings as well as whether Bond or Creswell should control the state organization. Generally party members from regions with heavy Negro populations like Baltimore, the Eastern Shore, and those few counties with Republican organizations in southern Maryland favored full Negro participation, arguing that even though not allowed to vote, Negroes could learn about politics at district meetings. To the Republicans of the northern and western parts of the state where there were few blacks, such arguments were spurious and embarrassing, for the inclusion of Negroes would mean that nonvoters determined the candidates and principles of the party and that Republicans would be even more closely attached to Negroes. If Negroes decided Republican policy, the argument went, what was to prevent women and children from participating at primary meetings?

The battle between Senator John Creswell and Hugh Bond for party control reinforced this policy disagreement. Creswell, quoting his mentor Henry Winter Davis, accused the Bond faction of premature agitation of the Negro issue: "They are like cocks that crow at midnight and only disturb those who are seeking their natural rest."[77] Convinced that he could make a viable organization based on federal patronage, Creswell pleaded for platforms which were not based on the "Negro issue," and which would "suit" northern states. Touted as a possible vice-presidential candidate and eventually named a cabinet officer in Ulysses S. Grant's administration, Creswell and his friends were accused of preferring to "sink the party rather than fail in accomplishing their purpose. Office! Office! seems to be the only inducement for them to enter zealously into the political arena."[78] According to Anna Ella Carroll, an influential if nonvoting Republican, Creswell had failed to obtain the endorsement of any local Republicans because he wanted "the party small in order to maintain leadership."[79]

To Bond and his small band of followers, it seemed that the Creswell faction denied the principles of justice. Hence, in the spring of 1868, Bond formed a new central committee, organized another

[77]Baltimore *American*, March 6, 1868.

[78]Cumberland *Union*, quoted in the Baltimore *American*, April 30, 1868.

[79]Carroll to Maryland Republican Senators, n.d., Carroll Papers, MHS.

convention, and sent a rival delegation to the Republican national convention in June. Like his gubernatorial canvass, Bond's campaign for Negro rights and his struggle to control the Republican party became an emotional crusade, supported by politically active blacks and a few white Marylanders, most of whom were veterans of the Union army. Followers of Creswell compared the Judge to men like Wendell Phillips "who assert doctrines or opinions not only impolitic but impracticable and whose impetuosity incapacitates them for leadership. They can agree with no one but themselves and we should confine their labors to the lecture room."[80] Lacking the political talent of compromise, Bond courageously tried to commit Republicans to Negro equality and thereby harmed his party, for most white Marylanders, disliking Creswell's tactics, despised Bond's principles.

Both wings of the party counted on the success of impeachment proceedings against Andrew Johnson and Senator Benjamin F. Wade's anticipated accession to the Presidency. Yet neither the disappointment following Johnson's acquittal in May nor the necessity of selling the presidential ticket of Ulysses Grant and Schuyler Colfax to the Maryland electorate healed the party split. Indeed the intense factional dispute continued unabated. A disgusted Republican later complained to a friend:

> The Republicans of Baltimore are now all upside down. Those who have possession of the Custom House, Post Office, and Internal Revenue here hunt down every man who believes Judge Bond is the true representative of Republican principles, and if they find him in office, they turn him out, and, if out, they keep him out and treat him as though he were a rank Loco-Foco until the breach has widened fearfully.[81]

By 1868 there were few Republican local organizations to stimulate political interest. Policy decisions, campaign tactics, and even convention organization became the province of the two state central committees, which sniped at each other in the pages of the Baltimore *American*, Cumberland *Union*, *Cecil Whig*, and Frederick *Examiner*. While the organization of the party lay in ruins, a discouraged Republican noted in a letter to Bond:

> The prejudices of the people must to some extent be consulted in all political movements if we desire to achieve speedy and permanent success. It is better for our leaders to be a little behind the popular movements if they desire to build up a strong and successful party, devoted to the advancement of all men, white and black alike. The would-be leaders of our party must

[80] Baltimore *American*, February 26, 1868.

[81] John Wright to George Boutwell, August 21, 1869, Vertical File, MHS.

> learn that first great lesson of implicit obedience to the wishes of their friends if they desire to build up a strong and successful party. . . . Some well-defined regulation must be adopted for the management of our party.[82]

Such a party found agreement only when attacking the opposition. In the view of both Republican factions, Democrats were "traitors who had started the war and who had rejected men whose patriotism set country above party."[83] While Republican conventions passed resolutions for congressional control of Reconstruction and against the perfidious Governor Swann, disloyal President Johnson, and corrupt Democratic party, such unanimous appeals could not mask internal disagreement over the future of either the Negro or the Maryland Republican party.

To Democrats these disagreements among the opposition were an added, but hardly an essential, benefit. In 1868 the powerful Maryland Democracy continued to control the political life of the state, a control to be relinquished only rarely and temporarily in the coming years. Again the ingredients of Democratic success—powerful local organizations, repetitive and attractive platforms, and experienced leadership—served the party well.

With an enthusiasm generated in part by the party's improved fortunes nationally, Maryland Democrats began the campaign early in the year. A variety of nominating conventions spurred political activity in wards and districts. In Baltimore the organization of a permanent headquarters on South Street served as a meeting place for the party faithful. Chartered "to support the Democratic ideals of Constitution and Union," this Democratic Association brought a number of speakers to Maryland. Weeks before the election, Baltimoreans heard appeals urging them to vote Democratic because "the abolition party of yesterday is the abolition party of today and ever in the history of the country has been a party of destruction. The only constitutional party is the Democratic party."[84] County machines, organized in many instances by county commissioners and clerks of the state courts,

[82]Henry Goldsborough to Bond, quoted in the Baltimore *American*, April 22, 1868.

[83]"Record of the Democratic Party, 1860–1865," Chrysmer Collection, Bel Air, Maryland.

[84]Baltimore *Daily Gazette*, September 23, 1868. By late July, the Association had 1,400 members, and by election day 2,500. See Jonathan Norris to Harry Norris, July 15, 1868, Norris Papers and *Act of Incorporation, Constitutional By-Laws, and Declaration of Principles of the Democratic Association of Baltimore City* (Baltimore: Torson and Rhea, 1868).

managed the campaign outside of Baltimore. The war had done nothing to change the power and authority these officials exerted, and commissioners still controlled the county administrative and political machines.[85] In a display of remarkable longevity, some officials had directed the county apparatus for over a decade. Faithful to the form of prewar political structure, county executive committees organized the spiral of mass meetings which served both to elect delegates to nominating conventions and coincidentally to stimulate party activity. According to one paper,

> the Democratic party entered on the present canvass after its accustomed fashion. Local and national committees and conventions have scattered political documents far and wide; they have engaged speakers; they have gotten up mass meetings; they have named the times for holding primary elections and have done what such bodies have done for the last 40 years.[86]

By September, the party had completed most of its nominations. Republicans despairingly noted the "old fossils' control of conventions . . . while young Democrats are assigned to back seats and conservatives ignored altogether," but Democrats, according to John Merryman, happily greeted political friends among whom their entire lives had been spent.[87] Reverdy Johnson's Senate seat, which he resigned in order to accept the ambassadorship to Great Britain, went not to the Democratic convert Thomas Swann, but to a loyal Democrat from western Maryland, William T. Hamilton, whose insistent emphasis on Anglo-Saxon superiority had earned him the gratitude of Democrats. The appearance of two former Unionist leaders—Swann and Blair—at the Democratic state convention signaled the end of conservative attempts to realign Maryland's party system. Although Swann later won a congressional nomination, he was, in the view of some, "a political orange, which the Democracy of the state squeezed and threw away,"[88] and while Blair served as a presidential elector, his position reflected the glory of the nomination of his brother, Francis P. Blair, Jr., for Vice President, rather than his own standing among Maryland Democrats.

Indeed, Maryland party leaders had fought the nomination of both Frank Blair and the Democratic presidential candidate, Horatio

[85]In two plebiscites held in 1867 to determine who should control the taxing power, the electorate in Kent and Harford counties overwhelmingly voted to keep this power in the hands of county commissioners. See William T. Kemp *et al.*, to Swann, May 15, 1867; Swann to County Committees, July 12, 1866, Swann Executive Papers.

[86]Baltimore *Daily Gazette*, September 21, 1868.

[87]Baltimore *Sun*, June 2, 1868; Baltimore *American*, July 24, 1868.

[88]Baltimore *American*, July 14, 1868.

Seymour, the New York governor during the Civil War; they preferred the Ohioan George H. Pendleton. For twenty-two ballots the entire Maryland delegation voted against Seymour in the Democratic National Convention held in New York City in July 1868. According to many delegates, Seymour had been too close to the Lincoln administration, and Blair, a Union General, had also served the Republicans too well. "No man," intoned one Maryland delegate, "should receive the nomination for presidency who does not stand squarely on the record of the past."[89] But national leaders, rejecting such conservatism, favored candidates who had a chance of election rather than those who displayed doctrinal consistency.

The issues the Maryland Democracy chose to bring before the public in 1868 were predictable. Old and revered slogans of Constitution and Union served both as reminders of the past and as attacks on the opposition. Just as Democrats had condemned Know-Nothings for their violations of the rights of Catholics and foreign-born before the war, just as they had attacked Unionists during the war for illegal arrests and elections, they now accused their opposition of violating the rights of southern states. "If the radicals continue in power four more years, the free institutions of the country will be subverted," predicted one candidate.[90] On the other hand, Democrats promised to uphold Constitution and Union by guaranteeing to each state its reserved rights. Familiar and repetitive appeals "to maintain the Union under the Constitution"[91] echoed from political stumps throughout Maryland. For pessimists, the 1868 election was "the last great trial for Constitutional Liberty on the continent and in the world."[92]

Clearly Maryland Democrats appealed to interests and issues of the past, which had now become concerns of the present. In a time of racial change, social dislocation, and economic uncertainty, Democratic county conventions expected "to preserve or rather restore those principles on which government was administered for over a half a century." References to the principles of Jeffersonian democracy joined paeans to Henry Clay, the ex-Whig, now claimed by Democrats who insisted that, if alive, Clay would be a member of their party.[93]

[89] Baltimore *Daily Gazette*, July 10, 1868.

[90] *St. Mary's Beacon* (Leonardtown), October 1, 1868.

[91] *Speech of Duncan McPherson before the Democratic Association of the City of Baltimore, August 18, 1868* (Baltimore: J. B. Reese, 1868).

[92] Jonathan Norris to Harry Norris, October 15, 1868, Norris Papers.

[93] Chestertown *Transcript*, September 12, 1868; Baltimore *American*, October 21, 1868.

Democrats of 1868 employed another of their traditional themes—fear of the Negro. Both as slave and free man, the Negro served as an effective and continuing campaign issue in Maryland politics. Before the war, Democrats accused the opposition of abolitionism; during the war the party complained of Unionist attempts to kidnap and then recruit slaves into the federal army; now after the war, Democrats found a compelling theme in Republican support for Negro voting and equality. "Shall this be a white man's government? Are you for a white man's government or a Negro dynasty?" asked Democrats.[94] In a reference to rebellions by blacks, the Cumberland *Alleganian* found "opponents organizing a magnificent edition of St. Domingo, Sudan, and Central Africa."[95] Even in western Maryland where there were few Negroes, such race-baiting was popular; an Allegany county convention unanimously resolved that "this government was made on the white basis by white men for the benefit of white men."[96]

Second in frequency only to attacks on Republicans, the issue of the Negro replaced the usual appeals in a presidential year to elect the top of the ticket.[97] In fact there is no better example of the attachment of the Democracy to the Negro than Maryland's 1868 campaign. In the words of the political satirist Petroleum Nasby, "the Democracy coodent git along without the nigger."[98] Anxious Republicans, divided on their own position on the Negro's future, complained that "if you take the nigger out of a Democratic speech, there is very little remaining."[99]

Only occasionally did Democrats introduce financial issues into the canvass. While some compared ubiquitous Republican tax collectors to the seventeen-year locusts currently ravaging the state, most

[94]Denton *Journal*, May 30, October 24, 1868. Democrats also accused the Republicans of hypocrisy. In a reference to that party's national plank on Negro suffrage which stated that in loyal states suffrage was a state matter but in the South a matter of guarantee by Congress, the *Beacon* wondered "what party forces Negro voting in the South, but is silent on the issue in the North." *St. Mary's Beacon* (Leonardtown), October 29, 1868.

[95]Cumberland *Alleganian*, November 6, 1868.

[96]*Ibid.*, October 23, 1868.

[97]I studied the partisan appeals in ten speeches given by Democrats during the campaign. Almost 40 percent of the content of these speeches was devoted to attacks on Republicans, Congress, and "Radical Reconstruction"; 28 percent to issues relating to Negroes; 15 percent to pleas to vote for Seymour and Democratic congressional candidates; 11 percent to financial issues; and 7 percent to miscellaneous topics.

[98]Locke, *Petroleum Nasby*, p. 483. Also quoted in the Baltimore *American*, January 24, October 29, 1868.

[99]*Cecil Whig* (Elkton), November 1, 1868.

candidates paid very little attention to gold prices, greenbacks, and redemption. Partly the result of an ambiguous national platform which accepted greenbacks where coin was not legally specified and partly the result of attention given more emotional issues, the avoidance of financial concerns permitted Democrats the luxury of campaigning without taking a specific position on potentially divisive economic issues.

The results of the 1868 election surprised no one. Democrats swept every county and added Maryland to the seven states Seymour won. The autonomous state party showed little chagrin at this national defeat, noting instead that the border states had remained loyal to the Democracy. It was enough to control Maryland and elect five congressmen. "Thank God," wrote one relieved Democrat, "old Maryland is all right."[100]

With statewide support, Seymour carried some of the traditional Unionist counties of the northwest. In southern Maryland and the Eastern Shore, Democrats gained over 80 percent of the vote, in Baltimore 70 percent.[101] Disciplined Democrats refused to split their tickets, and even the political renegade Thomas Swann, a congressional candidate, received only 7 percent fewer votes than Seymour. Because many former Unionists, particularly in Baltimore and the northwestern counties, refused to vote, only 80 percent of the registered voters actually cast ballots.

The Democratic victory in 1868 revealed the loyalty most Marylanders felt toward the political party which had controlled their state before the war. The war years had done nothing to shake this firm allegiance. Party leaders successfully cultivated such fidelity by adopting political patterns of the past. Thus local machines stimulated partisan activity by their continuing use of familiar appeals and tactics.

[100]Jonathan Norris to Harry Norris, November 7, 1868, Norris Papers.

[101]Correlations, on a county-by-county basis, reveal the consistent pattern of Maryland politics. There is a high correlation between the Democratic presidential vote in 1868 and the Democratic gubernatorial vote of 1867 (+.8496), the congressional vote of 1866 (+.7654), the presidential vote of 1864 (+.5938), and the 1860 Democratic vote for President (Breckinridge and Douglas) (+.5192). Correlations, on a county-by-county basis, also reveal that there were other areas just as consistently anti-Democratic. On a county-by-county basis there are positive correlations between the vote for Grant in 1868 and the Unionist vote for Bradford in 1861 (+.7381), the Unionist vote for Congress in 1861 (+.8146), the Unionist vote for the 1863 legislature (+.6491), the vote for Lincoln in 1864 (+.7563), the vote for Swann in 1864 (+.6423), the vote for Unionist Comptroller in 1864 (+.9389), and the vote for Bond in 1867 (+.9443). There were approximately 145,000 white Marylanders over 21 in 1868; 114,732 of these were registered, and 92,806 voted in the election of 1868. Baltimore *American*, November 19, 1868.

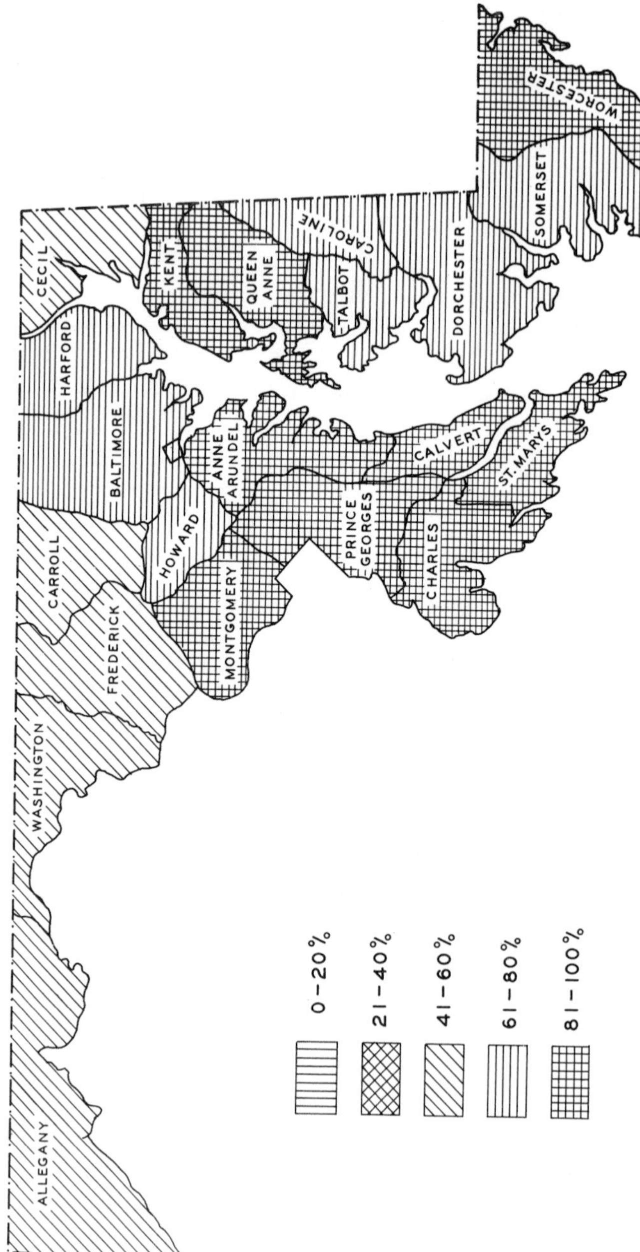

Map 4. *Geographic Distribution of the Democratic Vote for President in 1868*
Note: Wicomico = the county formed from Somerset and Worcester = 75% Democratic

Avoiding divisive problems, Democrats focused on the staples of past campaigns—the Negro, Constitution and Union, and the political opposition. In both the Constitutional Convention and the legislature, Democrats adhered closely to this same strategy. By 1868 the politics of the past had become, for Maryland, the politics of the future.

EPILOGUE

ITS PARTISAN FUTURE RESOLVED, Maryland life settled into predictable social and economic patterns. The war had done little to change politics and had not dramatically affected the demographic characteristics of a state small in size but still great in diversity. State population had increased 13 percent in the decade 1860-70,[1] with Baltimore and the northwestern counties accounting for most of the gain. The population of the tidewater counties remained almost stationary, and in some cases actually declined, as Negroes continued to move away from southern Maryland and the Eastern Shore. Many of these freedmen came to Baltimore, and the city's population consequently grew, as it had in previous decades, by nearly 20 percent. Several Baltimore wards, particularly those near the shipyards and city docks, quadrupled their black population, with the Ninth Ward experiencing a phenomenal 500 percent increase in the number of Negroes within its boundaries. Yet Baltimore still contained roughly the same proportion—one-third—of Maryland citizens as before the war and experienced little change in the racial and ethnic composition of its population.

Maryland's black population remained remarkably stable during the decade. In 1870 Negroes accounted for 22 percent of the state's total population, compared to 24 percent before the war. Despite the turmoil of emancipation and Reconstruction, six out of every ten Negroes still lived in the tidewater counties of southern Maryland and the Eastern Shore, and another two of every ten in Baltimore.

Manufacturing, industry, and commerce continued to center in Baltimore and the northwest, and in 1870, over 90 percent of the state's annual industrial production came from the region north of the Patuxent River, and nearly 75 percent from Baltimore city. This was the same proportion as before the war, and while the value of manufactured goods increased during the decade, the type of goods produced changed little. Thus iron foundries, flour and sugar mills, and clothing, cotton, and shoe factories still accounted for the bulk of the state's annual production.

Most Marylanders were still farmers, and the state's important cash crops continued to be tobacco, wheat, corn, and dairy products. While the typical Maryland farm was, as it had been in 1860, between 150 and 200 acres, the worth of these farms, the amount of land

[1]The following statistics are based on *The Statistics of the United States*, Ninth Census (Washington, D.C.: Government Printing Office, 1872).

under cultivation, and the value of the annual agricultural produce had increased, but at a decadal rate consonant with past growth.

If work was much the same as it had been in the past, so too were the favored recreations of Marylanders. Tournaments had survived the war and these popular affairs—symptomatic, according to a modern author, of a society with "a dislike of the present, and the here, and a yearning for the past and the elsewhere"[2]—flourished as costumed knights armed with lance and shield still competed in southern Maryland, the Eastern Shore, and some northern counties as well. In 1869, the Maryland Club baseball team, self-designated champion of the South, looked forward to competition with northern rivals. Farmers from the entire state still flocked to the livestock and agricultural displays of the Maryland Fair, a tradition since 1848, and in 1869, Walter W. Bowie, a cousin of Governor Bowie, compared the fair to a "brilliant panorama of the past. I feel like a traveler from a far country returned to the dearly loved home-scenes of my boyhood."[3] The German community continued to organize its popular Schuetzen—or riflery exhibitions—and for other Marylanders there were camp meetings, strawberry festivals, and the theater in Baltimore.

For those Marylanders who found politics a diversion, the state's political patterns seemed altogether viscous and immovable. As leaders of both parties agreed, only interference by Congress or passage of an amendment giving Negroes the vote could improve the fortunes of Republicans or diminish the control of Democrats. For Francis Thomas, the state's only Republican congressman and a lame duck by 1869, interference by Congress was essential if his party was even to survive. To encourage recalcitrant colleagues, Thomas presented endless petitions from Marylanders asking Congress "to adopt measures . . . by special legislation or by constitutional amendment to give to the people of the state a republican form of government."[4] Yet Congress showed little interest in undertaking such a policy. Most southern states had rewritten their Constitutions, and by 1869, seven of the eleven former Confederate states had satisfied requirements for readmission to Congress. There seemed little excuse for including

[2] Rollin G. Osterweis, *Romanticism and Nationalism in the Old South* (New Haven: Yale University Press, 1949), p. 15. For a description of one such tournament on Alexander Brown's estate in Baltimore county, see the Baltimore *Sun*, October 2, 1869.

[3] Baltimore *Sun*, October 29, 1869.

[4] *Congressional Globe*, 40th Cong., 3rd sess., 1869, 40, pt. 1:59; pt. 2:588.

Maryland under the jurisdiction of laws adopted for the return of disloyal states to the Union.

Instead, Republican congressional strategy now focused on the passage of an amendment to enfranchise Negroes. Such an addition to the Constitution would have little effect on politics in the North, where there were few blacks, or in the South where Negroes, aided by congressional legislation, were already voting, but in the border states, the proposed Fifteenth Amendment might change the political control of states like Maryland, Delaware, Kentucky, and Missouri.[5] To anxious Republicans like Hugh Bond, the amendment seemed necessary to protect both Negro rights and Republican fortunes. Thus it was with high expectations that Republican conventions in 1868 and 1869 called for the passage of such an amendment.

Not all Maryland Republicans, however, were so enthusiastic. Fearing that the cultivation of Negro voting implied commitment to racial equality in a state where prejudices ran deep, political realists prophesied that the support of black male suffrage would drive white Marylanders into the Democratic party. Even sympathetic newspapers like Cumberland's *Civilian and Telegraph* remarked on the increasing racial animosities in their counties, and the *Cecil Whig* charged that Democrats manipulated the suffrage issue to embarrass Republicans.[6] John Creswell, intent on his personal struggle for a small Republican party based on national patronage, recognized the need to placate Negrophobic fears of Marylanders by supporting universal amnesty for all white Southerners. In a series of letters to former Governor Bradford, Creswell wrote that he hoped he and Bradford, who opposed black suffrage, "could cooperate heartily as we had in the beginning days of the war."[7] Other Republicans made clear that while they supported Negro suffrage, they did not "mean to say that all men should be equal in every respect, for nothing could make two men alike."[8]

[5] For a careful study of the Fifteenth Amendment, see William Gillette, *The Right to Vote: Politics and the Passage of the Fifteenth Amendment* (Baltimore: Johns Hopkins Press, 1965) and for its impact in one state, see Felice Bonadio, *North of Reconstruction: Ohio Politics, 1865-1870* (New York: New York University Press, 1970.)

[6] *Civilian Telegraph* (Cumberland), August 7, 1870; *Cecil Whig* (Elkton), July 2, 1870.

[7] "Notes on John Creswell and Hugh Bond," 1869; "Notes on Negro Suffrage," October 1870; William Thomson to Bradford, October 9, 1870; Bradford to Creswell, November 7, 1870; Creswell to Bradford, November 28, 1870; Bradford speech given at Frederick, n.d., Bradford Papers, MHS.

[8] Baltimore *Sun*, October 14, 1869.

By 1869, Creswell had won the contest for control of Maryland's Republican party, and Grant appointed supporters of the Postmaster General to what newspapers offhandedly described as "the fat positions." According to the *Sun*, "the Bond wing has been completely flaxed." A number of old political "warhorses," many former Know-Nothings like James Ridgely, John Longnecker, and Charles Fulton, took over the post-office and custom-house patronage. Only one Bond man, Henry Goldsborough, received a federal position, and his appointment came, as the *Sun* was careful to point out, through the influence of one of Grant's personal friends, and not Bond.[9]

To Maryland Negroes, fearful of Creswell and his intentions toward them, the Fifteenth Amendment was cause for hope. Excluded in 1867 from many Republican local conventions and still denied the franchise, Negroes met in conventions to urge passage of the amendment by Congress and its ratification by three-fourths of the state legislatures. Resolutions adopted by a meeting of "colored" Republicans at Baltimore's Douglass Institute specified that "in view of the expected passage of the Fifteenth Amendment to the Federal Constitution, convention calls should go forth for a state convention of colored men to further the political reorganization of the state and the appointment of a colored Republican state central committee to look after the political interest of our own race in the counties of the state."[10]

Such activity was statewide and largely self-initiated, although Democratic papers insisted that they detected the hand of white Republicans: "Night and day they have not relaxed their energies to instruct the Negroes in their duty to the Radical party and they have largely succeeded in inducing them to join clubs pledged to support Radical nominees."[11] Negro leaders, like Isaac Myers, the Baltimore caulker and labor leader, traveled throughout the state lecturing and organizing. Insistent that Negroes support the Bond faction of the Republican party and not accept positions under the national administration as "bootblacks and lackeys," black leaders demanded an equal voice in party affairs. A Negro from Annapolis, Daniel Draper, cautioned members of his race "to avoid the white Republican who would cordially take the hand of the colored man in the dark, but would refuse to recognize them in broad daylight." Echoing both fear

[9] *Ibid.*, April 9, 14, 1869.

[10] *Ibid.*, March 26, 1869.

[11] Margaret Callcott, *The Negro in Maryland Politics, 1870–1912* (Baltimore: Johns Hopkins Press, 1969), pp. 23–24.

of white purposes and recognition of Negro strength, a black physician, Dr. Henry Brown, pointed out that "the colored Republicans of Maryland, 40,000 strong, hold the rod over the head of 30,000 white Republicans and ere long they will wield their power."[12]

Such statistics frightened the state's powerful Democratic party. According to the Washington *Star*, "the Democracy of Maryland have been in some anxiety of mind lest under action of the Fifteenth Amendment, . . . their majority large as it has been, will be swamped. It is estimated that the Republican vote of the state, swelled by the new colored vote, will be at least 70,000. The democratic vote there last year was 62,000."[13] Such predictions were not lost on party leaders, who began a campaign to defeat Negro suffrage.

The most effective opponents of the Fifteenth Amendment were Maryland's Democratic senators and congressmen. In a long speech given on the floor of the Senate, George Vickers, a Democrat from the Eastern Shore, summed up his party's opposition. Arguing that the proposed amendment denied the constitutional privilege of states to run their own elections, Vickers insisted that "if states once surrender to Congress the right to control suffrage, they cease to be independent states." Such constitutional objections were secondary to the Senator's fear of black suffrage on racial grounds. Denying the Declaration of Independence was anything more than "abstract enunciations," Vickers lapsed into the harsh racism so pervasive in his native state:

> It is hardly magnanimous . . . to fix this law of suffrage upon those who do not desire it because this fragrant black race does not grow well in the frosty soil of New England nor in northern latitudes. This District [of Columbia] may be called the botanical political experimental garden. . . . [I wish] the two honorable Senators from Massachusetts were present also so that they might inhale the delightful odor. Such proximity in public conveyances is alike offensive to the taste, instinct, judgment, and olfactories of the citizens.

Vickers followed with a lesson in ethnography for his fellow senators. Concluding that mankind was indeed divided into distinct varieties and races, the senator maintained, as did his party, that "this was a white man's government."[14]

Such strongly held constitutional and racial objections did not completely obscure the partisan nature of Vickers' disapproval of the constitutional amendment. Pointing out the inconsistency of Republi-

[12] Baltimore *Sun*, June 2, 1869.

[13] Quoted in the Baltimore *Sun*, July 12, 1869.

[14] *Congressional Globe*, 40th Cong., 3rd sess. 1869, 40, pt. 2:905.

cans on black suffrage, Vickers pridefully acknowledged what Maryland Democrats had long known:

> . . . the Democratic party is not a progressive party because the Constitution is not progressive; the principles of the Constitution are now just as they were when they came from the hands of our fathers; they are plain, explicit, and well-defined; and a party which stands upon the Constitution cannot in relation to constitutional questions, be a progressive party.[15]

Such impassioned arguments were unavailing, and in late February, the Fifteenth Amendment passed Congress by the requisite two-thirds, Vickers and all the Maryland delegation, except Francis Thomas, voting nay.[16] Now the amendment went to the state legislatures, where the Democrats needed only ten states to defeat ratification.

Throughout 1869, Maryland newspaper nervously kept count of the number of states that ratified the amendment. There was, however, no doubt of the position the Maryland legislature would take, and in February 1870, the all-Democratic legislature rejected the Fifteenth Amendment, seventy-six against, and none in favor. Yet when it became obvious in the spring of 1870 that twenty-eight states would ratify and that Negro voting, buttressed by a federal enforcement act, would become a reality, the Democratic state central committee, in a dramatic and eminently practical reversal, supported a revised registration law that allowed Negro registration.[17] Such tactics foreshadowed the occasional Democratic strategy of appealing to the Negro vote.

The expectation of black voting also led to heightened racial animosity within the state. Even before the first Negro had voted, lynchings increased, and rumors of a Ku Klux Klan organization circulated throughout the state. Yet such extra-legal associations never had much impact in Maryland, and the reason was obvious. With the government firmly in the hands of Democratic "Bourbons"—so-called because their opponents accused them, as Napoleon did the French royal family, of neglecting present and future for the past—Maryland

[15] *Ibid.*

[16] For a detailed study of the process of ratification, see Gillette, *Right to Vote*, pp. 46–78, and the same author's "Anatomy of a Failure: Federal Enforcement of the Right to Vote in Border States," in *Radicalism, Racism and Party Realignment: The Border States during Reconstruction*, ed. Richard O. Curry (Baltimore: Johns Hopkins Press, 1969), pp. 265–304.

[17] Baltimore *American*, March 29, 1870.

was already redeemed by those who believed in a white man's government.[18]

On April 8, 1870, Elijah Quigley, a black man from Towson, placed his ballot in a Baltimore county voting box. It was fitting that this first Negro vote in sixty years should be cast in a local election for county commissioners.[19] By fall, a surprising number of Negroes—35,000—had registered for the congressional elections, and the full impact of black voting power was soon felt when several southern Maryland counties with heavy Negro populations went Republican. This election of 1870 ushered in a new era in state politics. For the remainder of the nineteenth century, Marylanders would confirm what one paper called "the lease of power which the Democratic party enjoys,"[20] but new concerns, new constituents, and even new ways of party organization would transform the "politics of continuity."

[18] *Easton Star*, June 16, 1868. A letter to Oden Bowie in the Executive Papers indicated that there were Klansmen near Hagerstown. [?] to Oden Bowie, April 4, 1871, Bowie Executive Papers, Hall of Records, Annapolis, Md.

[19] Callcott, *Negro in Maryland Politics*, p. 3; Chestertown *Transcript*, April 9, 1870.

[20] Baltimore *Sun*, November 6, 1869.

APPENDIXES

APPENDIX A

Relationships between Variables and Election Returns: Coefficients of Correlation

In this study the relationship between social and economic variables and voting returns by party on a county-by-county basis is given as a coefficient of correlation. A coefficient of correlation of +1.00 indicates a perfect direct relationship. A coefficient of −1.00 indicates a perfect inverse relationship. Significant relationships are indicated when the coefficient is greater than plus or minus .50. The Pearson product-moment formula is used here to calculate the coefficients of correlation. The formula is:

$$R = \frac{N(\text{sum of } xy) - (\text{sum of } y)(\text{sum of } x)}{\sqrt{N(\text{sum of } x^2) - (\text{sum of } x)^2}\ \sqrt{N(\text{sum of } y^2) - (\text{sum of } y)^2}}$$

where R is the coefficient of correlation, x is the deviation from the average in one variable, y is the deviation from the average in the other variable, and N is the number of cases. Unless otherwise noted, the correlations in this study are based on percentages, rather than raw figures, of election returns and social and economic data from counties and Baltimore city. Despite the desirability of studying smaller units, it is impossible to find social and economic information for election districts or wards, except for those from Baltimore in the 1850s.

Correlations can only suggest possible relationships between social variables and election returns; they do not reveal causal connections or linear relationships. As W. S. Robinson and more recently Walter Burnham have pointed out, ecological correlations must be used with caution. Nonetheless, this statistical tool remains useful in pointing out factors involved in voting behavior which other nonstatistical methods overlook, and in the case of Maryland politics, coefficients substantiate relationships apparent from other sources. See Walter Dean Burnham, "Quantitative History: Beyond the Correlation Coefficient; A Review Essay," *Historical Methods Newsletter* 4 (March 1971): 62-66.

APPENDIX B

Roll-Call Analysis

Throughout I have used the following criteria for the selection of roll calls: (1) the degree of participation. Two-thirds of the Maryland House of Delegates had to vote on the roll call for it to be included. (2) Important issues as determined by contemporary interest. Thus roll calls debated in the daily and weekly press were included. I then established various substantive categories such as economic, procedural, and sumptuary roll calls and chose a similar number of roll calls for each category in each legislature. Obviously, I am less interested in the abstract figures—that is, the fact that the index of cohesion in 1860 among Eastern Shore delegates was 65—than I am in the comparison of this figure with earlier and later legislatures.

I have also used the index of likeness as a measure of inter-party difference. This index measures the difference between two groups in their response to a roll call and is the complement of the difference between the percentage voting "yes" in two parties measured on a scale from zero to one hundred.

First developed by Stuart Rice in the 1920s, roll-call analysis has been used by numerous political scientists and historians including Julius Turner in *Party and Constituency: Pressures on Congress*, rev. Ed. (Baltimore: Johns Hopkins Press, 1970), and more recently, Joel Silbey in *The Shrine of Party: Congressional Voting Behavior, 1841-1852* (Pittsburgh: University of Pittsburgh Press, 1967). As with any such quantitative technique, there are dangers in depending too heavily on roll-call analysis. The technique should, I believe, be used over a period of time to diminish the possibility of distortion in the selection of roll calls.

APPENDIX C

Explanation of Cluster Bloc Analysis

Cluster bloc or pair agreement analysis was first described by Stuart Rice in the 1920s. It has not been widely used because of the amount of labor involved, but now the use of computers reduces this labor and makes such analysis feasible. Using a program developed by Jim Nathanson of the Johns Hopkins University Computer Center, I was able to compare the voting records of legislators in each Assembly from 1858 to 1870. The essential data in cluster bloc analysis are the percentages of agreement on roll calls, and the purpose of the scores is to measure the amount of agreement between legislators. Such a technique helps to reveal party cohesiveness as well as the existence of blocs within a party.

Roll-Call Number	1	2	3	4	5
Henry Stockbridge	Y	A	N	Y	A
Dennis Claude	N	N	N	Y	A

Voting Key: Y = yea; N = nay; A = absent
Pair agreement = 2/5 = 40%

For another example of the use of this technique see Allan Bogue, "Bloc and Party in the U.S. Senate: 1861-1863," *Civil War History* 13 (1967): 221-41.

APPENDIX D
Tables

APPENDIX D

Table D-1
Average Index of Cohesion on 48 Selected Roll Calls in Legislatures, 1858-1867

Regions and parties	1858	1860	1861	1862	1864	1865	1867
Northern and western counties	66	60	58	66	58	61	60
Eastern Shore	67	65	60	64	64	66	77
Southern Maryland	64	70	77	75	74	85	80
Baltimore	60	68	93	60	69	72	71
Democratic party	73	75	77	80	86	86	85
Know-Nothing party	74	70	73				
Union party				72	70	68	85

Note: Because of the criteria used in the selection of roll calls, these indexes of cohesion are not necessarily a good indication of party behavior within the entire legislative session, and they should not be compared to figures for other legislatures or Congress. A random sample of roll calls would have produced even higher indexes of cohesion (and higher indexes of party likeness). The significance of these figures lies in their comparative statement about the regional and political behavior of legislators over a period of time.

Table D-2
Age of 106 Democratic and 95 Know-Nothing Leaders in 1859

Age	Democrats	Know-Nothings
20-29	12	7
30-39	29	12
40-49	23	13
50-59	19	31
60-69	2	21
Over 70	3	1
Unknown	18	10

Sources: Manuscript Census Returns, Maryland, Eighth Census, 1860, National Archives, Washington, D.C.; newspapers, biographical dictionaries, and the Dielman File, MHS.

Note: Leaders chosen in both parties held elective and appointive offices, and thus include congressmen, state officials, and delegates as well as members of the state and county central committees. The holders of important patronage jobs, such as the collector of customs and the manager of the post office in Baltimore, are included in the sample.

Table D-3
Property of 106 Democrats and 95 Know-Nothing Leaders in 1859

Value of Property	Democrats	Know-Nothings
$ 0-$ 1,999	3	4
2,000- 4,999	6	12
5,000- 13,999	11	16
14,000- 19,999	19	16
20,000- 39,999	21	18
40,000- 49,999	13	9
Over $50,000	15	10
Unknown	18	10

Sources: Same as those for Table D-2.
Note: Sample is same as that in Table D-2.

Table D-4
Slaveholding among 106 Democratic and 95 Know-Nothing Leaders in 1859

Number of Slaves	Democrats	Know-Nothings
1-4	8	9
5-9	12	4
10-19	9	0
20-49	3	3
50-100	4	0
Over 100	2	0
Unknown or having no slaves	68	79

Sources: Same as those for Table D-2.
Note: Sample is same as that in Table D-2.

Table D-5
Occupations of 106 Democratic and 95 Know-Nothing Leaders in 1859

Occupation	Democrats	Know-Nothings
Farmer	25	20
Planter[a]	13	2
Lawyer	25	18
Merchant-Shopkeeper	3	11
Physician	9	7
Mechanic	5	6
Manufacturer	6	10
Miller	0	3
Miscellaneous	2	8
Unknown	18	10

Sources: Same as those for Table D–2.

Note: Sample is same as that in Table D–2.

[a]The term "planter" usually refers to owners of large tobacco farms. Occasionally it was used by the owners of large holdings who did not grow tobacco, and it seems to be a self-conferred title, particularly popular among southern Marylanders and residents of the Eastern Shore.

Table D-6

Cluster Bloc Analysis on 49 Roll Calls in the Special Session of the Legislature, 1861

	Brune	War-field	Pitts	Harri-son	Thom-as	Wallis	Scott	Sangs-ton	Winans	Morfit	Kessler	Brining	Ford	Bryan	Durant	Morgan	Chap-lin	Coudy
Brune[a]		100	100	100	97	98	98	97	100	97	80	75	87	98	99	98	80	77
Warfield[a]			100	100	97	98	98	97	99	97	85	76	88	95	99	98	80	77
Pitts[a]				100	97	98	98	97	99	98	83	78	81	96	99	98	80	77
Harrison[a]					100	98	98	97	99	98	80	75	87	98	99	98	80	77
Thomas[a]						99	97	98	92	90	88	77	84	80	96	97	78	60
Wallis[a]							93	100	95	93	84	78	76	87	88	92	87	76
Scott[a]								98	95	96	88	68	86	91	93	89	89	75
Sangston[a]									95	94	90	70	83	87	86	90	67	77
Winans[a]										98	78	63	83	90	91	93	80	78
Morfit[a]											86	79	81	90	89	91	78	73
Kessler[b]												89	90	78	75	83	87	78
Brining[b]													90	81	75	81	86	82
Ford[b]														69	80	75	75	80
Bryan[c]															86	65	70	50
Durant[c]																96	88	85
Morgan[c]																	80	90
Chaplin[d]																		57
Coudy[d]																		

Source: Journal of the Proceedings of the House of Delegates, Extra Session, 1861 (Frederick: Elihu Riley, 1861).

Note: This analysis reveals the agreement scores of Baltimore legislators among themselves and with Democratic representatives from other sections. The agreement scores between the Baltimore legislators were considerably higher than those among other legislators, including those from southern Maryland.

[a]Baltimore legislator.

[b]Legislator from northern or western Maryland.

[c]Legislator from southern Maryland.

[d]Legislator from the Eastern Shore.

Table D-7
Age of 85 Unionist and 60 States' Rights Leaders in 1861

Age	Unionists	States' Rights
20-29	6	2
30-39	18	5
40-49	25	16
50-59	16	16
60-69	7	11
70-79	1	2
Unknown	12	8

Sources: Same as those for Table D-2.
Note: Leaders include members of the state central committee and county executive committees.

Table D-8
Property of 85 Unionist and 60 States' Rights Leaders in 1861

Value of Property	Unionists	States' Rights
$ 0-$ 1,999	6	2
2,000- 4,999	8	4
5,000- 13,999	12	7
14,000- 19,999	26	13
20,000- 39,999	9	12
40,000- 49,999	5	9
Over $50,000	7	5
Unknown	12	8

Sources: Same as those for Table D-2.
Note: Sample is same as that in Table D-7.

Table D-9
Slaveholding among 85 Unionist and 60 States' Rights Leaders in 1861

Number of Slaves	Unionists	States' Rights
1-4	6	9
5-9	4	12
10-19	4	6
20-49	0	5
50-99	1	5
100-499	1	3
Over 500	0	0
Unknown or having no slaves	69	20

Sources: Same as those for Table D-2.
Note: Sample is same as that in Table D-7.

Table D-10
Occupations of 85 Unionist and 60 States' Rights Leaders in 1861

Occupation	Unionists	States' Right
Farmer	13	14
Planter	2	8
Lawyer	18	11
Merchant-Shopkeeper	13	5
Physician	5	5
Clerk	4	2
Businessman	11	3
Newspaper editor	3	2
No occupation	4	2
Unknown	12	8

Sources: Same as those for Table D-2.
Note: Sample is same as that in Table D-7.

Table D-11
Age of 45 Unconditional Unionist and 44 Conservative Unionist Leaders in 1863

Age	Unconditional Unionists	Conservative Unionists
20-29	6	3
30-39	10	6
40-49	9	10
50-59	12	15
60-69	7	8
70-79	1	2

Sources: Same as those for Table D-2.

Note: Sample is based on the state central committees of the two factions in 1863. Both committees had 50 members, although I found information on only 45 Unconditional Unionists and 44 Conservative Unionists.

Table D-12
Property of 45 Unconditional Unionist and 44 Conservative Unionist Leaders in 1863

Value of Property	Unconditional Unionists	Conservative Unionists
$ 0-$ 1,999	3	2
2,000- 4,999	5	4
5,000- 13,999	13	12
14,000- 19,999	13	13
20,000- 39,999	7	10
40,000- 49,999	3	2
Over $50,000	1	1

Sources: Same as those for Table D-2.
Note: Sample is same as that in Table D-11.

Table D-13
Slaveholding among 45 Unconditional Unionist and 44 Conservative Unionist Leaders in 1863

Number of Slaves	Unconditional Unionists	Conservative Unionists
1-4	2	1
5-9	6	4
10-19	3	5
20-49	1	4
50-99	0	2
Over 99	0	0
Unknown or having no slaves	33	28

Sources: Same as those for Table D-2.
Note: Sample is same as that in Table D-11.

Table D-14
Eleven Democratic and Unionist Delegates' Percent Agreement Scores on 48 Roll Calls in the 1864 Legislature

	Westcott	Tolsen	Biggs	Trail	Stockbridge	Boswell	Carrico	Claude	Iglehart	Fawcett	Handy
(U) Westcott											
(U) Tolsen	76										
(U) Biggs	77	48									
(U) Trail	88	65	97								
(U) Stockbridge	70	64	85	85							
(U) Boswell	74	61	75	82	78						
(D) Carrico	33	20	24	27	24	11					
(D) Claude	35	47	13	25	19	19	97				
(D) Iglehart	43	71	25	32	31	18	96	93			
(D) Fawcett	46	71	25	25	28	34	89	96	86		
(D) Handy	45	65	26	36	30	38	93	95	93	81	

Source: Journal of the Proceedings of the House of Delegates, 1864 (Annapolis: Richard P. Bayley, 1864).
Note: Legislators were chosen at random. (U) designates a Unionist; (D), a Democrat. Both Westcott and Tolsen were identified by the press as Conservative Unionists.

Table D-15
Prewar Political Allegiance of 106 Democratic Leaders in 1866

Democrats	Unknown	Know-Nothings
67	36	3

Sources: Manuscript Census Returns, Ninth Census, 1870, Maryland, National Archives, Washington, D.C.; newspapers, biographical dictionaries, and the Dielman File, MHS.

Note: Leaders include members of the state central committee, elected representatives in Congress and the state legislature, and members of county executive committees.

Table D-16
Property of 106 Democratic Leaders in 1866

Value of Property	Democrats
$ 0-$ 1,999	3
2,000- 4,999	13
5,000- 13,999	23
14,000- 19,999	38
20,000- 39,999	10
40,000- 49,999	4
Over $50,000	3
Unknown	12

Sources: Same as those for Table D-15.
Note: Sample is same as that in Table D-15.

Table D-17
Occupations of 106 Democratic Leaders in 1866

Occupation	Democrats
Farmer	23
Planter[a]	10
Lawyer	14
Merchant-Shopkeeper	5
Attorney	3
Physician	6
Clerk	5
Businessman	6
Blue Collar[b]	7
Educator	1
Sheriff	1
Newspaper editor	3
Mechanic	4
Military	2
No Occupation	4
Unknown	12

Sources: Same as those for Table D-15.

Note: Sample is same as that in Table D-15.

[a]The distinction between planter and farmer is not explained in the Manuscript Census.

[b]The blue-collar category, while an anachronistic term, describes a hatter, master carver, barber, and four clerks.

Table D-18
Cluster Bloc Analysis Revealing Agreement Scores among 3 Unionists, 5 Conservatives, and 5 Democrats on 48 Roll Calls in the 1867 Legislature

	McCulley	Baker	Buhrman	Ford	Boswell	Evans	Kerr	Turner	Miller	Hammond	Knott	Horsey	Jump
(U) McCulley													
(U) Baker	93												
(U) Buhrman	93	100											
(C) Ford	43	34	38										
(C) Boswell	46	36	33	81									
(C) Evans	38	30	31	65	72								
(C) Kerr	36	27	25	72	87	70							
(C) Turner	46	29	28	88	92	61	93						
(D) Miller	42	35	36	90	88	72	81	59					
(D) Hammond	51	32	41	85	94	76	88	93	85				
(D) Knott	35	21	25	90	89	70	99	93	85	89			
(D) Horsey	26	27	26	81	91	80	99	82	81	80	90		
(D) Jump	50	29	33	87	80	73	84	92	93	89	93	92	

Source: Journal of the Proceedings of the House of Delegates, 1867 (Annapolis, Henry A. Lucas, 1867).

Note: (U) designates a Unionist; (C), a Conservative; (D), a Democrat.

The five "Conservatives" were chosen because they were identified in the press as Conservative leaders who joined Democrats in 1867. Other legislators were chosen at random from the Unionist and Democratic parties.

Table D-19
Age of 106 Democratic and 100 Republican Leaders in 1868

Age	Democrats	Republicans
20–29	7	16
30–39	10	30
40–49	15	24
50–59	22	8
60–69	34	9
70–79	6	5
Unknown	12	8

Sources: Same as those for Table D-15.

Note: Leaders include elected officials in 1867–68 (congressmen, senators, state legislators, etc.) and members of county or state executive committees in 1867–68.

Table D-20
Property of 106 Democratic and 100 Republican Leaders in 1868

Value of Property	Democrats	Republicans
$ 0–$ 1,999	3	1
2,000– 4,999	17	16
5,000– 13,999	26	28
14,000– 19,999	26	25
20,000– 39,999	18	11
40,000– 49,999	3	8
Over $50,000	1	3
Unknown	12	8

Sources: Same as those for Table D–15.
Note: Sample is same as that for Table D–19.

Table D-21
Occupations of 106 Democratic and 100 Republican Leaders in 1868

Occupation	Democrats	Republicans
Farmer	23	20
Planter	10	5
Lawyer	15	18
Merchant-Shopkeeper	5	8
Attorney	3	5
Physician	6	7
Clerk	5	6
Businessman	6	9
Blue Collar	7	6
Newspaper editor	3	4
Mechanic	4	1
Military	3	0
No Occupation	4	3
Unknown	12	8

Sources: Same as those for Table D–15.
Note: Sample is same as that for Table D–19.

BIBLIOGRAPHICAL ESSAY

Manuscript Collections

Lacking the manuscript collections available in other states, historians have neglected Maryland. In place of extensive collections of private papers elsewhere, the Maryland historian finds frequent mention of hurried trips to Washington—which vitiated any need for correspondence—as well as occasional talk of papers purposefully destroyed during the Civil War (as in the case of William Preston). Furthermore, a number of family papers are still privately owned and access to them is difficult.

The most important papers for the purposes of this study were those of the Maryland governors of the period—Thomas Hicks, Augustus Bradford, Thomas Swann, and Oden Bowie. While the executive papers of these men are in the Hall of Records, Annapolis, some of the private correspondence of the first three is in the Maryland Historical Society; in the case of Thomas Swann, both public and private papers are privately owned. Other important collections are those of William Preston, the Glenn family, Samuel Harrison, James Pearce, Reverdy Johnson, Brantz Mayer, Benjamin Howard, Harry Norris, Hugh Bond, and John Thomas in the Maryland Historical Society; the Simon Gratz and Samuel P. Chase papers in the Historical Society of Pennsylvania; the Robert Todd Lincoln Collection of Abraham Lincoln Papers and the papers of Andrew Johnson, Ulysses Grant, Montgomery Blair, John A. J. Creswell, and Edward McPherson in the Library of Congress; the Blair-Lee Collection in the Princeton University Library, as well as the letters of Montgomery Blair to Samuel Barlow in the Henry E. Huntington Library, San Marino, California; and the letters of Henry Winter Davis in the Samuel Francis Du Pont Papers in the Eleutherian Mills Historical Library, Wilmington, Delaware. There are important collections which relate to Maryland politics in the Southern Historical Collection in the University of North Carolina Library, the Duke University Library, and the University of Virginia Library. The John P. Kennedy Papers in the Peabody Library, Baltimore, Maryland are also a rich manuscript source for understanding the politics of the 1850s and 1860s.

Official Documents and Statistical Sources

To some extent, official documents can be used to supplement meager manuscript collections. Among those used for this study are the *Congressional Globe*, the Manuscript Census Returns of the Eighth and Ninth Censuses, as well as various official compendiums of the censuses such as Joseph C. G. Kennedy's *Preliminary Report on the Eighth Census, 1860* (Washington, D.C.: Government Printing Office, 1862), and R. S. Fisher, *Gazetteer of the State of Maryland, Returns of the 7th Census of the United States* (Baltimore: J. S. Waters, 1852). Both the House and Senate of the Maryland legislature published a *Journal* of their proceedings for every session as well as a volume of *Documents* relevant to the session. This *Journal* does not include the debates on various bills, although it does provide the voting record of delegates on roll calls. *The Proceedings and Debates of the Constitutional Convention of 1864* are very complete, as are some county records such as "The Minutes of the Meetings of the County Commissioners," the latter usually found in the county courthouses throughout the state. Official communications of the governors are in the Executive Letterbooks at the Hall of Records, although Swann's Letterbooks are still privately owned. Official election returns are also in the governor's papers, and I have used these returns for my statistical tabulations. I have also used the U.S. Department of Interior's biennial guide to federal employees called the *United States Official Register* for 1859, 1861, 1864, 1867, and 1869 (Washington, D.C.: Government Printing Office), the *War of the Rebellion: A Compilation of the Official Records of the Union and Confederate Armies* (128 vols.; Washington, D.C.: Government Printing Office, 1880-1901), and the Letters of Application and Recommendation, which are on microfilm in the Department of State records in the National Archives. There are other important papers relating to Maryland in the National Archives. Among them are the Maryland Investigation, Papers of the House of Representatives, 1867 (Record Group 233); the Middle Department, U.S. Army Commands (Record Group 98); Papers of Henry Warfield and the Baltimore *Daily Exchange* in the Civil War Papers (Record Group 59), and the extensive Freedmen's Bureau Records (Record Group 105), all in the National Archives.

Newspapers

It has become fashionable to deride newspapers as historical sources, and in many cases they are indeed inaccurate and misleading. Yet without the newspaper, the Maryland historian would lack an essential guide to the history of the nineteenth century. In Baltimore, there were four important dailies during the 1860s—the *Sun*, *Daily*

Gazette, American, and *Clipper*. Each Maryland county was served by at least one weekly newspaper. Although there are incomplete files of some of these papers, many of them served as useful sources, especially the *Cecil Whig* and *Cecil Democrat* (Elkton), the Chestertown *Transcript*, the *Southern Aegis* (Bel Air), the Port Tobacco *Times*, the Frederick *Examiner* and *Herald*, the *St. Mary's Beacon* and *St. Mary's Gazette* (Leonardtown), the *Baltimore County Advocate* (Towson), and the *Mountain Valley Register* (Middletown). I have supplemented these papers with readings from the New York *World* and *Herald* and the two German language dailies published in Baltimore, *Der Deutsche Correspondent* and *Baltimore Wecker.*

Local Histories

Although local and county histories are numerous, they frequently reflect specialized genealogical and antiquarian interests. Among the best are J. Thomas Scharf, *History of Maryland from the Earliest Period to the Present Day*, 3 vols. (1879; reprint ed., Hatboro, Pa.: Tradition Press, 1967) and Matthew Page Andrews, *History of Maryland: Province and State* (1929; reprint ed., Hatboro, Pa.: Tradition Press, 1965). Both Scharf and Andrews are classic examples of the pro-Democratic, anti-Republican political bias which pervades most of the writing on Maryland during the Civil War and Reconstruction periods. Every Maryland county has a history, and there are several of Baltimore City. I found the most useful to be J. Thomas Scharf, *History of Baltimore City and County* (Philadelphia: J. H. Everts, 1884), and his *History of Western Maryland* (Philadelphia: L. H. Everts, 1882); Will H. Lowdermilk, *History of Cumberland* (Washington, D.C.: J. Anglim, 1878), and Thomas J. C. Williams, *History of Frederick County, Maryland* (Frederick: L. K. Titsworth & Co., 1910) and his *History of Washington County* (Chambersburg, Pa.: J. M. Runk and L. R. Titsworth, 1906). The Williams history of Frederick and Washington counties includes biographical information on prominent citizens which I wish was available for other counties.

There are a variety of descriptive accounts, mainly travelers' reminiscences, relevant to the mid-nineteenth century. See Ralph Semmes, *Baltimore as Seen by Visitors, 1783-1860* (Baltimore: Maryland Historical Society, 1953); "A Maryland Tour in 1844, Diary of Isaac Van Bibber," *Maryland Historical Magazine* 39 (1944): 237-68; and Henry Stockbridge, "Baltimore in 1846," *Maryland Historical Magazine* 6 (1911): 20-34.

Biographies

Like the general history of their state, individual Marylanders have also been neglected. Bernard C. Steiner's *Life of Henry Winter Davis* (Baltimore: John Murphy & Co., 1916) is badly outdated, but there are two studies currently in progress which will undoubtedly fill the gap in our understanding of the Baltimore congressman. Steiner also served as the biographer of *Reverdy Johnson* (Baltimore: Norman, Remington Co., 1914), but any future biographers of Johnson will undoubtedly hesitate before undertaking the study of a man with one of the more illegible hands in American history. The most notable studies of individual Marylanders include Philip Bohner, *John Pendleton Kennedy, Gentleman from Baltimore* (Baltimore: Johns Hopkins Press, 1961); Carl Brent Swisher, *Roger B. Taney* (New York: Macmillan Co., 1936); Samuel Tyler, *Memoir of Roger Brooke Taney* (Baltimore: John Murphy & Co., 1872); Walker Lewis, *Without Fear or Favor: A Biography of Chief Justice Roger Brooke Taney* (Boston: Houghton Mifflin, 1965); and William E. Smith's magisterial *The Francis Preston Blair Family in Politics* (New York: Macmillan Co., 1933). It is worth noting that there are no biographies of Maryland governors during the period, although George Radcliffe has done a careful job on Thomas Hicks during the secession crisis in his *Governor Thomas H. Hicks of Maryland and the Civil War*, Johns Hopkins University Studies in Historical and Political Science, ser. 19 (Baltimore: Johns Hopkins Press, 1901). The most helpful unpublished works are Elizabeth M. Grimes, "John Angel James Creswell" (master's thesis, Department of History, Columbia University, 1939); Michael Catherine Hodgson, Sr., "The Political Career of John Angel James Creswell" (master's thesis, Department of History, Catholic University, 1951); Mary Agnes Kelly, C.D.P., "Montgomery Blair, Postmaster General in the Cabinet of Abraham Lincoln" (master's thesis, Catholic University, 1956); and Nancy Miller, "Thomas Swann: Political Acrobat" (master's thesis, Virginia Polytechnic Institute, 1969). The *Maryland Historical Magazine* has printed a number of short articles on prominent Marylanders, including Bernard Steiner's "Brantz Mayer" 5 (1910): 1-18, and the same author's "James Alfred Pearce" 16 (1921): 319; 17 (1922): 33-177, 269, 348; 19 (1923): 13, 162.

For capsule biographies of prominent Marylanders there are a number of biographical directories. The most complete are *The Biographical Cyclopaedia of Representative Men of Maryland and the*

District of Columbia (Baltimore: National Biographical Publishing Co., 1879); Heinrich E. Bucholz, *Governors of Maryland* (Baltimore: William and Wilkins, 1908); and Wilbur F. Coyle, *The Mayors of Baltimore* (reprinted from the Baltimore Municipal Journal in book form, 1919). I have also used various Baltimore City registers to supplement these directories, and I have found the Dielman File at the Maryland Historical Society, a vertical file of newspaper clippings on prominent Marylanders, extremely helpful in the task of amassing biographical information about political leaders.

Master's Theses and Dissertations

There are a number of excellent unpublished theses and dissertations that relate to Maryland history. Among them are Richard Fuke, "The Breakup of the Union Party" (master's thesis, University of Maryland, 1965), a careful study of the disruption of the Union party after the war; William Evitts, "A Matter of Allegiances, Maryland from 1850 to 1861" (Ph.D. diss., Johns Hopkins University, 1971); William Catton, "The Baltimore Business Community and the Secession Crisis, 1860-1861" (master's thesis, University of Maryland, 1952), and the same author's *John W. Garrett of the Baltimore and Ohio: A Study in Seaport and Railroad Competition, 1820-1874* (Ann Arbor, Mich.: University Microfilms, 1959); John Stabler's tedious but exhaustive study of "The Constitutional Union Party: A Tragic Failure" (Ph.D. diss., Columbia University, 1954); Charles Clark, "Maryland Politics during the Civil War" (Ph.D. diss., University of North Carolina, 1940); and finally Milton L. Henry, "Henry Winter Davis" (Ph.D. diss., Louisiana State University, 1972).

Recent Histories of Maryland

There are several recent studies of Maryland history which deserve mention. First, Charles Wagandt's *The Mighty Revolution: Negro Emancipation in Maryland, 1862-1864* (Baltimore: Johns Hopkins Press, 1964) is a lively, descriptive account of how the slaves were freed in Maryland. Wagandt has recently completed a short narrative account of Maryland during Reconstruction published in Richard O. Curry, ed., *Radicalism, Racism and Party Realignment: The Border States during Reconstruction* (Baltimore: Johns Hopkins Press, 1969).

Wagandt deserves great credit for his discovery of a number of privately owned manuscript collections, which he ferreted out in some cases by completing the genealogy of various nineteenth-century leaders and calling on their descendants. Margaret Callcott's *The Negro in Maryland Politics, 1870-1912* (Baltimore: Johns Hopkins Press, 1969) is a careful study of black politics based largely on newspapers and statistics, and William Gillette's *The Right to Vote: Politics and the Passage of the Fifteenth Amendment* (Baltimore: Johns Hopkins Press, 1965) is an account of the process of ratification of the Fifteenth Amendment. William S. Myers has written two somewhat dated studies, one on the Constitution of 1864 and the other, *The Self-Reconstruction of Maryland, 1864-1867*, Johns Hopkins Studies in Historical and Political Science, ser. 27 (Baltimore: Johns Hopkins University Press, 1909). I have also found John and Lawanda Cox's study of *Politics, Principle and Prejudice, 1865-1866: Dilemma of Reconstruction America* (New York: Free Press of Glencoe, 1963), a great help in understanding Montgomery Blair's effort at forming a National Union Party.

Studies of Maryland Negroes

The state's Negroes have suffered the same scholarly neglect accorded almost every other area of Maryland history. There are two standard volumes, Jeffrey R. Brackett, *The Negro in Maryland: A Study of the Institution of Slavery*, Johns Hopkins University Studies in Historical and Political Science, extra vol. 5 (Baltimore: Johns Hopkins University, 1889), and James M. Wright, *The Free Negro in Maryland, 1634-1860*, Columbia University Studies in History, Economics and Public Law, vol. 97, (New York: Columbia University Press, 1921). See also Elwood Bridner, Jr., "The Fugitive Slaves of Maryland," *Maryland Historical Magazine* 66 (1971): 33-49, and M. Ray Della, "The Problems of Negro Labor in the 1850's," *Maryland Historical Magazine* 66 (1971): 14-32.

Political Studies

It is no longer profitable to study political parties of the past without some recognition of the concepts and techniques used by modern political scientists to analyze twentieth-century parties. I have found a number of such studies helpful, including Maurice Duverger, *Political Parties, Their Organization and Activity in the Modern State* (New York: Wiley, 1963); Julius Turner, *Party and Constituency: Pressures on Congress*, Johns Hopkins University Studies in Historical and Political Science, ser. 69, rev. ed. (Baltimore: Johns Hopkins Press, 1970); Angus Campbell *et al., The Voter Decides* (Evanston: Row, Peterson, 1954); Angus Campbell *et al., The American Voter* (New York: John Wiley & Sons, 1960); Stuart Rice, *Quantitative Methods in Politics* (New York: Alfred A. Knopf, 1928). While Turner and Rice delineate various new techniques, Duverger and Campbell present new concepts that can be used to study any political party. There are a number of recent studies that successfully apply these new techniques to the nineteenth-century political party, including William N. Chambers and Walter D. Burnham, eds., *The American Party System* (New York: Oxford University Press, 1967); and William N. Chambers, *Political Parties in a New Nation: The American Experience, 1776-1809* (New York: Oxford University Press, 1963).

INDEX

Library of Congress Cataloging in Publication Data

Baker, Jean H
The politics of continuity.

(The Goucher College series)
Bibliography: p.
1. Political parties—Maryland—history.
2. Maryland—Politics and government—1865-1950.
3. Maryland—Politics and government—Civil War.
I. Title.
JK2295.M32B34 329.02 72-12354
ISBN 0-8018-1418-9

THE JOHNS HOPKINS UNIVERSITY PRESS

This book was composed in Baskerville text and Garamond display
by Jones Composition Company, Inc., from a design by Laurie Jewell.
It was printed by Universal Lithographers, Inc., on S. D. Warren's
60-lb. Sebago, in a text shade, regular finish, and bound by
L. H. Jenkins, Inc., in Columbia Bayside linen.